# Missouri Course Le[v

Principles of Constitutional Democracy

1.A.1   Identify important principles in the Declaration of Independence, such as unalienable rights and government by consent of the governed

1.A.2   Identify important principles in the Constitution including limited government, rule of law, majority rule, minority rights, separation of powers, checks and balances

1.A.3   Identify important principles in the Bill of Rights such as basic rights and freedoms (for rights listed see Amendments 1-8; for rights not listed see Amendment 9)

Principles and Processes of Governance Systems

2.C.1   Distinguish between powers and functions of local, state and national governments

Missouri, United States and World History

3a.A.1   Summarize the viability and diversity of Native American cultures before Europeans came

3a.C.1   Outline the discovery, exploration and early settlement of America

3a.D.1   Explain the American Revolution, including the perspectives of patriots and loyalists and factors that explain why the American colonists were successful

3a.F.1   Investigate the causes and consequences of Westward Expansion, including: Texas and the Mexican War; Oregon Territory; California Gold Rush

3a.F.2   Examine cultural interactions among these groups from colonial times to Civil War: Native Americans; Immigrants from Europe; Africans brought to America

3a.I.1   Identify political, economical and social causes and consequences of the Civil War and Reconstruction

Economic Concepts and Principles

4.A.1   Apply the following economic concepts: scarcity; supply and demand; trade-offs (opportunity cost)

4.E.1   Identify the role of technology in our economy and how our economy has changed from an agricultural economy to an industrial economy

4.F.1   Interpret the past, explain the present and predict the future consequences of economic decisions

Elements of Geographical Study and Analysis

5.A.1   Use geographic research sources to acquire information and answer questions

5.A.2   Construct maps

5.B.1   Locate cities of Missouri and the United States

5.B.2   Locate states and major topographic features of the United States

5.B.3   Locate and describe real places, using absolute and relative location

5.C.1   Identify physical characteristics, such as climate, topography, relationship to water and ecosystems

5.C.2   Identify human characteristics, such as people's education, language, diversity, economies, religions, settlement, patterns, ethnic background and political system

5.F.1   Identify different kinds of regions in the United States

5.H.1   Identify major patterns of population distribution, demographics and migrations in the United States

5.J.1   Use geography to interpret the past, explain the present and plan for the future (e.g., physical processes that continue to reshape the earth)

Relationships of Individuals and Groups to Institutions and Traditions

6.E.1   Identify how a person becomes a member of a group or institution and what factors influence inclusion or exclusion from a group

6.I.1   Identify how ideas, concepts and traditions have changed over time in the United States

Tools of Social Science Inquiry

7.A.1   Select, investigate, and present a topic using primary and secondary resources, such as oral interviews, artifacts, journals, documents, photos and letters

7.B.1   Use maps, graphs, statistical data, timelines, charts and diagrams to interpret, draw conclusions and make predictions

7.B.2   Create maps, graphs, timeline, charts and diagrams to communicate information

7.C.1   Distinguish between fact and opinion and recognize bias and points of view

7.D.1   Use technological tools for research and presentation

7.G.1   Identify, research and defend a point of view/ position

MISSOURI
Macmillan/McGraw-Hill TIMELINKS

The United States

PROGRAM AUTHORS

James A. Banks
Kevin P. Colleary
Linda Greenow
Walter C. Parker
Emily M. Schell
Dinah Zike

CONTRIBUTORS

Raymond C. Jones
Irma M. Olmedo

 Macmillan/McGraw-Hill

Early Years

PROGRAM AUTHORS

James A. Banks, Ph.D.
Kerry and Linda Killinger
  Professor of Diversity Studies
  and Director, Center for
  Multicultural Education
University of Washington
Seattle, Washington

Kevin P. Colleary, Ed.D.
Curriculum and Teaching Department
Graduate School of Education
Fordham University
New York, New York

Linda Greenow, Ph.D.
Associate Professor and Chair
Department of Geography
State University of New York at
  New Paltz
New Paltz, New York

Walter C. Parker, Ph.D.
Professor of Social Studies Education,
University of Washington
Seattle, Washington

Emily M. Schell, Ed.D.
Visiting Professor, Teacher Education
San Diego State University
San Diego, California

Dinah Zike
Educational Consultant
Dinah-Mite Activities, Inc.
San Antonio, Texas

CONTRIBUTORS

Raymond C. Jones, Ph.D.
Director of Secondary Social Studies
  Education
Wake Forest University
Winston-Salem, North Carolina

Irma M. Olmedo
Associate Professor
University of Illinois-Chicago
College of Education
Chicago, Illinois

HISTORIANS/SCHOLARS

Rabbi Pamela Barmash, Ph.D.
Associate Professor of Hebrew Bible
  and Biblical Hebrew and Director,
  Program in Jewish, Islamic and Near
  Eastern Studies
Washington University
St. Louis, Missouri

Thomas Bender, Ph.D.
Professor of History
New York University
New York, New York

Ned Blackhawk
Associate Professor of History and
  American Indian Studies
University of Wisconsin
Madison, Wisconsin

Chun-shu Chang
Professor of History
University of Michigan
Ann Arbor, Michigan

Manuel Chavez, Ph.D.
Associate Director, Center for Latin
  American & Caribbean Studies,
  Assistant Professor, School of
  Journalism
Michigan State University
East Lansing, Michigan

Sheilah F. Clarke-Ekong, Ph.D.
Professor of Anthropology
University of Missouri-St. Louis
St. Louis, Missouri

Lawrence Dale, Ph.D.
Director, Center for Economic
  Education
Arkansas State University
Jonesboro, Arkansas

Mac Dixon-Fyle, Ph.D.
Professor of History
DePauw University
Greencastle, Indiana

Carl W. Ernst
William R. Kenan, Jr., Distinguished
  Professor
Department of Religious Studies
Director, Carolina Center for the
  Study of the Middle East and Muslim
  Civilizations
University of North Carolina
Chapel Hill, North Carolina

Brooks Green, Ph.D.
Associate Professor of Geography
University of Central Arkansas
Conway, Arkansas

Sumit Guha, Ph.D.
Professor of History
Rutgers
The State University of New Jersey
New Brunswick, New Jersey

Thomas C. Holt, Ph.D.
Professor of History
University of Chicago
Chicago, Illinois

Richard E. Keady, Ph.D.
Professor, Comparative Religious
  Studies
San Jose State University
San Jose, California

RFB&D learning through listening — Students with print disabilities may be eligible to obtain an accessible, audio version of the pupil edition of this textbook. Please call Recording for the Blind & Dyslexic at 1-800-221-4792 for complete information.

The McGraw·Hill Companies

Macmillan McGraw-Hill

Send all inquires to:

Macmillan/McGraw-Hill
8787 Orion Place
Columbus, OH 43240-4027

MHID 0-02-151785-1

ISBN 978-0-02-151785-5

Printed in the United States of America.

1 2 3 4 5 6 7 8 9 10   071/043   13 12 11 10 09 08

The United States
Early Years
CONTENTS

Reference Section

Skills and Features

Introduction To . . .

Introduction

EXPLORE The Big Idea

Essential Question
What information and skills can help you learn about social studies?

FOLDABLES™ Study Organizer

Organizing Information
Make and label a Trifold Book Foldable. Write the words **What I Know, What I Want To Know,** and **What I Learned** at the top of each section. Fill in the **What I Know** and **What I Want To Know** sections before you read the Introduction. Fill in the **What I Learned** section as you read the Introduction.

What I know

What I Want to Know

What I Learned

Eight Strands of Social Studies

MISSOURI COURSE LEVEL EXPECTATIONS
7.G.1

THINKING ABOUT SOCIAL STUDIES

Social studies is the study of people and the world we live in.

The Social Studies Strands

Since the topic of social studies is so large, it is divided into different parts. These parts, called strands, help us organize and understand social studies. Each strand teaches us something about the world. Thinking about how the eight strands influence each other builds our understanding of the world in the past and today. The circle graph below shows the eight strands of social studies you will learn about in this book.

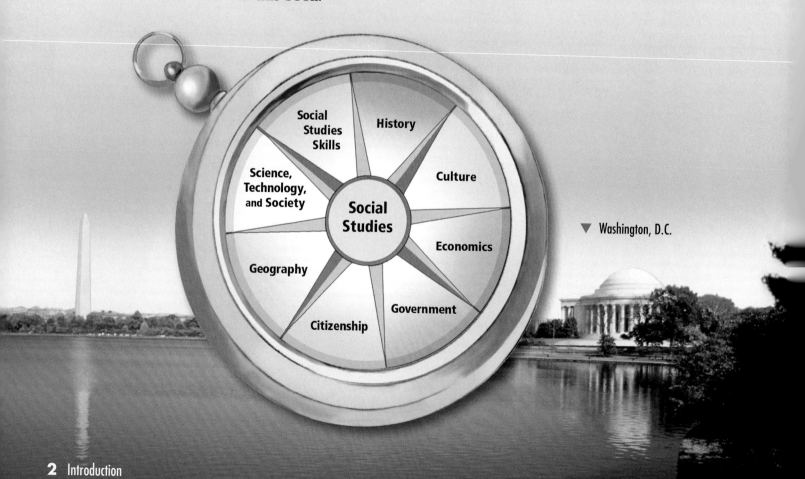

Social Studies Skills

History

Science, Technology, and Society

Culture

Social Studies

Economics

Geography

Government

Citizenship

▼ Washington, D.C.

History

History is the study of the past using **artifacts** and records from people who lived long ago. Artifacts are human-made objects, such as pottery, clothing, and tools. Studying history often helps us understand what is happening today.

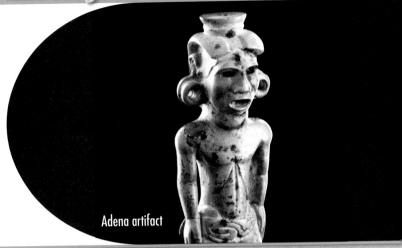
Adena artifact

Culture

The beliefs, customs, and daily routines of a group of people are called **culture**. An individual can belong to more than one culture. The culture of the United States is a mixture of the cultures of all the people who live here.

Chinese New Year Parade

Economics

In social studies, economics means how people use natural resources, money, and knowledge to produce goods and services. In the past, the American economy depended on farming and manufacturing. Today finance and technology are large parts of the economy.

Outdoor vegetable stand

Government

United States Congress

Government is the set of rules used to organize how people live together. The Constitution is the foundation for the United States government. Our country is a democratic republic. In the United States, everyone, including people in power, must obey the Constitution.

Citizenship

Students saying the Pledge of Allegiance

Citizenship describes the rights and responsibilities of people in a system of government. The Bill of Rights gives all Americans certain rights. An important part of citizenship in the United States is participating in government, especially through voting.

Geography

The United States

Geography is the physical environment and the way it influences people's lives. Geography can affect people's jobs, health, education, culture, and available resources.

Science, Technology, and Society

In social studies, the science, technology, and society strand studies the ways that advancements in science, changes in technology, and the introduction of new ideas influence people's lives. For example, recent advances in technology have drastically changed how people communicate with one another.

Cell phones have changed how we communicate.

Social Studies Skills

Social studies skills are skills that will help you better understand social studies and the world around you. In addition, you can use these skills in other subjects, such as language arts and science. These skills will help you become a more effective reader, writer, and thinker.

Reading maps is a social studies skill.

Putting It All Together

The eight social studies strands are all connected to one another. Each is an important part of this subject. As you learn about social studies, remember to make connections to other things you have learned. That way, you will have a better understanding of how the world works.

In the pages that follow, you will learn more about some important social studies skills. These skills are useful because they are a way to help you comprehend, or understand, social studies. They also show that the strands are connected to each other and the other subjects that you study.

Finally, they will help you think about what you read in this textbook and consider how it relates to your life.

QUICK CHECK

Select one of the Social Studies strands. Write a paragraph about how this strand can help you understand how the world works.

Reading Informational Text

HERE'S A TIP

Vocabulary words in this book are highlighted. The definitions are in the text and the glossary at the back of the book.

READING FOR UNDERSTANDING

Studying social studies is more than just remembering names and dates. Understanding what you read is also important.

When reading **informational texts,** or texts that explain information, you must think about what you are reading. This means that while reading the information, you should ask questions similar to these:

- What happened?
- When did it happen?
- How did it happen?

- Why did it happen?
- Where did it happen?
- Who was involved?

Using Your Textbook

Your textbook has many tools to help you think about what you are reading. Each of the units has an essential question. This is a question you will answer as you read the unit. Each unit also has a reading skill and Foldable to help you organize your thoughts as you read. The skill and Foldable will focus your attention on details that will help you understand the essential question.

Within the units, each lesson has a bookmark that lists the vocabulary words, the reading skill, a graphic organizer, and the learning standards for that lesson.

Point of View

As you study history, it is important to consider **point of view**, or how people see the world. Many things can shape point of view such as gender, ethnicity, age, and wealth. People's experiences and culture can also influence their point of view. As a reader, you must consider all points of view when forming conclusions about history.

For example, in the late 1700s, Great Britain and the British colonies in North America became involved in a war called the American Revolution. During this time two groups of colonists, Loyalists and Patriots, had different opinions about the war.

Loyalists were colonists who believed separating from England would harm businesses in the colonies. England was the main buyer of colonial goods at the time. Loyalists feared that without British support, colonial businesses would fail.

In contrast, Patriots thought England was controlling colonial trade. They believed that breaking away from England's control would allow them to develop trade with other countries to make greater profits.

Knowing these two points of view can help you better understand the mood in the colonies during the American Revolution.

QUICK CHECK

What have you learned about the mood in the colonies during this time based on the points of view of Loyalists and Patriots?

▼ Explaining your point of view can help solve problems.

MISSOURI COURSE LEVEL EXPECTATIONS
7.A.1, 7.C.1, 7.G.1

Analyzing Sources

DIFFERENT SOURCES

You must closely examine a source in order to understand it.

Sources from the Past

As you study social studies, you will use sources of information to understand events in the past. By using a variety of sources, you will gain a wide view of historical events.

Many times, you will come across many sources about the same topic. These sources may have the same information. Sometimes, though, you may find that the information differs. If that happened, what should you do?

Start by looking closely for opinions. An **opinion** is a statement that tells what a person thinks, believes, or feels. The author's opinions may influence his or her interpretation of events. It is important to separate opinions from **facts** in order to understand a source. A fact is information that is known to be true.

When you analyze a source, you also need to think about the author's purpose. Does the author want to inform, persuade, or motivate the audience? This will change the way the source is written.

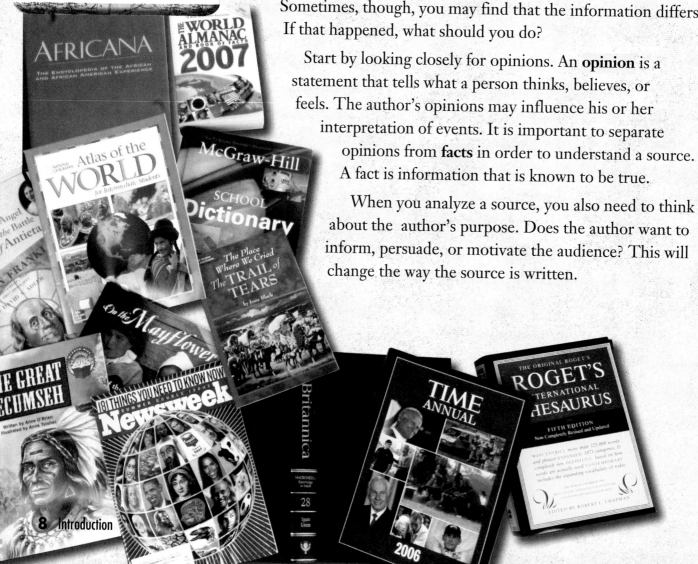

Credibility

When sources disagree about the details of events in history, it can sometimes be hard to decide what to believe. A critical reader must decide on the **credibility,** or correctness, of sources of information.

You can judge credibility by asking questions about the source. Is the source an eyewitness account from someone who was there, or was it written by someone who didn't see the event? Is the source a historian who knows about the topic?

Read part of a speech given by Patrick Henry in 1775 about British control of the colonies.

> **"**There is no retreat but in submission and slavery! Our chains are forged! The war is inevitable—and let it come! . . . I know not what course others may take; but as for me, give me liberty or give me death!**"**

▲ Patrick Henry

Henry thought that the British were treating the colonists unfairly and that war was the only option. Henry was an eyewitness to the events leading to the Revolutionary War. This means the speech is credible.

Computers make searching for information easier.

Finding More Information

Another way to check a source's credibility is by comparing it to other sources. To look for more information on the same topic, you can use key words. **Key words** are important words or phrases that are used to describe pieces of information.

Use key words about the topic you are studying to search other sources for more information. If you find the same details, the original source becomes more credible.

CAUTION

Be sure to carefully check credibility when using Internet sources. The Internet is not regulated, or controlled. This means that opinions sometimes look like facts.

TYPES OF SOURCES

In social studies you will read, use, and analyze a variety of sources. They are either primary sources or secondary sources.

Primary Sources

Think about the activities in which you have participated today. If you wrote an e-mail or a note to a friend, you created a **primary source** about your life. A primary source is a first-hand account of an event or an artifact created during the period of history being studied. Throughout your textbook you will read and write about primary sources.

To decide if a source is a primary source, you should look at the author, date, details, and language of the source. The letter below is an example of a primary source.

July 21, 1776
Boston

Last Thursday . . . I went . . . to Kings Street to hear the proclamation for independence . . . When Col(onel) Crafts read . . . great attention was given to every word. As soon as he ended . . . every face appeared joyful.

—Abigail Adams

Examples of Primary Sources
- letters
- diaries and journals
- photographs
- official records
- artifacts

Secondary Sources

Did you know that you are reading a **secondary source** right now? A secondary source is an account of the past created by someone who was not an eyewitness to the event.

Secondary sources usually combine information from many different sources. They can be interpretations of past events.

Sometimes they summarize a specific time or event in history. Read the encyclopedia entry below to see an example of a secondary source.

QUICK CHECK

Suppose you read a poem written last year. The poem describes life in colonial New England. Is the poem a primary or secondary source? How do you know?

CAUTION

Some sources, such as books, newspapers, and maps, can be either primary or secondary. You have to look at when the source was created in order to decide on the source's type.

Thomas Paine

1737–1809, political writer. Born in England, Paine came to the American colonies in 1774. In January 1776, he wrote *Common Sense*, a best-selling pamphlet that helped to inspire colonists to unite against British rule. He also wrote a series of essays called *The American Crisis*, which encouraged colonists to continue the American Revolution despite hardships.

Examples of Secondary Sources

- textbooks
- encyclopedias
- biographies
- books written after the time period

VOCABULARY

problem solving p. 12

decision making p. 13

**MISSOURI COURSE
LEVEL EXPECTATIONS**
7.G.1

Problem Solving

A STEP-BY-STEP APPROACH

There will be times in your life when you need to solve a problem. Sometimes these are simple problems. Occasionally you will come across a problem that doesn't have an easy answer. There may be more than one way for you to approach the problem. Then what should you do?

Solving a problem is a big responsibility. **Problem solving** is finding an answer to a difficult issue.

Begin problem solving by identifying the problem. Gather information about what caused the situation. List all of your options, or ways of solving the problem. Carefully consider the possible results of each option. Then choose a solution and try it out. Afterward, evaluate, or decide, if you were successful.

The Broken Plate Dilemma

Step 1

Identify the Problem
While I was visiting my grandmother, I broke her special cookie plate. Now I am not sure what to do.

Step 2

Gather Information
It is one of her favorite things. It is old. I shouldn't have been playing with it.

Step 3

List All Your Options
1. I can pretend I didn't break it.
2. I can tell her what happened and offer to replace it.

Decision Making: Choices

Not every decision you make will involve a problem. **Decision making** usually involves choosing between two or more things and may have little effect on others. For example, should you have eggs or cereal for breakfast?

When you make a decision, you should focus on the goal you want to accomplish. Consider how your options will help you reach that goal. Whenever you have a decision to make, you can use the steps on the bottom of the page to help you decide what to do.

QUICK CHECK

Why is it important to list all of your possible options when solving a problem?

▲ Working together can help solve problems.

Step 4

Choose a Solution and Do It

1. If I don't tell her, she will be upset that I wasn't honest.

2. If I do tell her, she will be sad, but I won't feel guilty and I can replace it.

I will tell her.

Step 5

Evaluate: Was the Problem Solved?

She was sad. I feel bad that I broke the plate. But she was glad I told her, and we will buy a new one this weekend.

I solved the problem.

If your plan wasn't successful, TRY AGAIN!

Note: You may need to go back and choose or think of another option.

VOCABULARY

historian p. 14

oral history p. 14

research p. 14

data p. 15

**MISSOURI COURSE
LEVEL EXPECTATIONS**
7.B.1, 7.B.2, 7.D.1

Communicating Research

SHARING WHAT YOU'VE LEARNED

Historians, people who study the past, examine clues and records from people who lived long ago. They also study artifacts and **oral history**, or information that is spoken rather than written down.

Historians share their **research**, or information they have discovered about the past, in different ways. Some write books or create museum exhibits. Others make documentaries or movies.

As a student, you may be asked to research a topic and share your findings with others. There are many ways to communicate research:

- Write a report
- Give a speech
- Create a poster
- Make a diorama
- Paint a picture
- Create a chart or graph
- Make a computer presentation
- Write a play, poem, or song
- Create a graphic organizer
- Write a newspaper article

These girls are doing research at the library.

Communicating Data

Sometimes the information you need to share with others is best shown in the form of a chart or graph. This type of information is called **data**, or facts, from which inferences or conclusions can be made.

There are many different charts and graphs you can use to show data. It is very important to choose the best chart or graph for the specific type of information you are presenting. The table below describes six of the most common charts and graphs.

Charts and Graphs

Name	Description	Picture
line graph	• Tracks changes over time • Shows how pieces of information are related	
table	• Organizes words and numbers to make finding information easy	
bar graph	• Shows relationships between groups of information	
diagram (or flowchart)	• Shows the movement of information or steps in a process	
circle graph	• Shows how something can be divided into parts	
time line	• Shows the order in which events took place	

! CAUTION

No matter what chart or graph you choose, be sure to label it. Include all important information, such as a title, labels, scale, and data.

QUICK CHECK

What is the purpose of a diagram or flowchart?

The Big Idea Activities

What information and skills can help you learn about social studies?

Write About the Big Idea

Expository Essay
Use the completed Trifold Book Foldable to help you write an expository essay that answers the Big Idea question, *What information and skills can help you learn about social studies?* Begin your essay with a paragraph that summarizes what you already knew about social studies. Add a paragraph that explains what you wanted to learned about social studies. End with a concluding paragraph that summarizes the information you learned in the Introduction.

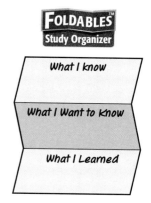

Go on a Scavenger Hunt

Previewing informational text can help prepare you for what you are about to read. Go on a scavenger hunt through this book to find at least one example of a social studies strand. Share your example with your classmates. Explain why the example you found fits the strand. Could your example fit into another strand?

As you read through the book, keep looking for examples of all eight social studies strands.

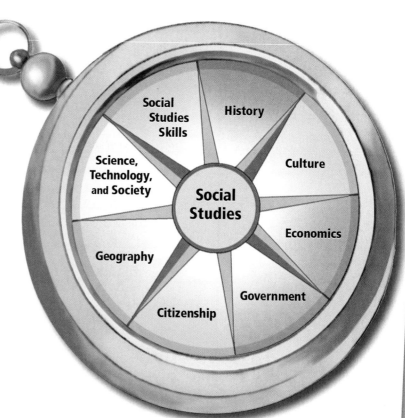

The Ancestral Pueblo built their homes into the sides of cliffs at Mesa Verde.

EXPLORE The Big Idea

Essential Question
How do people adapt to where they live?

FOLDABLES™ Study Organizer

Compare and Contrast
Make and label a Two-tab Foldable book before you read this unit. Label the tabs **Hunter-Gatherers** and **Farming Cultures**. Use the Foldable to organize information as you read.

Hunter-Gatherers

Farming Cultures

LOG ON
For more about Unit 1 go to
www.macmillanmh.com

NATIVE PEOPLES OF NORTH AMERICA

PEOPLE, PLACES, AND EVENTS

Maya Artifact

Navajo Woman

Central America

250 | Maya cities arise in Mexico and Guatemala

Southwest

1200 | Navajo settle in the Southwest

| 200 | 400 | 600 | 800 |

In about A.D. 250, **Maya** cities arose in the rain forests of Mexico and **Central America**.

Today you can visit ruins of ancient Maya cities such as Tikal and Chichén Itzá.

The **Navajo** people settled in the **Southwest** in about A.D. 1200.

Today the Navajo follow many of their traditional customs.

Mississippian Artifact

Mississippi River Valley

1300 | Cahokia is abandoned

Iroquois Chief

Northeast

1451 | Iroquois Confederacy adopts early constitution

 1000   1200   1400   1600

Cahokia, a large city built by **Mississippian Mound Builders**, was deserted by about 1300.

Today you can see Cahokia's largest mounds at a park near Collinsville, Illinois.

In 1451 the five nations of the **Iroquois Confederacy** adopted the "**Great Law of Peace,**" an early constitution.

Today many members of the Confederacy live in New York.

19

Lesson 1

VOCABULARY

archaeologist p. 21

glacier p. 21

civilization p. 22

irrigation p. 24

adobe p. 24

READING SKILL

Compare and Contrast
Copy the chart below. As you read, fill it in with facts about the Ancestral Pueblo and the people of Cahokia.

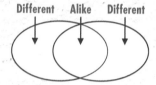

Different   Alike   Different

MISSOURI COURSE LEVEL EXPECTATIONS

3a.A.1, 5.A.1, 5.C.1, 5.C.2, 5.J.1, 6.I.1, 7.B.1, 7.B.2

Settling the Americas

Hunter-gatherers attack an Ice Age mastodon.

Visual Preview

How did early people adapt to life in North America?

A Hunter-gatherers followed animals into North America by land and water.

B The Olmec and Maya developed farming in Mexico and Central America.

C The Hohokam, Ancestral Pueblo, and Mound Builders settled in North America.

D The people of Cahokia built a large agricultural society in North America.

20

A THE FIRST HUNTER-GATHERERS

Suppose you had to travel a long distance thousands of years ago, and you could only paddle along a coastline or walk across land. What plants and animals might you eat along the way? There were no grocery stores, so you would have to find your own food.

The first Native Americans followed animals that supplied their food and clothing. When animals moved, people moved after them. In some regions a hunting trip could take days, so people ate a lot of plants. They gathered wild berries, mushrooms, and grasses. That's why we call them hunter-gatherers.

Archaeologists are people who study the tools, bones, and remains of ancient people. Some archaeologists think that hunter-gatherers first reached North America from Asia between 15,000 and 30,000 years ago. No one can say for sure when the first people arrived in the Americas.

Coastal and Land Routes

During the Ice Age, water froze into thick sheets of slow-moving ice called **glaciers**. Glaciers held so much water that ocean levels dropped and land appeared in some places. Over time, a land bridge appeared that joined Asia and the Americas. We call this the Beringia Land Bridge.

Many archaeologists believe the first people to arrive in North America crossed the land bridge from Asia and followed a water route along the Pacific Ocean. Archaeologists have found remains that show people may have reached the tip of South America. Other hunter-gatherers arrived in North America from Asia about 12,000 years ago. Archaeologists believe these early humans settled across the Americas.

QUICK CHECK

Compare and Contrast How were the lives of hunter-gatherers different from the lives of people today?

▼ Archaeologists study remains at a settlement of early people in South America.

EARLY PEOPLES OF MEXICO

About 10,000 B.C. the last Ice Age ended, and Earth's climate grew warmer. Ice Age mammals, such as mammoths and mastodons, could not survive in warmer weather. Humans had to start growing food when they could not hunt or gather enough to survive.

No one knows how farming first started. We do know that in the Americas it started in Mexico. By about 7000 B.C., people in Mexico and Central America were raising three crops: maize (also called corn), beans, and squash.

As in the Fertile Crescent of Asia, farmers in the Americas produced surpluses—more food than they needed. Some people now were free to specialize. They became traders, builders, or potters, for example. Over time, large specialized societies developed and became **civilizations** —populations that shared systems of trade, art, religion, and science.

The Olmec

In about 1200 B.C., the Olmec civilization developed in the steamy rain forests of southern Mexico. Olmec culture spread along trade routes across Mexico and Central America. One of the wealthiest centers of the Olmec was La Venta, which produced rubber, tar, and salt. La Venta had a large

▼ This Maya pyramid, the Temple of Five Stories, is located in Mexico.

fishing industry. Its people were the first to make food from a wild bean known as *cacao*—chocolate. Today the Olmec culture is famous for enormous stone head carvings found in Mexico. The Olmec also developed a calendar and were likely the first American people to understand the concept of zero.

The Maya

In about 2600 B.C., the Maya arose in the same region as the Olmec. Both groups settled in southeastern Mexico and Central America. From about A.D. 250 to 900, the Maya became a powerful civilization. Like the Olmec, the Maya had scientists who created calendars and studied the stars. The Maya also developed a system of mathematics and a form of writing called hieroglyphs.

The Maya were talented artists and builders. Workers built stone pyramids and temples to honor their hundreds of gods. These buildings can still be seen today. The Maya also built stone palaces, roads, and ball courts. Maya cities such as Chichén Itzá, Tikal, and Copán had populations of several thousand people.

Over time, the population outgrew the food supply. People moved out of the cities in search of food. The Maya civilization lost power by A.D. 900, but the people did not disappear. Today more than 6 million Maya live in Mexico, Belize, and Guatemala.

QUICK CHECK

Compare and Contrast How were the Olmec and Maya alike?

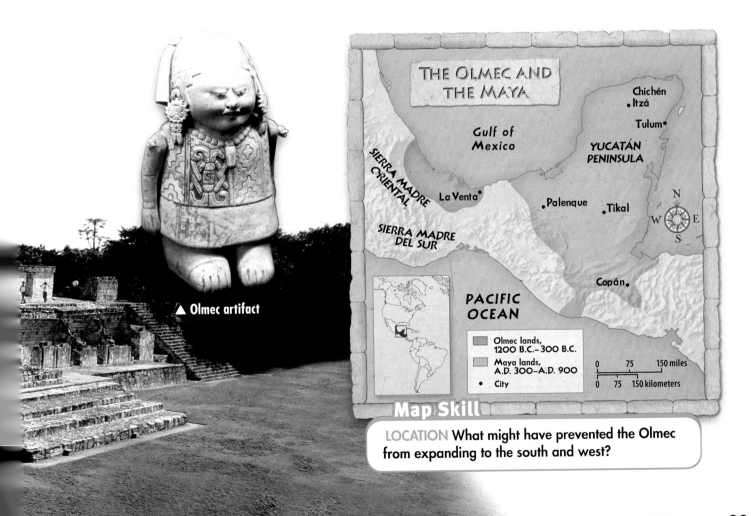

▲ Olmec artifact

THE OLMEC AND THE MAYA

Chichén Itzá

Tulum

Gulf of Mexico

YUCATÁN PENINSULA

SIERRA MADRE ORIENTAL

La Venta

Palenque

Tikal

N
W   E
S

SIERRA MADRE DEL SUR

Copán

PACIFIC OCEAN

Olmec lands, 1200 B.C.–300 B.C.
Maya lands, A.D. 300–A.D. 900
City

0   75   150 miles
0   75   150 kilometers

Map Skill

LOCATION **What might have prevented the Olmec from expanding to the south and west?**

If you could go back thousands of years and fly over southwest North America, you would see narrow waterways flowing through the desert and cities built into cliffs. If you could fly over the Mississippi River valley, you would see large round hills built by humans.

The Hohokam

In about A.D. 300, a group known as the Hohokam settled in the desert of present-day Arizona. The Hohokam grew maize, beans, squash, and cotton in this hot, dry region. How did they do it? They used **irrigation** to guide water from rivers to their fields. Irrigation supplies dry land with water through pipes and ditches. Using sharpened sticks and stone hoes, Hohokam workers dug canals, or human-made waterways, to carry water many miles.

The Hohokam also trapped rabbits, birds, and snakes. They ate wild desert plants, such as cactus and prickly pear.

With little stone or wood for building, the Hohokam built homes from **adobe**—bricks made of mud and straw. These homes were built partly underground in pits. Building underground helped to keep the homes cool during the day and warm at night.

Ancestral Pueblo

In about A.D. 700, a people called the Ancestral Pueblo settled in the Southwest. They lived in dwellings that looked like apartment buildings built into the sides of cliffs. These dwellings had special rooms called kivas for meetings or religious purposes.

▼ The Taos Pueblo is located in New Mexico.

The **Adena** of the Ohio River valley were the first mound builders. The earliest mounds were tombs. The dead were placed in log rooms in the mounds. Tools and other items for use in the next world were placed beside the body.

Adena Artifact

The natural world was the center of Ancestral Pueblo beliefs. Historian John Upton Terrell said,

❝The [Ancestral Pueblo] see themselves as woven into . . . the winds, the stars, and the moon. . . .❞

Like the Hohokam, the Ancestral Pueblo planted maize, beans, and squash. They used dry farming, a method that caught rain and melted snow in stone-lined pits. They then used this water on their crops.

Mound Builders

Other North American civilizations developed in river valleys of the Midwest. Over a period of about 1,000 years, civilizations arose in the Ohio and Mississippi River valleys. The people are called mound builders because of the cone-shaped hills and animal-shaped earthworks they built.

In about 200 B.C., the Hopewell were the first civilization to settle in the Mississippi River valley. Many Hopewell mounds can be seen today across the Midwest. Some were burial mounds, and others were used for religious ceremonies.

Another civilization, called the Mississippian culture, developed in about A.D. 700. Like the other mound-building cultures, they buried their dead in mounds. They also used their mounds as places to watch the movements of the sun and stars.

QUICK CHECK

Compare and Contrast How were the shelters of the Hohokam and Ancestral Pueblo different?

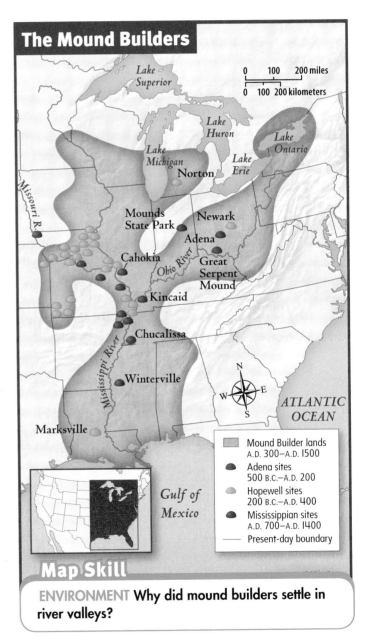

The Mound Builders

Lake Superior
Lake Huron
Lake Michigan
Lake Erie
Lake Ontario
Missouri R.
Norton
Mounds State Park
Newark
Adena
Cahokia
Ohio River
Great Serpent Mound
Kincaid
Chucalissa
Mississippi River
Winterville
Marksville
Gulf of Mexico
ATLANTIC OCEAN

0 100 200 miles
0 100 200 kilometers

Mound Builder lands
A.D. 300–A.D. 1500

Adena sites
500 B.C.–A.D. 200

Hopewell sites
200 B.C.–A.D. 400

Mississippian sites
A.D. 700–A.D. 1400

Present-day boundary

Map Skill

ENVIRONMENT **Why did mound builders settle in river valleys?**

The greatest Mississippian city was Cahokia, built near present-day St. Louis, Missouri. By A.D. 1100 Cahokia's population was about 20,000, making it one of the largest cities in the world at the time. Villages stretched around the city in all directions. High log fences, called palisades, protected the villages.

Like other agricultural societies, the people of Cahokia needed to know about the patterns of the seasons. Archaeologists have found the remains of a great circle of tree trunks outside Cahokia. They believe farmers planted these to act as a giant sundial.

Scientists do not agree about what happened to the people of Cahokia. Some say climate change, wars, or disease may have driven people out of the city. By 1300 Cahokia was empty.

QUICK CHECK

Compare and Contrast How did the Adena, Hopewell, and Mississippian peoples use earth mounds?

▼ Cahokia was one of the largest cities in the world in A.D. 1100.

Check Understanding

1. **VOCABULARY** Write a sentence about people who study ancient groups. Use three of the vocabulary terms below.

   archaeologist civilization adobe
   glacier   irrigation

2. **READING SKILL Compare and Contrast** Use your chart from page 20 to write a paragraph comparing the Ancestral Pueblo with the people of Cahokia.

3. **Write About It** Write a paragraph that tells how the Hohokam adapted to their environment.

26

Chart and Graph Skills

Read Parallel Time Lines

VOCABULARY

time line

B.C.

A.D.

B.C.E.

C.E.

century

circa

parallel time line

A **time line** lists events in history. Some time lines use the abbreviation B.C. It stands for "before Christ." The letters A.D. are for years after the birth of Christ. Some time lines use B.C.E., which stands for "before the Common Era," and C.E., which means "common era." Time lines can be divided into time periods. A **century**, or 100 years, is one time period. The word **circa** means "around" or "about." It is used when an exact date is not known.

The time line below is a **parallel time line**. Parallel time lines show two sets of dates and events on the same time line.

Learn It

Read the parallel time line below.

● The time line begins in the year 1500 B.C. and ends at A.D. 1000.

● The Olmec events took place in 1300 B.C., 900 B.C., and 300 B.C. The Maya events happened in 800 B.C., 300 B.C., A.D. 250, A.D. 500, and A.D. 900.

Try It

Use the time line to answer the questions.

● Which culture developed first, the Olmec or the Maya? Explain your answer.

● Which events on the time line happened around the same time?

Apply It

● Make a time line of your life. Then add events that have taken place in the United States during your lifetime.

Parallel Time Line: Early Peoples of North America

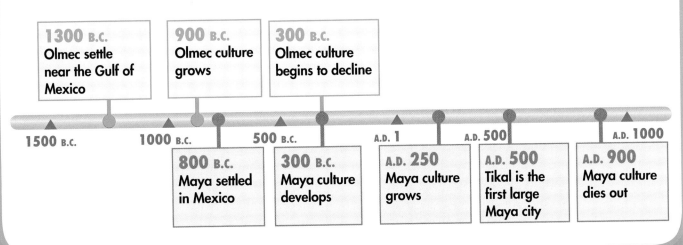

1300 B.C.
Olmec settle near the Gulf of Mexico

900 B.C.
Olmec culture grows

300 B.C.
Olmec culture begins to decline

1500 B.C.   1000 B.C.   500 B.C.   A.D. 1   A.D. 500   A.D. 1000

800 B.C.
Maya settled in Mexico

300 B.C.
Maya culture develops

A.D. 250
Maya culture grows

A.D. 500
Tikal is the first large Maya city

A.D. 900
Maya culture dies out

VOCABULARY

totem pole p. 30

potlatch p. 31

READING SKILL

Compare and Contrast
Copy the chart below. As you read, use it to compare and contrast the Inuit and Tlingit.

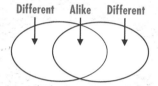

Different   Alike   Different

MISSOURI COURSE LEVEL EXPECTATIONS

3a.A.1, 5.A.1, 5.C.1, 5.C.2, 5.J.1, 6.E.1, 6.I.1, 7.B.1

NATIVE AMERICANS OF THE WEST

Whales were important to Native American economies in the West.

Visual Preview How did the environments of the West affect the lives of Native Americans?

A The Inuit hunted whales to use for food, tools, weapons, and cooking oil.

B The Tlingit used nearby forests to make canoes, totem poles, and masks.

A VARIED LANDS AND PEOPLE

For Native Americans in the West, environment helped form culture. The West is a region of great diversity—from the extreme cold of the Arctic to the hot, dry deserts of southern California. Cultures developed according to the climate and natural resources of the surroundings.

The Inuit in Alaska had to find ways to live in the bitterly cold Arctic. They kept warm by building pit houses made of stone and covered with earth. When they went on hunting trips, men built igloos, temporary shelters of snow blocks. In warm weather, hunters made tents from wooden poles and animal skins. The Inuit hunted walruses, seals, fish, and whales. They used the skins for clothing and turned bones into tools and weapons.

The California Desert

Life in the desert of southern California was different from life in the Arctic. Groups such as the Cahuilla and Paiute used desert plants, including roots and cactus berries, for food. They also grew crops using irrigation. The Cahuilla, for example, dug wells in the desert sand and packed sand around the wells, creating small lakes. They used the lakes to water fields of maize, squash, beans, and melons.

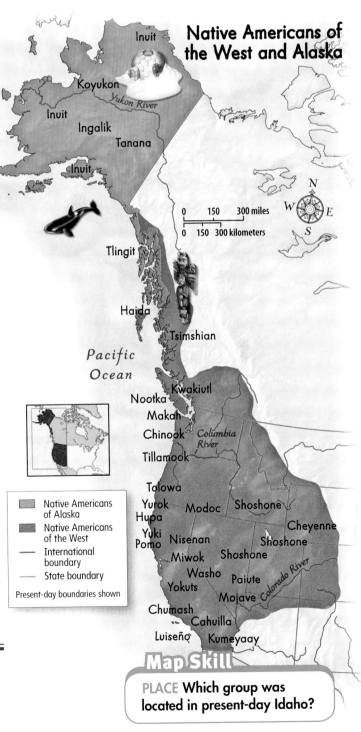

Native Americans of the West and Alaska

Inuit
Koyukon
Yukon River
Inuit
Ingalik
Tanana
Inuit

Tlingit

Haida

Tsimshian

Pacific Ocean

Kwakiutl
Nootka
Makah
Chinook *Columbia River*
Tillamook

Tolowa
Yurok Modoc Shoshone
Hupa
Yuki
Pomo Nisenan Shoshone
Miwok Shoshone
Washo Paiute *Colorado River*
Yokuts
Mojave
Chumash
Cahuilla
Luiseño Kumeyaay

Cheyenne

Legend:
- Native Americans of Alaska
- Native Americans of the West
- International boundary
- State boundary

Present-day boundaries shown

Map Skill

PLACE **Which group was located in present-day Idaho?**

QUICK CHECK

Compare and Contrast How are the Inuit different from Native Americans of the California desert?

Like Native Americans in other regions, those in the Pacific Northwest used only enough plants and animals to survive. The region was rich in natural resources, so its groups often did not need to farm. The rocky, narrow coastline and offshore islands of this region provided wild plants and fish, especially salmon.

Native Americans used stone axes to cut fir and cedar trees. They hollowed out logs to make canoes as long as 60 feet—perfect for hunting seals and whales in the Pacific Ocean. Logs were also carved into boxes, dishes, spoons, and masks.

Celebrations

Pacific Northwest groups also used wood to make **totem poles**. Totem poles are carved logs that are painted with symbols, called totems, of animals or people. Totem poles often told stories of important family members or celebrated special events.

Potlatch dancer

Citizenship

Be a Leader

Have you ever thought of being a leader? In 1945 Tlingit civil rights leader Elizabeth Peratrovich was responsible for a civil rights law that gave Native Americans equal rights. Leaders are able to identify problems and find solutions. Consider being a leader in your community or school.

Write About It Identify a problem in your community or school. Then write an essay about how you would work with others to find a solution.

The Tlingit continue to use the abundant resources of the sea and forests. Tlingit women are known around the world for their fine baskets made from cedar trees. Tlingit men continue the traditional wood carving and painting of totem poles, canoes, and face masks.

Tlingit carver

When totem poles were raised, a family sometimes held a **potlatch**. Potlatches are special feasts at which guests, not hosts, receive gifts. The host might give hundreds of gifts at the feast, which could last for several days. In return, the host received the respect of the community. As in the past, potlatches today bring people together for important family events such as the birth, death, or marriage of a family member.

The Wealth of the Tlingit

The Tlingit settled in the Pacific Northwest. Like other people in the region, they got most of their food and goods from the sea. The Tlingit traveled by canoe to trade their surplus, or extra, goods with other groups along the coast. This extensive system of trade made the Tlingit wealthy. In the 1700s the Tlingit lived in an area that stretched about 400 miles along the coast between Mount St. Elias in southeastern Alaska and what is now the Portland Canal in British Columbia. The Pacific Ocean's warm North Pacific Current kept the

weather mild and wet. These conditions made it easy to get food and wood, so the Tlingit often had free time to develop trades and crafts.

The Tlingit used this time to become skilled craftworkers. They used tree bark and other materials to weave colorful blankets and made sturdy baskets. The Tlingit also built wooden plank houses large enough to hold several related families. Totem poles stood in front of some houses. The Tlingit still live in Alaska today.

QUICK CHECK

Compare and Contrast How was the way the Tlingit adapted to their environment different from other Native American groups?

Check Understanding

1. **VOCABULARY** Write a sentence for each vocabulary term below.

   totem pole   potlatch

2. **READING SKILL Compare and Contrast** Use your chart from page 28 to write about the Inuit and Tlingit.

3. **Write About It** Write about how geography affected the lives of Native Americans in the West.

VOCABULARY

migrate p. 34

hogan p. 35

READING SKILL

Compare and Contrast
Copy the chart below. As you read, use it to compare and contrast the Pueblo and Navajo.

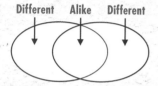

Different   Alike   Different

MISSOURI COURSE LEVEL EXPECTATIONS

3a.A.1, 5.A.1, 5.C.1, 5.C.2, 5.J.1, 6.I.1, 7.B.1

PEOPLE OF THE SOUTHWEST

A Pueblo deer dance celebration

Visual Preview

How did the desert environment affect people's lives?

A Pueblos are made of adobe, which protects the homes from extreme heat and cold.

B The Navajo learned how to use sheep for food and wool.

32

A THE PUEBLO

The Ancestral Pueblo you read about in lesson one are believed to be related to later Pueblo groups. Like their ancestors, the Pueblo had to adapt to where they lived to survive.

Can you imagine farming in a place that receives only a few inches of rain each year? The Pueblo—like their ancestors—figured out how to farm in the desert. They used a method called dry farming.

The Amazing Pueblo Farmers

Dry farming uses tiny dams and canals to direct water to beans, squash, and cotton crops. The Pueblo also learned how to grow a special maize plant with long roots that could reach water deep underground. The Hopi and Zuni are two Pueblo groups shown on the map below.

PLACES

The **Taos Pueblo** is over 1,000 years old. The multistoried buildings are made of adobe. Today you can visit the Taos Pueblo where shops sell pottery, silver jewelry, and leather goods.

Taos Pueblo

Pueblo Homes

The Pueblo built homes called pueblos out of adobe. The Spanish used the word pueblo to describe both the people and their homes. Adobe protects homes from extreme heat or cold. Pueblos looked like apartment buildings, except that the first floor of most pueblos had no doors or windows. To get in and out of a pueblo, people climbed a ladder to a door in the roof. By lifting the ladder up and placing it on the roof, they were protected from unwanted guests.

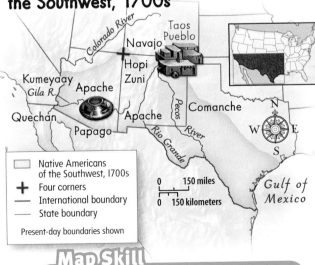

Native Americans of the Southwest, 1700s

Colorado River
Taos Pueblo
Navajo
Hopi
Zuni
Kumeyaay
Gila R.
Apache
Quechan
Apache
Papago
Pecos River
Comanche
Rio Grande
Gulf of Mexico

N W E S

0   150 miles
0   150 kilometers

☐ Native Americans of the Southwest, 1700s
+ Four corners
— International boundary
— State boundary
Present-day boundaries shown

Map Skill

LOCATION **Which rivers are on or near Apache lands?**

QUICK CHECK

Compare and Contrast **How were the Pueblo similar to the Ancestral Pueblo?**

THE NAVAJO

Thousands of years ago, the Navajo, or Diné, were hunter-gatherers in parts of present-day Alaska and Canada. The Navajo began to **migrate**, or move, to northern New Mexico by the late 1200s.

Today the Navajo are the largest non-Pueblo people in the Southwest. Many live in the Four Corners area, where the states of Utah, Colorado, Arizona, and New Mexico meet.

Learning from the Pueblo

In order to survive, the Navajo knew they had to adapt ideas and practices from their Pueblo neighbors. Like the Pueblo, the Navajo used dry farming to grow crops in the dry land. They also wove cotton to make cloth. Both the Navajo and the Pueblo are known for their fine silver and turquoise jewelry. Turquoise is a blue stone that is found only in the Southwest and in western South America.

◀ A Navajo grandmother teaches her granddaughter how to weave a blanket.

Navajo hogan →

Navajo Living

The Navajo lived in **hogans**, which are dome-shaped homes for one family. The hogans are made with log or stick frames that are covered with mud or sod. They have a smoke hole in the roof to release the smoke from a fire. Traditional hogans have six or eight sides and face east to catch the first rays of dawn.

The Navajo captured sheep from the Spaniards in the 1600s. These animals became an important part of Navajo culture. Many Navajo people became shepherds. The meat provided food, and weavers made wool into clothes and blankets.

The Navajo believed in a balance to the Earth that they called *hozho*, or "walking in beauty." To maintain hozho, the Navajo sing songs or chants. One song says, "All is beautiful before me, All is beautiful behind me, All is beautiful above me, All is beautiful around me."

QUICK CHECK

Compare and Contrast **In what ways are pueblos different from hogans?**

▲ Turquoise squash blossom necklace

Check Understanding

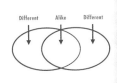

1. **VOCABULARY** Write about the Navajo using these vocabulary words.

   migrate   **hogan**

2. **READING SKILL Compare and Contrast** Use your chart from page 32 to write about the Pueblo and Navajo.

   Different   Alike   Different

3. **Write About It** Write about how the Pueblo or Navajo learned to live in the Southwest.

VOCABULARY

teepee p. 37

lodge p. 37

travois p. 38

coup stick p. 39

READING SKILL

Compare and Contrast
Copy the chart below. As you read, use it to compare and contrast life on the Plains before and after the arrival of horses.

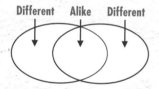

Different   Alike   Different

MISSOURI COURSE LEVEL EXPECTATIONS

3a.A.1, 5.A.1, 5.C.1, 5.C.2, 5.J.1, 6.E.1, 6.I.1, 7.A.1, 7.B.1

NATIVE AMERICANS OF THE PLAINS

This painting shows the excitement of a buffalo hunt.

Visual Preview | **How did the natural resources of the Plains impact Native Americans?**

A Hunting bison provided food, clothing, and shelter.

B During the winter, the Lakota made clothing, tools, and calendars.

A THE OPEN PLAINS

Imagine looking into the distance, seeing only land and blue sky. The Great Plains is a vast, nearly flat region where you can see for miles. The land has powerful winds, blistering summer heat, and cold winters.

Native Americans began to settle on the Great Plains in about 1300. They hunted for food on foot. They used bows and arrows and stampeded animals into traps. Some groups farmed near rivers.

Horses Arrive

By the 1700s, wild horses had spread from the Southwest to the Great Plains. Once tamed, they changed the lives of people there. Men hunted on horseback, and many groups traded with faraway groups. As a result, groups such as the Lakota, Crow, Pawnee, and Cheyenne prospered on the Plains.

Where the Bison Roam

Between 40 million and 100 million bison roamed the Great Plains in the 1700s. They provided food and clothing. Some groups used bison skin to make **teepees**. Teepees are cone-shaped homes made with long poles covered with animal hides.

Some Plains groups stayed in one place and lived in large earthen **lodges**. Lodges are homes made of logs covered with grasses, sticks, and soil. A fire in a central fireplace provided heat and light.

QUICK CHECK

Compare and Contrast In what ways are teepees different from lodges?

Native Americans of the Plains, 1700s

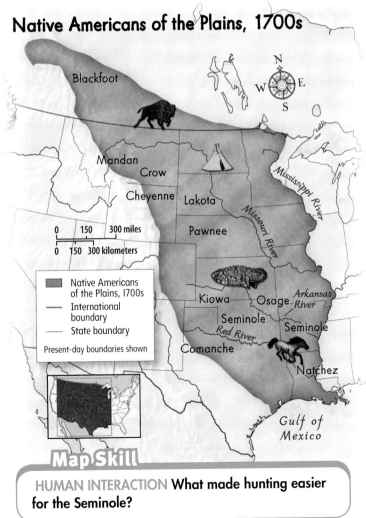

Native Americans of the Plains, 1700s
International boundary
State boundary
Present-day boundaries shown

Blackfoot
Mandan
Crow
Cheyenne
Lakota
Pawnee
Missouri River
Mississippi River
Kiowa   Osage   Arkansas River
Seminole
Red River   Seminole
Comanche
Natchez
Gulf of Mexico

0   150   300 miles
0   150   300 kilometers

Map Skill

HUMAN INTERACTION **What made hunting easier for the Seminole?**

Fire was not only used to cook bison meat, it was also used in the hunt. Some hunters often set grass fires to frighten a herd into a stampede. Often hundreds of animals would rush over a cliff, falling to their deaths. The hunters would then gather the meat and skins that they needed. Plains people used a **travois** to carry the meat and skins back to camp.

A travois is a sled-like device that is dragged by people or animals. At first, dogs were trained to pull the travois. Later, horses did the job.

Keeping Records

Would you go outside if it was 20 degrees below zero? The Lakota did not. Instead they used the long, cold winter months to stay close to a fire. There they made clothes, weapons, or tools. They also made illustrated calendars called winter counts.

When the Lakota settled in a camp for the winter, they met to decide the most important events of that year. These events were painted as picture symbols in a circle on bison hide. The history of the Lakota is read counter-clockwise, moving left, from the center of the circle. Study the winter count on this page.

Primary Sources

This winter count was created by a Lakota named Lone Dog. It is a copy of the original, which was destroyed in a fire. The symbols are read in a counter-clockwise spiral. The key tells the meaning of some of the symbols. How does the winter count help you understand Lone Dog's life?

An 1800–1871 Winter Count by Lone Dog

 1800–1801
Europeans bring striped blankets

 1845–1846
30 Lakota killed by Crow Indians

 1845–1846
There is plenty of meat

Write About It Write a journal entry giving more details about an event shown on the winter count.

The **Spanish brought horses** with them to North America in the 1500s. Some horses got away and lived in the wild. In the 1600s, the Pueblo were using horses in the Southwest. By the 1700s horses had moved into the Great Plains, forever changing the lives of the people who lived there.

Horses arrive

In most Plains cultures, a child's first success was given public recognition. For example, Blackfoot boys who won shooting matches were allowed to wear feathers in their hair like older men. Children were also praised for showing qualities that were admired, such as being generous and speaking well.

QUICK CHECK

Compare and Contrast Why were the skills taught to boys different from those taught to girls?

Learning Life Skills

Parents taught their children useful skills early in life. On the Great Plains, parents taught their children good listening skills by telling them stories and singing songs about their culture. Boys were taught to hunt and shoot. They learned, for example, to track small game such as rabbits and birds. They used small bows and arrows to shoot these moving targets. Later they took part in shooting matches and practice battles. Boys also learned the value of courage. One way they showed courage was to touch an enemy without killing him. To do this, they used a special pole called a **coup stick**. Coup is the French word for "strike" or "hit."

Girls learned different skills. They learned to sew by making doll clothes, using the sinews from bison as thread. Sinews are tendons that connect muscle to bone. Girls were also given toy teepees to set up while their mothers set up the family teepees. Older girls learned how to use scraping tools to clean animal skins. The skills taught to children on the Great Plains would prepare them for different tasks as adults.

Check Understanding

1. **VOCABULARY** Write a story about a day in a village of Native Americans on the Great Plains using the vocabulary terms below.

teepee	travois
lodge	coup stick

2. **READING SKILL Compare and Contrast** Use your chart from page 36 to write about Plains groups.

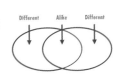

3. **Write About It** How did Native Americans on the Great Plains adapt to the environment?

People of the Eastern Woodlands

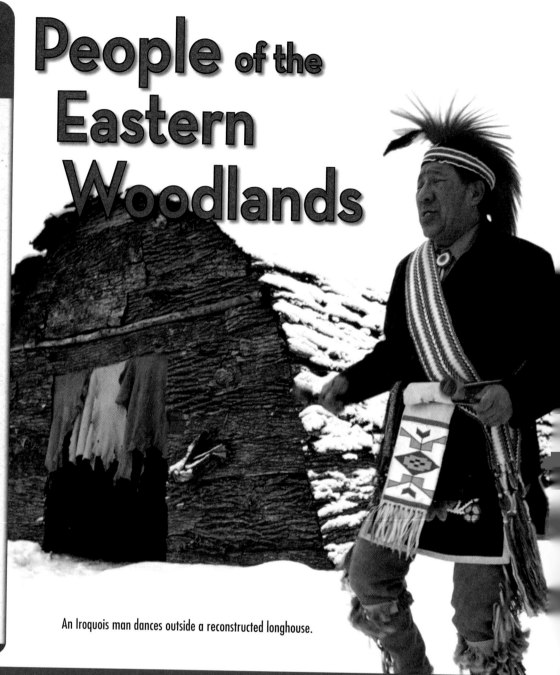

An Iroquois man dances outside a reconstructed longhouse.

VOCABULARY

slash-and-burn p. 41

longhouse p. 43

wampum p. 43

Creek Confederacy p. 44

clan p. 44

Iroquois Confederacy p. 45

READING SKILL

Compare and Contrast
Copy the chart below. As you read, use it to compare and contrast the Iroquois and the Creek.

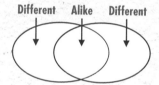

Different   Alike   Different

MISSOURI COURSE LEVEL EXPECTATIONS

3a.A.1, 5.A.1, 5.C.1, 5.C.2, 5.J.1, 6.E.1, 6.I.1, 7.A.1, 7.B.1

Visual Preview

How did the environment shape Eastern Woodlands cultures?

A People hunted forest animals and grew maize, squash, and beans.

B The Iroquois used materials from the forests to build their homes.

C Groups worked together to protect and govern themselves.

A LAND RICH IN FORESTS

Did you know that North America was once called Turtle Island? The Iroquois named it that because they believed Sky Woman fell out of the sky and the Great Turtle caught her, causing an island to form.

The Iroquois include five groups, the Cayuga, the Mohawk, the Oneida, the Onondaga, and the Seneca. These groups share many cultural traits, such as language. When the Iroquois settled in present-day New York, the area was covered with thick forests. They said the forests were so thick that a squirrel could jump from tree to tree for a thousand miles without touching the ground. Forest animals, such as deer, provided woodland groups with food and clothing.

Farming the Land

Because the forests were so thick, many groups in the Eastern Woodlands practiced a type of farming called **slash-and-burn**. They cut down, or slashed, trees. They then burned the undergrowth to clear room for crops. Ash from the burned vegetation helped to make the soil fertile. After a crop had been harvested, they left the plot empty for several years. The next year another plot was cleared and planted. This method helped keep the soil from wearing out.

Each spring most groups planted the "Three Sisters" of maize, squash, and beans. In autumn crops were harvested, dried, and stored for the winter.

QUICK CHECK

Compare and Contrast Compare slash-and-burn farming with dry farming.

Native Americans of the Eastern Woodlands, 1600s

Native Americans of the Eastern Woodlands, 1600s
— International boundary
— State boundary
Present-day boundaries shown

0   150   300 miles
0   150   300 kilometers

Map Skill

LOCATION **Which river created a natural boundary for Native Americans of the Eastern Woodlands?**

Archaeologists believe the Creek of the southern woodlands are descendants of the Mississippian mound-building people. When a Creek town reached a population of about 400 to 600 people, about half the population would move to a new site.

CREEK

Creek Villages

▶ The Creek (known as the Muskogee today) arranged their towns around a large council house or "Chokofa." Family homes were wattle-and-daub huts, which are made from poles and covered with grass, mud, or thatch.

Creek Art

▶ The Creek decorated their pots with wooden stamps. They pressed the carved stamps into pottery while it was still wet.

Celebrations

▶ Both the Creek and Iroquois celebrated the Green Corn Festival, honoring the summer's first maize crop.

The Iroquois of the northern woodlands usually built their villages on the tops of steep-sided hills. The steep slopes formed natural defenses for the village. A high log fence was commonly built along the edge of a village for added protection.

QUICK CHECK
Compare and Contrast **How are Creek and Iroquois villages different?**

IROQUOIS

Iroquois Villages

▶ The Iroquois call themselves Hodenosaunee. In Iroquoian this means "people of the **longhouse**." Longhouses were large enough for several families and were made of bent poles covered with sheets of bark. The longest longhouse is thought to have been 334 feet. That's longer than a football field!

Iroquois Art

▶ The Iroquois made fine beadwork, called **wampum**. Wampum is polished beads made from shells that are woven together. It was used in ceremonies or as gifts.

Sports

▶ Both the Iroquois and the Creek played lacrosse. lacrosse sometimes settled disagreements among groups.

Archaeologists group Native Americans in many ways. One way is by language. Find the language family of the Creek in the chart on this page. Native Americans can also be grouped by how they governed themselves. Some groups formed confederacies. A confederacy is a union of people who join together for a common purpose.

Creek Government

To protect themselves from enemies, the Creek formed the **Creek Confederacy**. Most of the groups in the confederacy spoke Muskogean languages. The groups also shared customs, such as the Green Corn Festival.

The Creek Confederacy divided its towns into war towns (red) and peace towns (white). Red towns declared war, planned battles, and held meetings with enemy groups. White towns passed laws and held prisoners. During periods of war, however, even people in peace towns joined in the fighting. When a new town formed, it maintained close ties to other towns. This kept the Creek Confederacy united.

Iroquois Society

Iroquois women were leaders of their society and did most of the farming. They decided how land would be used and who would use it. Women were the heads of their **clans.** A clan is a group of families that share the same ancestor. The head of each clan was called a clan mother. No important decision could be made without the approval of the clan mother. Although the leaders of each village were men, it was the clan mothers who chose them—and could also remove them.

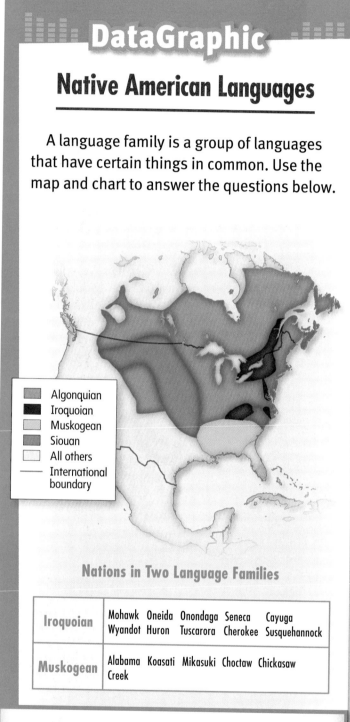

DataGraphic

Native American Languages

A language family is a group of languages that have certain things in common. Use the map and chart to answer the questions below.

Algonquian
Iroquoian
Muskogean
Siouan
All others
International boundary

Nations in Two Language Families

Iroquoian	Mohawk Oneida Onondaga Seneca Cayuga Wyandot Huron Tuscarora Cherokee Susquehannock
Muskogean	Alabama Koasati Mikasuki Choctaw Chickasaw Creek

Think About Languages

1. In what part of the present-day United States were the Mikasuki located?

2. What traits do you think the groups in the same language family shared?

Deganawida

longhouse

Deganawida asking a group to join the
Iroquois Confederacy ▶

Iroquois Government

When the Iroquois people were a small
group, they worked together to solve
disagreements. When their numbers began
to grow, arguments broke out among clans.
According to Iroquois history, two Iroquois
leaders, Deganawida and Hiawatha, saw that
fighting was destroying their people. In the
1500s, the two leaders urged the Iroquois to
work together for peace.

In about 1570, five Iroquois groups joined
together to form the **Iroquois Confederacy**,
also known as the Iroquois League. Its goal
was to maintain peace among the five Iroquois
groups, or nations. After the Tuscarora moved
to New York from North Carolina in 1722,
the Confederacy was called Six Nations. The
Confederacy is still active today.

QUICK CHECK

Compare and Contrast **How were the Creek and
Iroquois confederacies different?**

Check Understanding

1. **VOCABULARY** Write a sentence using the
   word about farming from the list below.

   slash-and-burn   wampum

   longhouse   Creek Confederacy

2. **READING SKILL Compare
   and Contrast** Use your chart
   from page 40 to write about
   the people of the Eastern
   Woodlands.

   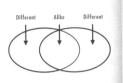
   Different   Alike   Different

3. **Write About It** How did Native
   Americans farm in the forests of the
   Eastern Woodlands?

EXPLORE
The
Big
Idea

Vocabulary

Number a paper from 1 to 4. Beside each number, write the word from the list below that matches the description.

potlatch   travois

migrate   slash-and-burn

1. A sled-like device used to transport goods

2. A method of clearing land for farming

3. To move from one place to another

4. A special feast at which the guests receive gifts

Comprehension and Critical Thinking

5. How did the geography of the Tlingit region help them trade with other groups?

6. **Reading Skill** How was the Creek Confederacy different from the Iroquois Confederacy?

7. **Critical Thinking** How did the environment of the Southwest affect the groups that lived there?

8. **Critical Thinking** In what way did trade help Native Americans?

Skill

Use Parallel Time Lines

Write a complete sentence to answer each question.

9. Which culture developed first, the Hohokam or Ancestral Pueblo?

10. Which two events happened at the same time on the time line?

Hohokam Events

circa 300
Hohokam culture begins

circa 1100
Peak of Hohokam culture

circa 1500
Hohokam culture ends

300   600   900   1200   1500

circa 700
Ancestral Pueblo culture begins

circa 1100
Peak of Ancestral Pueblo culture

circa 1300
Ancestral Pueblo culture ends

Ancestral Pueblo Events

MAP Test Preparation

Directions Read the passage. Then answer Numbers 1 through 3.

Native American culture is determined by the environment. The arctic is extremely cold. By contrast, the dry deserts of southern California are very hot. Native American cultures in these areas adapted to the climate and natural resources of the surroundings.

The Inuit in Alaska found ways to live during the bitterly cold arctic winters. On hunting trips, men built igloos, temporary shelters made from snow blocks. During warm weather, hunters made tents from wooden poles and animal skins. The Inuit hunted walruses, seals, and fish.

1 **What is paragraph 2 mainly about?**

○ how the Arctic is very cold

○ how the Inuit survived

○ Native American culture

○ the deserts of California

2 **Read the sentence: "Each culture adapted to the climate and natural resources of their surroundings." Which of the following words is a synonym for the word surroundings as used in the above sentence?**

○ environment

○ life

○ change

○ feelings

3 **Where could you look for more information about the Inuit?**

Write your answer on a separate piece of paper.

How do people adapt to where they live?

Write About the Big Idea

Descriptive Essay
Use the Unit 1 Foldable to help you write a descriptive essay that answers the Big Idea question, *How do people adapt to where they live?* Be sure to begin your essay with an introduction. Use the notes you wrote under each tab in the Foldable for details to support each main idea. Be sure to describe how the group's location affected its way of life.

FOLDABLES™
Study Organizer

Hunter-Gatherers

Farming Cultures

Make a Model Shelter

Make a model of one of the Native American shelters you read about in the unit.

1. Choose a shelter that you would like to live in.

2. Use your textbook and additional research to choose the best materials to construct your shelter.

3. You may choose to make only the exterior of the shelter or a diorama of the interior.

When you have finished your model, write a paragraph describing why you would like to live in the shelter. Include facts and a description about the shelter you have created.

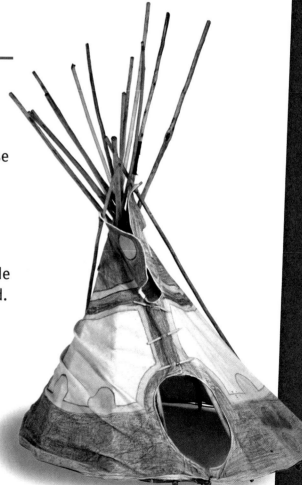

EXPLORE The Big Idea

Essential Question
What happens when different cultures first meet?

FOLDABLES™
Study Organizer

Cause and Effect
Make and label a Concept Map Foldable book before you read this unit. Across the top write **When different cultures meet.** Label the three tabs **Before, During,** and **After.** Use the Foldable to organize information as you read.

When different cultures meet

Before	During	After

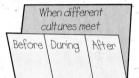

LOG ON

For more about Unit 2 go to
www.macmillanmh.com

The *Niña*, the *Pinta*, and the *Santa María* set sail on the Atlantic Ocean.

Exploration and Colonization

PEOPLE, PLACES, AND EVENTS

Marco Polo

Silk Road

1295 | Marco Polo describes China

Christopher Columbus

San Salvador

1492 | Columbus lands on San Salvador

1250	1350	1450

In 1295 **Marco Polo** returned to Venice and described China for the first time to amazed Europeans.

Today you can visit cities that were once major trading posts along the **Silk Road**.

In 1492 **Christopher Columbus** landed in North America, but he thought he had reached Asia!

Today a stone monument on **San Salvador** marks the place where Columbus landed.

Moctezuma II

Tenochtitlán

1502

Moctezuma II comes to
power in Tenochtitlán

Massasoit

Massachusetts

1621

Wampanoag and Pilgrims
celebrate Thanksgiving

1550

1650

1750

Moctezuma II ruled the Aztec from
Tenochtitlán, a city of more than 200,000
people.

Today Mexico City, Mexico, is built on the site
of Tenochtitlán.

In 1621 **Massasoit** and other Wampanoag
joined the Pilgrims at Plymouth Plantation for a
Thanksgiving celebration.

Today you can celebrate Thanksgiving at a
modern-day Plymouth Plantation.

THE WORLD Expands

Vikings were the first explorers from Europe to reach North America.

VOCABULARY

profit p. 54

barter p. 54

merchant p. 54

navigation p. 57

READING SKILL

Cause and Effect
Copy the chart below. As you read, fill in information about the European exploration of Asia and North America.

Cause	→	Effect
	→	
	→	
	→	

MISSOURI COURSE LEVEL EXPECTATIONS
4.F.1, 5.A.1, 5.B.3, 5.C.2, 5.J.1, 6.I.1, 7.A.1, 7.B.1

Visual Preview

How did events in Europe affect exploration?

A Vikings sailed along Europe's coasts and rivers and reached North America.

B Europeans learned about Asian inventions from travelers and traders.

C New navigation tools opened trade to Africa and Asia.

D Bartolomeu Dias and Vasco da Gama sailed to Asia for trade.

A THE MIDDLE AGES

About 1,500 years ago, Europe was divided into small kingdoms that were often at war. Most people were poor farmers who rarely left the villages where they were born. Their worlds were very small.

During the Middle Ages, few Europeans knew anything about Asia or Africa—or even about nearby kingdoms. The Middle Ages are a period of European history that ranges from A.D. 500 to 1500. It came between the end of ancient Rome and the beginning of the age of exploration.

Northern Traders and Raiders

The first people of the Middle Ages to travel to distant regions were the Norse, or "north people," who lived in what are today Denmark, Sweden, and Norway. They were skilled sailors who traveled through Europe by ocean and rivers. Their ships carried furs, fish, and timber. The Norse traded those items for oil, spices, and goods from Europe and western Asia.

Norse sailors often acted more like pirates than traders. They are also called Vikings, from the Norse word for "raiders." Viking raids terrified the people of Europe for centuries.

Around A.D. 1000, Viking explorers became the first Europeans to reach North America. They sailed west and built settlements in Iceland and Greenland. Historians believe that disease and battles with native peoples caused settlers to abandon the settlements. As a result, the Viking exploration of North America remained unknown for centuries.

QUICK CHECK

Cause and Effect Why were the Norse also known as Vikings?

▲ Old maps showed sea monsters in unknown ocean regions.

Ⓑ TRADE AND TRAVEL

During the Middle Ages, travel was dangerous and difficult. Most roads were only muddy paths. Yet some Europeans crossed the continent and traveled east on foot, on horseback, or on sailing vessels.

The Crusades

In 1095 thousands of Europeans prepared for a long journey to Jerusalem in western Asia. The city had great religious importance to Jews, Christians, and Muslims.

In 1096 the first of many wars for control of Jerusalem began. European Christians hoped to capture Jerusalem from the Muslim Turks who ruled it. These wars were known by those in Europe as the Crusades. The Crusaders captured Jerusalem, but wars for control of the city continued for centuries.

Trade and Merchants

The Crusades gave Europeans greater contact with Asia. Many Europeans who joined the Crusades returned with items that were unknown in Europe, such as silk or spices. These returning travelers found that Europeans were willing to pay a lot for items such as cotton, pepper, and cinnamon. They became traders who made a **profit** by charging more than they paid for products. Profit is the money that remains after the costs of running a business.

Soon, a new class of people formed called **merchants**. Merchants made their living from buying and selling goods. Some merchants exchanged goods for other goods, rather than for money. This system is called **barter**.

The Travels of Marco Polo

In 1295 a family of merchants named Polo returned to Venice after many years away. They had traveled thousands of miles across Asia, visiting places no European had ever seen. They had lived as guests in the palace of the ruler of China. One member of the family, Marco Polo, had left at 17 years old and was 43 when he returned.

In China, the Polos saw items unknown in Europe, including paper money and gunpowder. They ate foods that were unknown in Europe, such as noodles. Back in Venice, Marco Polo described the wonders he had seen. A writer named Rustichello wrote down his stories in a book known today as *The Travels of Marco Polo*. The book's description of the world beyond Europe inspired many Europeans to look for new routes to Asia.

PLACES

The city of **Venice** is built on small islands in northeast Italy. In Marco Polo's time, the city was a center for trade between Europe and western Asia. At that time, it was the wealthiest city in Europe.

Venice

Marco Polo's route · Silk Road · City

EUROPE
Genoa Venice
Constantinople
Black Sea
Caspian Sea
Trabzon
Tabriz
Bukhara
Mediterranean Sea
PERSIA
HINDU KUSH
ASIA
GOBI
Khanbalik (Beijing)
CHINA
Yangchow
HIMALAYA
Quanzhou
ARABIA
Red Sea
Persian Gulf
AFRICA
40°N
20°N
20°N
INDIA
Arabian Sea
Bay of Bengal
South China Sea
10°N
10°N

The Travels of
Marco Polo
1271 to 1295

0   500   1,000 miles
0   500   1,000 kilometers
50°E   60°E   70°E   80°E   90°E

Map Skill

MOVEMENT **Why did trading centers in Europe develop on large bodies of water?**

Trade with Asia

From about A.D. 100 until the 1300s, Chinese traders brought silk to western Asia. From there it was brought to Europe by merchants. The traders traveled on a famous route called the Silk Road, which connected Asia and Europe. Besides silk, the traders brought spices and jewels along this route.

Traveling between Europe and Asia was difficult. European merchants first had to travel by boat to reach western Asia. Then they traveled by land across the deserts of central Asia. It was a dangerous journey that could take years. If someone could find a new route to Asia, it would save time and money.

QUICK CHECK

Cause and Effect **How did the arrival of silk and spices from Asia help the merchant class to arise?**

▲ Marco Polo became famous for the stories of his travels across Asia and his years living in China.

© NEW TRADE ROUTES

Europe and Asia were not the only important centers of trade in the 1400s. Africa was also an important trading center. Many parts of Africa were rich in natural resouces. Salt from North Africa was bartered for gold from West African kingdoms. At that time, salt was as valuable as gold because it kept meat from spoiling. The wealth of African kingdoms drew traders from western Asia who were Muslims.

African Kingdoms

As more Muslim traders came to West Africa, many West Africans became followers of Islam. Trade links were formed with merchants in Arabia. In the 1350s, the ruler of a kingdom called Mali traveled to the Muslim holy city of Mecca in Arabia. Along the way, the ruler gave away so much gold that the metal lost its value for ten years. Another African kingdom, Songhai, was larger than all of Europe in the 1400s.

African kingdoms fought among themselves in the 1400s. War weakened most kingdoms. Then, the discovery of gold in the Americas ended African control of Europe's gold supply. Europeans began to enslave Africans in the 1500s, and the great kingdoms collapsed.

A School for Sailors

In the 1400s, Portugal was a small country on the Atlantic coast of western Europe. It was far from Asia, but close to Africa. At that time, land routes to Asia were controlled by Portugal's enemies. Prince Henry of Portugal believed that ships could sail south along the western coast of Africa to reach Asia.

European explorers had not followed this route before. Prince Henry was eager to gain a share of Asia's wealth for Portugal. He also believed that trade with African kingdoms would grow if new sea routes were followed.

▲ Chinese compasses

LAPIS POLARIS MAGNES

▲ An important tool in navigation was the astrolabe. It helped sailors measure the height of the sun and the stars above Earth. Sailors used the astrolabe to find their location north or south of the Equator.

▲ Navigators work at Prince Henry's school

Prince Henry invited experts in mapmaking, shipbuilding, and mathematics to his palace. He set up a school where experts worked on problems of **navigation,** finding direction and following routes at sea.

Sailors guessed their latitude north of the Equator by locating the North Star. However, south of the Equator, sailors could no longer see the North Star. The Chinese compass, which pointed north, became an important navigation tool south of the Equator.

Maps were another technology that helped explorers. Mapmaking experts taught Portuguese captains to make maps of the lands they would explore. Later, these maps would be valuable tools because they showed the safest routes to follow along the African coast.

QUICK CHECK

Cause and Effect How did Portugal's location lead the country to explore sea routes to Asia?

Ⓓ VOYAGES AROUND AFRICA

Portuguese shipbuilders also developed a new ship, the caravel. It had both square and triangle-shaped sails. These sails allowed it to change direction and catch the wind more easily than older ships.

By 1460 Prince Henry's caravels had sailed along more than 2,000 miles of the African coastline. In 1488 Bartolomeu Dias became the first European to sail around the southern tip of Africa, known as the Cape of Good Hope. This brought him to the Indian Ocean.

Dias never reached India. Another Portuguese explorer, Vasco da Gama, sailed across the Indian Ocean and landed at Calicut, India, on May 20, 1498.

QUICK CHECK

Cause and Effect How did the invention of the caravel help Portuguese explorers?

Check Understanding

1. **VOCABULARY** Write one sentence that uses at least two of these words.

   profit   barter
   merchant   navigation

2. **READING SKILL Cause and Effect**
   Use your chart from page 52 to write a paragraph explaining how the Crusades helped connect Europe and Asia.

3. **Write About It** Write about how trade may have helped to change European attitudes toward other cultures.

◄ Caravels carried explorers over long distances.

Map and Globe Skills
Use Latitude and Longitude Maps

VOCABULARY

global grid
latitude
longitude
absolute location
relative location
parallel
meridian
Prime Meridian

Some maps divide the Earth into a **global grid**, or set of crisscrossing lines. The two sets of lines are called **latitude** and **longitude**. Lines going from east to west are called latitudes. Lines going from north to south are called longitudes. Latitude and longitude are measured in units called degrees. The symbol for degrees is °. The **absolute location** of a place is where latitude and longitude lines cross.

Another way to determine the location of a place is by using **relative location**. Relative location describes where a place or region is located in relation to another. For example, the relative location of the United States is north of Mexico.

Learn It

- A line of latitude is called a **parallel**. Parallels measure distance north and south of the Equator. The Equator is 0° latitude. Lines of latitude north of the Equator are labeled **N.** Those south of the Equator are labeled **S.**

- A line of longitude is called a **meridian**. Meridians measure distance east and west of the **Prime Meridian**. The Prime Meridian is 0° longitude. Meridians that are east of the Prime Meridian are labeled **E.** Meridians west of the Prime Meridian are labeled **W.**

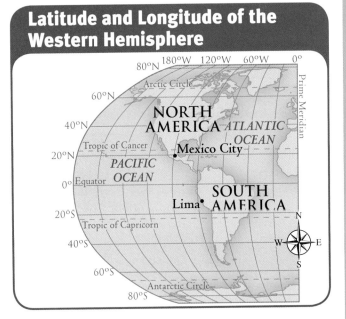

Latitude and Longitude of the Western Hemisphere

Try It

- Locate Mexico City. Which line of latitude is closest to this city?

- Locate Lima in South America. Which line of longitude is closest to this city?

Apply It

- Find the longitude and latitude lines that are closest to your community.

- Which city is closer to your community in longitude, Mexico City or Lima?

VOCABULARY

expedition p. 61

colony p. 63

Columbian Exchange
p. 64

READING SKILL

Cause and Effect
Copy the chart below.
As you read, fill in the
actions of Spanish
explorers and the results.

Cause	→	Effect
	→	
	→	
	→	

**MISSOURI COURSE
LEVEL EXPECTATIONS**

3a.C.1, 3a.F.2, 4.F.1, 5.A.1, 5.C.2,
5.J.1, 6.I.1, 7.B.1

SPANIARDS REACH THE AMERICAS

Columbus lands in
North America.

Visual Preview

How did Spanish explorers change the Americas?

A Queen Isabella
paid for Columbus
to find a new route to
the Indies in 1492.

B Columbus's
voyage led to
trade with the Taíno
people of San Salvador.

C The Columbian
Exchange brought
new goods to Europe
and the Americas.

SAILING WEST TO THE INDIES

European explorers in the 1400s knew the world was large, but they had no idea how large. How could they? Up to this time, they had traveled only to the East.

European explorers were only interested in reaching one place—the Indies. Today we call the region Asia. As you have read, the dream of wealth inspired many explorers to take the risky year-long journey across the Mediterranean Sea, around Africa, and across the Indian Ocean. But one explorer sailed in a different direction. His name was Christopher Columbus.

A New Direction

Oceans were the highways of the 1400s. As a result, countries located on the Atlantic Ocean or the Mediterranean Sea became world powers. Two of these powers, Spain and Portugal, were eager to send **expeditions** to the Indies. An expedition is a journey made for a certain purpose such as exploration.

A skilled sailor from Italy named Christopher Columbus approached the rulers of Portugal and Spain with his idea. He wanted to lead an expedition to the Indies—but he wanted to sail in the

Queen Isabella

"wrong" direction. Columbus believed that sailing west for about 3,000 miles would bring him to the Indies. The trip would be faster than the year-long voyage around Africa, he claimed.

Portugal's king wasn't interested in Columbus's idea. The rulers of France and England had no interest either. Finally, Queen Isabella and King Ferdinand of Spain agreed to pay for ships for Columbus. On August 3, 1492, Columbus left Spain with three ships—the *Niña*, the *Pinta*, and the *Santa María*. Columbus kept two logs, or records, of the voyage. In one log, he recorded the exact distances the ships sailed each day. In the second log, he recorded shorter distances. Some historians believe that Columbus used the second log to mislead other explorers. He wanted to keep his route secret.

QUICK CHECK

Cause and Effect Why did countries located on oceans become world powers?

B REACHING THE AMERICAS

Through August and September of 1492, Columbus's ships sailed across the Atlantic Ocean. Food and water had almost run out when they sighted land on the horizon on October 12.

Today we know that Columbus had reached San Salvador. It is one the Bahama Islands, part of North America. But Columbus believed he had reached the Indies. His crew got a warm welcome from people who paddled out to greet the ships. They carried fresh fruits unlike any the Europeans had ever seen. Columbus called these people "Indios," which is Spanish for "Indians," believing that he had reached his goal. However, the people called themselves the Taíno.

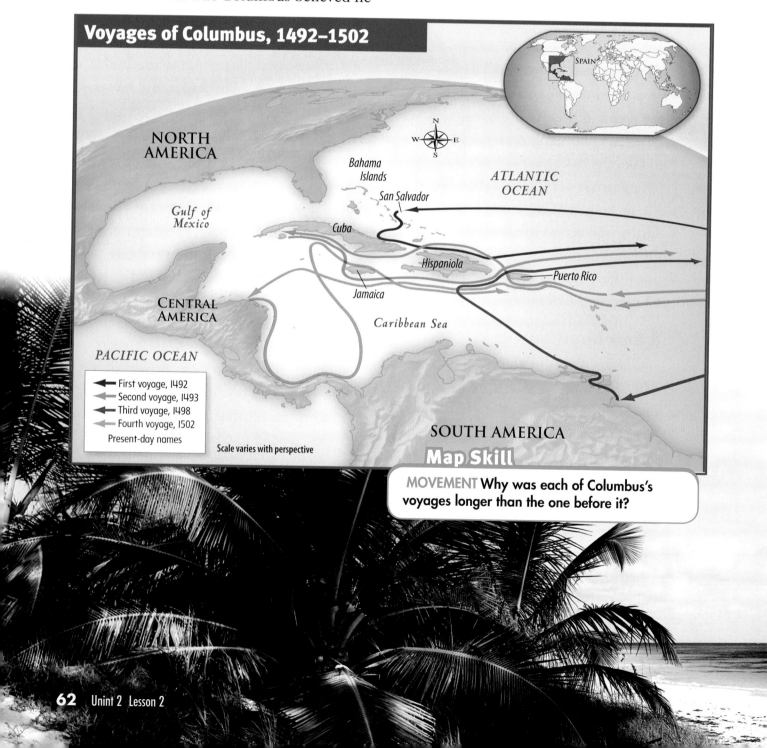

Voyages of Columbus, 1492–1502

SPAIN

NORTH AMERICA

Bahama Islands

San Salvador

ATLANTIC OCEAN

Gulf of Mexico

Cuba

Hispaniola

Puerto Rico

Jamaica

CENTRAL AMERICA

Caribbean Sea

PACIFIC OCEAN

→ First voyage, 1492
→ Second voyage, 1493
→ Third voyage, 1498
→ Fourth voyage, 1502
Present-day names

Scale varies with perspective

SOUTH AMERICA

Map Skill

MOVEMENT **Why was each of Columbus's voyages longer than the one before it?**

The Taíno

The first meeting between the Spaniards and the Taíno was friendly. The Taíno gave food and gifts to the newcomers to show friendship. In return, Columbus gave the Taíno glass beads and brass bells. Columbus described his gifts as:

things of small value, in which they took . . . pleasure and became so much our friends it was a marvel.

—CHRISTOPHER COLUMBUS

They may have been friends at first, but a century later, disease and violence had destroyed the Taíno. They left no written records. Most of what we know about the Taíno comes from artifacts and Spanish journals. We know that the Taíno cut large canoes from tree trunks. These handmade boats could carry more than 30 people. The Taíno used spears to catch fish. They grew cotton, tobacco, maize, yams, and pineapple. The Taíno also contributed several words to English that you probably know, including hammock and hurricane.

A New Colony

Columbus stayed in what he called the Indies for only a few months. He sailed to other islands in the present-day Caribbean Sea, but he did not find the riches he expected. Taking some Taíno with him, he returned to Spain. When he reported on his expedition, King Ferdinand and Queen Isabella asked Columbus to return to the Caribbean to claim more land.

In 1493 Columbus landed on the island of Hispaniola with more than 1,500 people to set up a Spanish **colony**. A colony is a settlement far from the country that rules it. Today two countries—Haiti and the Dominican Republic—are located on the large island. Columbus made four voyages to the Americas and the Caribbean. On his third voyage, he reached the South American mainland for the first time. He died in 1506, still believing he had reached the Indies.

QUICK CHECK

Cause and Effect How did the arrival of the Spanish change the lives of the Taíno people?

EVENT

Columbus believed he had landed in the Indies. An explorer who followed Columbus claimed that the lands were unknown to Europeans. His name was **Amerigo Vespucci**. On a map made in 1507, a German geographer labeled the land "America," in honor of Vespucci.

Amerigo Vespucci

ACROSS THE ATLANTIC OCEAN

The meeting between the Taíno and Columbus led to what is known today as the **Columbian Exchange**. To exchange means to give something in return for something else. The Columbian Exchange was the movement of people, plants, animals, and diseases across the Atlantic Ocean. It worked out well for Europeans. They were introduced to new foods from the Americas, such as tomatoes and corn. These foods improved the diet of Europeans.

The exchange also introduced food and animals to the Americas. Animals from Europe changed life in America. As you have read, horses changed the way the Native Americans hunted. Cattle and pigs became new food sources. Wool from sheep brought changes to the clothing people wore. Unfortunately,

THE COLUMBIAN EXCHANGE

The Columbian Exchange changed life on both sides of the Atlantic Ocean. Study the charts below.

Products Exchanged, 1500s

From the Americas		To the Americas		
Food	Animals	Food	Animals	Tools
Tomatoes	Turkeys	Wheat	Horses	Wheels
Corn	Squirrels	Rice	Sheep	Plows
Potatoes	Muskrats	Bananas	Pigs	
Sweet Potatoes		Onions	Cattle	
Pineapple		Sugar	Goats	
		Coffee		
		Oranges		
		Peaches		
		Melons		

Europeans and their animals brought germs and diseases that were unknown in the Americas. Smallpox, measles, and other diseases from Europe spread quickly. By 1600, millions of native peoples across the Americas had died.

QUICK CHECK

Cause and Effect How did food from North America change the diet of people in Europe?

Check Understanding

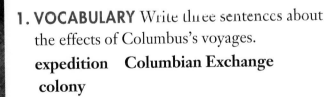

1. **VOCABULARY** Write three sentences about the effects of Columbus's voyages.

    **expedition   Columbian Exchange
     colony**

2. **READING SKILL Cause and Effect** Use your chart from page 60 to write a paragraph about the effects that animals from Europe had on Native Americans after 1492.

Cause	→	Effect
	→	
	→	
	→	

 EXPLORE The Big Idea 3. **Write About It** What changes occurred in Europe after Columbus's voyages?

Spanish Exploration and Conquest

Lesson 3

VOCABULARY

empire p. 67

conquistador p. 67

READING SKILL

Cause and Effect
Copy the chart below. As you read, fill in the actions of the Spanish and the results.

Cause	→	Effect
	→	
	→	
	→	

MISSOURI COURSE LEVEL EXPECTATIONS

3a.C.1, 3a.F.2, 5.A.1, 5.C.2, 5.J.1, 6.I.1, 7.B.1

Tenochtitlán, the Aztec capital, was built on islands in Lake Texcoco. Causeways, or land bridges, led to the mainland.

Visual Preview

How did the arrival of Spanish explorers change Native American empires?

A The Aztec capital fell after attacks by Spaniards and other enemies.

B The Spanish set out to conquer the Inca, the largest empire in South America.

C Spanish soldiers, led by Francisco Pizarro, conquered the Inca Empire.

THE AZTEC EMPIRE

A

If someone asked you to name the greatest city in the world, what city would you name? If you asked Spanish explorers in 1520, chances are good that many of them would have said that Tenochtitlán was the greatest city in the world.

Tenochtitlán was the capital of the Aztec Empire. An **empire** is a large area in which different groups of people are controlled by one ruler or government.

By 1500 more than 200,000 people lived in Tenochtitlán, making it one of the largest cities in the world. The Aztec controlled about 6 million people.

Cortés Lands in Mexcio

In 1519 the Spaniard Hernan Cortés landed in Mexico with more than 500 **conquistadors**. Conquistador is the Spanish word for conqueror. Several enslaved Africans were among his party. Native people had never seen men with black or white skin. They had never heard guns fired. And they had never seen horses. The Spanish struck fear among the Native people.

Cortés reached Tenochtitlán in November 1519. Moctezuma II, the Aztec ruler, welcomed the Spaniards. But Cortés took Moctezuma prisoner and demanded gold for the king's freedom. The Aztec refused and violence broke out. Moctezuma was killed. Cortés and his men were driven away. But the Spaniards left behind a deadly weapon—smallpox.

Months later, smallpox had killed more than 100,000 Aztec. Cortés returned and destroyed Tenochtitlán. The Spanish capital, Mexico City, was built on the ruins of the Aztec capital.

QUICK CHECK

Cause and Effect Why was Cortés able to return to conquer Tenochtitlán after being driven out?

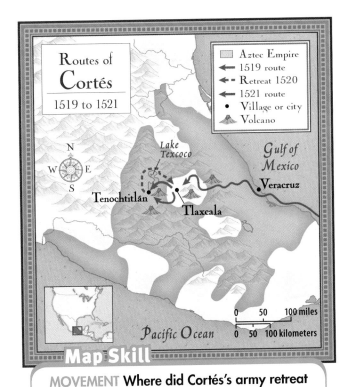

Routes of Cortés 1519 to 1521

Aztec Empire
← 1519 route
←- Retreat 1520
← 1521 route
• Village or city
▲ Volcano

Lake Texcoco

Gulf of Mexico

Veracruz

Tenochtitlán

Tlaxcala

Pacific Ocean

0 50 100 miles
0 50 100 kilometers

Map Skill

MOVEMENT **Where did Cortés's army retreat to in 1521?**

ⓑ THE INCA EMPIRE

After the conquest of the Aztec Empire, the Spanish set out to conquer the land to the south. They did not know that another empire—the wealthiest in the world—ruled much of South America. This was the Inca Empire.

At the height of its power, the Inca Empire extended more than 2,500 miles along the western coast of South America. This is about the distance from New York City to Phoenix, Arizona.

Linked by Highways

Most of the Inca Empire was located in the Andes mountain range. The capital of the empire, Cuzco, in present-day Peru, was built at an altitude of 11,000 feet. A system of paved stone roads leading out from Cuzco formed a highway system that tied the empire together. Today Cuzco is one of the highest cities on Earth.

Information was carried along the roads by messengers who were able to run 50 miles a day. They carried knotted strings, called quipus, to help remember information. The Inca used quipus to keep records. String colors stood for objects to be counted. For example, red strings stood for soldiers, and yellow strings measured maize crops. Quipus were an important tool for communicating information, especially as the empire grew larger.

The Inca Empire

ANDES MOUNTAINS

Amazon River

Cajamarca

Cuzco

SOUTH AMERICA

PACIFIC OCEAN

ANDES MOUNTAINS

ATLANTIC OCEAN

N W E S

| 0 | 300 | 600 miles |
| 0 | 300 | 600 kilometers |

■ Inca Empire
• City

Map Skill

LOCATION **Which city would Spanish explorers most likely enter first? Why?**

Inca Society

Inca society was like European society in some ways. Rulers and religious leaders were the highest class. Instead of paying taxes with money, the Inca provided services, such as repairing roads, digging canals, and building temples for several months each year. Workers received clothing and food for their work. Inca women were required to weave one piece of clothing for the workers each year.

Although the Inca did not use money, gold and silver were important to the society. Gold was called "the sweat of the sun," and silver was called "the tears of the moon." Inca craftworkers made cups, bowls, and plates from these precious metals. These were used mainly by the rulers, nobles, and priests. After the arrival of the Spanish, few of these gold and silver objects remained.

QUICK CHECK

Cause and Effect Why were highways an important part of the Inca Empire's rise to power?

The ruins of Machu Picchu are high in the Andes of Peru.

This painting shows Pizarro, the Spanish conquistador, capturing Atahualpa, the Inca ruler, at the battle of Cajamarca.

Ⓒ THE FALL OF THE INCA

In 1531 Spanish conquistador Francisco Pizarro landed on the west coast of South America with about 180 men and about 30 horses. At the time Pizarro arrived, the Inca Empire was collapsing. The highway system that allowed messengers to travel easily had allowed disease to spread quickly. Smallpox had entered the empire from Mexico several years earlier. Thousands of Inca people had died, including the Inca ruler, Wayna Capac. After his death, a civil war broke out between his sons, Atahualpa and Huascar, for control of the empire.

Atahualpa controlled the northern part of the empire. He had heard reports about Pizarro's arrival, but he was not worried. Pizarro had only 180 men. The war with Huascar was a more serious problem.

Pizarro reached the Inca town of Cajamarca in 1532. His soldiers knew they were greatly outnumbered by the Inca. One Spanish soldier wrote:

> **"**All were full of fear, for we were so few, and so deep into the land, with no hope of rescue.**"**

Pizarro and Atahualpa

Atahualpa heard reports of Pizarro's arrival. However, Atahualpa didn't send troops against the Spanish. They remained camped outside the city. Atahualpa sent a message to Pizarro, inviting him to meet in the city. Pizarro entered Cajamarca and hid his men around the main square. After the Inca entered the square, Pizarro gave a signal. Guns exploded from doorways and windows. Spaniards on horseback rode into the square, swinging steel swords. Thousands of Atahualpa's men were killed. Pizarro himself took the Inca ruler prisoner.

To earn his freedom, Atahualpa offered to fill a huge room with gold and silver. For months, gold and silver objects arrived from all corners of the empire. But Pizarro was dishonest and refused to release the Inca ruler. When the room was filled, he killed Atahualpa. Then he melted down the precious metal objects into bars of gold and silver to send back to Spain. That's why so few objects remain from the glory days of the Inca Empire—Pizarro turned them into money. By 1540 Spain controlled one of the largest empires in the world.

▶ The bird and the pipe-playing figure are Inca artifacts. Spaniards melted down most Inca artifacts.

QUICK CHECK

Cause and Effect How was the Inca Empire weakened before Pizarro arrived?

Check Understanding

1. **VOCABULARY** Write one sentence to show a relationship between the two words below.

   empire   **conquistador**

2. **READING SKILL Cause and Effect** Use your chart from page 66 to show how the Spanish desire for gold destroyed the Aztec and Inca empires.

Cause	→	Effect
	→	
	→	
	→	

3. **EXPLORE The Big Idea Write About It** How did Spanish exploration change Central and South America?

71

VOCABULARY

frontier p. 73

missionary p. 75

enslave p. 75

mestizo p. 76

READING SKILL

Cause and Effect

Copy the chart. As you read, fill it in with causes and effects of Spanish exploration of North America.

Cause	→	Effect
	→	
	→	
	→	

MISSOURI COURSE LEVEL EXPECTATIONS

3a.C.1, 3a.F.2, 4.F.1, 5.A.1, 5.C.2, 5.J.1, 6.I.1, 7.A.1, 7.B.1

SPAIN'S OVERSEAS EMPIRE

De Soto explored the Southeast.

Visual Preview

How did Spain's growing empire impact life in North America?

A In the early 1500s, Spaniards explored Florida in search of Gold.

B In the 1500s, Spaniards explored the Southwest and expanded colonies.

C Spaniards, Native Americans, and Africans lived in the Spanish colonies.

A SPANISH IN NORTH AMERICA

Weighed down by guns and armor, hundreds of men came ashore in blazing heat. In search of gold and adventure, the conquistadors paved the way for Spanish settlers.

For the Spanish, North America was a **frontier** in the 1500s. A frontier is the far edge of a settled area. Modern-day Florida was one early frontier for the Spaniards.

"Place of Flowers"

In 1513 Juan Ponce de León led an expedition in search of a Fountain of Youth that was said to be on an island north of Cuba. He landed near what is today St. Augustine, Florida. He named the land *La Florida*—"place of flowers."

Search for Gold

In 1539 Hernando de Soto landed in Florida with hundreds of men and animals. He explored the present-day southeastern United States. He never found gold. Instead, diseases carried by his men and animals killed thousands of Native Americans.

QUICK CHECK

Cause and Effect How did false stories bring Spanish explorers to Florida?

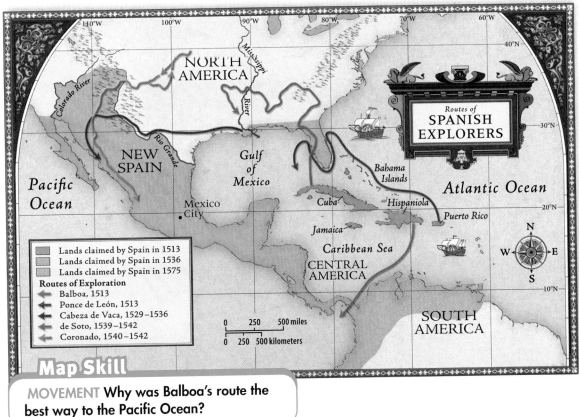

Routes of
SPANISH
EXPLORERS

Lands claimed by Spain in 1513
Lands claimed by Spain in 1536
Lands claimed by Spain in 1575
Routes of Exploration
Balboa, 1513
Ponce de León, 1513
Cabeza de Vaca, 1529–1536
de Soto, 1539–1542
Coronado, 1540–1542

0   250   500 miles
0   250   500 kilometers

Map Skill

MOVEMENT **Why was Balboa's route the best way to the Pacific Ocean?**

▼ Coronado explored the Southwest.

ⓑ NEW SPAIN EXPANDS

Spanish conquistadors continued to explore the frontier in other parts of North America. With each expedition, disease carried by the men and their animals spread quickly among Native Americans.

Explorers in the Southwest

In 1528 Spanish conquistador Álvar Núñez Cabeza de Vaca sailed north from Cuba. A hurricane wrecked his ship on the coast of present-day Texas. Cabeza de Vaca and his men lived in a Native American village for four years. In 1536 they arrived in Mexico City after walking through present-day Texas, New Mexico, and Arizona.

In 1540 Francisco Vásquez de Coronado led an expedition of Spaniards, Africans, and Native Americans across what is now the southwestern United States. He claimed large areas of land for Spain. Coronado and his men were the first Europeans to see the Grand Canyon, located in present-day Arizona.

Colonists Arrive

By 1550 Spain controlled two large territories in the Americas. In South America, the Spanish called the territory Peru. The territory that included Mexico and most of Central America was called New Spain.

As growing numbers of Spaniards settled in New Spain, Spanish rulers took tighter control of the new colony. Rulers gave encomiendas, or large areas of land, to colonists who were loyal to them. The land included many Native American villages. Native Americans were forced to work for the Spanish landowners. On the encomiendas, many Native Americans died from starvation, disease, and overwork.

Primary Sources

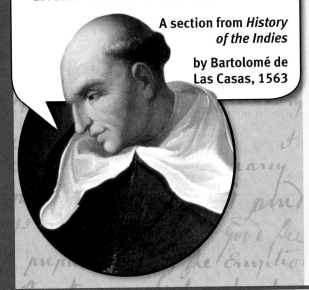

Not only have [Native Americans] shown themselves to be very wise peoples . . . providing for their nations . . . and making them prosper in justice, they have equaled many diverse nations of the world . . .

A section from *History of the Indies*

by Bartolomé de Las Casas, 1563

Write About It Write a letter to de Las Casas explaining what effect his words have on your feelings about Native Americans.

Some colonists spoke out against the treatment of Native Americans. One was Bartolomé de Las Casas. De Las Casas was a **missionary**—a person who tries to persuade people to accept new religious beliefs. De Las Casas's opinions about the Native Americans were different from the opinions of many Spaniards. Read his opinion above.

Africans in New Spain

Spanish explorers brought the first **enslaved** Africans to Mexico. To enslave people is to force them to work against their will. Enslaved Africans were not brought to New Spain in large numbers until many thousands of Native Americans had died. As more encomiendas were settled, more workers were needed.

By 1550, more than 5,000 enslaved Africans were working in the fields of encomiendas in New Spain. Enslaved Africans also worked in the silver mines of New Spain. At the ports of Veracruz and Acapulco, enslaved Africans often loaded silver and other precious metals onto ships bound for Spain.

In the 1570s, some enslaved Africans and Native Americans rebelled. Some rebels were defeated, but others escaped to areas far from the encomiendas where they could be free. After escaping, enslaved Africans and Native Americans built their own communities. These settlements came to be called maroon communities. One leader of a rebellion was an African named Yanga, who had been a king in his homeland. In 1570 Yanga and his followers escaped to the mountains around Veracruz. They built a town called San Lorenzo de los Negros.

▼ A statue of Yanga

QUICK CHECK

Cause and Effect Why did the growth of encomiendas bring enslaved Africans to Mexico?

ⓒ SOCIETY IN NEW SPAIN

New Spain Social Pyramid

Viceroy

Peninsulares

Criollos

Mestizos

Native Americans and Enslaved Africans

Chart Skill

Which groups were at the bottom of the pyramid?

By the middle of the 1500s, three different groups of people—Native Americans, Spanish, and Africans—had created a new society. Its leader was New Spain's ruler, the viceroy. Below him were Spaniards from Spain, called Peninsulares. Below them were people born in New Spain of Spanish parents, called Criollos. Below this group were **mestizos**, people who were both Spanish and Native American. At the bottom of the pyramid were Native Americans and enslaved Africans, forced to work without wages.

From 1600 to 1680, the Spanish built over 20 settlements in New Mexico. These settlements became important centers for missions, where priests tried to convert Native Americans, and for mining natural resources.

In the 1680s the Spanish built settlements in the part of New Spain that is now the state of Texas. They also built settlements along the coast of the Pacific Ocean. By 1800 the Spanish controlled much of what is now Texas, New Mexico, Arizona, and California.

QUICK CHECK

Compare and Contrast How were mestizos different from Spaniards?

Check Understanding

1. **VOCABULARY** Write a short play about the meeting of the two people in the list below. Use the other vocabulary words in the play.

   frontier   enslave
   missionary   mestizo

2. **READING SKILL Cause and Effect** Use the cause and effect chart on page 72 to help you write a paragraph about the change that occurred after the Spanish explored North America.

Cause	→	Effect
	→	
	→	
	→	

3. **Write About It** What do you think happened when the Native Americans and Spanish settlers met for the first time?

Chart and Graph Skills

Compare Line and Circle Graphs

VOCABULARY

line graph
circle graph

When European explorers arrived in the Americas, both Native American and European cultures experienced change. One way you can measure changes is to use **line graphs** and **circle graphs**. A line graph shows a change over time. A circle graph shows how something can be divided into parts. All of the parts together make up a circle. Circle graphs are also called pie graphs because the parts look like slices of pie.

Learn It

- To find out what information a graph contains, look at its title.

- Study the labels on a graph. Labels on a line graph appear along the bottom of the graph and along the left side. Labels on a circle graph explain the subject.

Try It

- Look at the line graph. What was the Taíno population of Hispaniola in 1570?

- Look at the circle graph. Which group made up the largest part of the population of Hispaniola in 1570?

Apply It

- Summarize the line graph's information about the Taíno people on Hispaniola.

- Summarize the circle graph's information about the people of Hispaniola in 1570.

- Summarize what both graphs tell you about the meeting of different cultures.

Taíno Population of Hispaniola, 1496-1570

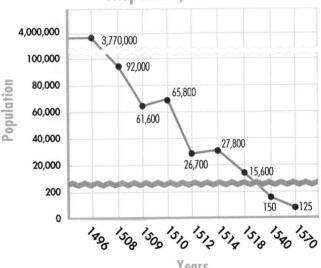

Population of Hispaniola, 1570

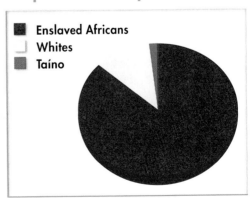

■ Enslaved Africans
□ Whites
■ Taíno

Lesson 5

VOCABULARY

Northwest Passage
p. 79

merchant company
p. 80

READING SKILL

Cause and Effect
Copy the cause and effect chart below. As you read, list the causes and effects of the search for the Northwest Passage.

Cause	→	Effect
	→	
	→	
	→	

MISSOURI COURSE LEVEL EXPECTATIONS

3a.C.1, 3a.F.2, 4.F.1, 5.A.1, 5.C.2, 5.J.1, 6.I.1, 7.B.1

SEARCHING FOR THE NORTHWEST PASSAGE

Dutch ships such as these brought explorers to the Americas and Asia.

Visual Preview

How did the search for the Northwest Passage affect people?

A Europeans learned about North America while exploring the east coast.

B Henry Hudson explored the Hudson River and traded with the Lenni Lenape.

A EUROPEANS SAIL WEST

Trade with Asia brought huge profits for European countries that were trading silk, spices, and other goods. Sailing east around Africa, however, took months. Was there a quicker way to reach Asia?

In the 1490s and 1500s, many Europeans believed there was a water route across North America. They believed this route connected the Atlantic to the Pacific Ocean. This shortcut, which no one was sure existed, was called the **Northwest Passage**.

Explorations in North America

You have read how ships had to sail around Africa to reach Asia. European rulers thought that finding a Northwest Passage would help them reach Asia in much less time than the African route. In 1497 the king of England hired an Italian, John Cabot, to find this shorter route to Asia. Cabot sailed west and sighted land at Newfoundland, an island off the coast of Canada.

Cabot did not find a Northwest Passage, but he came upon something valuable. He found an area of the Atlantic Ocean southeast of Newfoundland. These waters were so crowded with fish that sailors scooped them into baskets dropped over the sides of their ships. Soon, some colonists would make a lot of money shipping dried fish to Europe.

In 1524 France hired an Italian explorer named Giovanni da Verrazano to continue the search for a Northwest Passage. Verrazano explored the east coast of North America. He reached the New York Harbor and the mouth of what would later be called the Hudson River. Even though he didn't find the Northwest Passage, Verrazano discovered one of the most important rivers in North America.

QUICK CHECK

Cause and Effect What effect did Cabot's voyage have on Europeans?

Giovanni da Verrazano ▶

THE SEARCH GOES ON

All of Europe was abuzz with talk of a Northwest Passage. Merchants realized that if the Northwest Passage were found, they could make huge profits. Dutch merchants began to lead the way.

A New Kind of Company

In 1602 Dutch merchants founded the first **merchant company**. This company was a group of business people who shared the costs of a trading voyage. They would also share the profits from the spices brought back from Asia. The question was, would they see a profit? It was a huge risk.

One merchant company that was willing to take the risk was the Dutch East India Company. In 1609 it hired an English sea captain, Henry Hudson, to find a shortcut to Asia. Hudson believed that North America was only about 70 miles wide. He also believed that the Northwest Passage was located north of Virginia. He sailed along the Atlantic coast of North America. In August Hudson explored Chesapeake and Delaware Bays. Neither of these waterways was the Northwest Passage.

▲ Henry Hudson

When Hudson reached New York Harbor, he mapped it and traded with the local Native Americans, the Lenni Lenape. But the relationship between the Dutch and the Lenni Lenape was not always peaceful. Hudson's crew wrote of battles.

Hudson sailed about 150 miles north on the river that flowed into the harbor, thinking he had found the Northwest Passage. He soon discovered that it contained freshwater. Hudson's reports of rich soil and resources would encourage the Dutch to start a colony there.

Exploring Hudson Bay

On Hudson's second voyage in 1610, he explored what is now Hudson Bay while searching for the Northwest Passage. As winter set in, his ship, the *Discovery*, froze in the ice. When spring came, Hudson tried to continue his voyage. By this time, his crew was tired of the harsh conditions aboard ship. They had been living on moldy bread and rotten meat. The threat of mutiny, or naval revolt, filled the air. The crew did not kill Hudson, but they

The Hudson River ▼

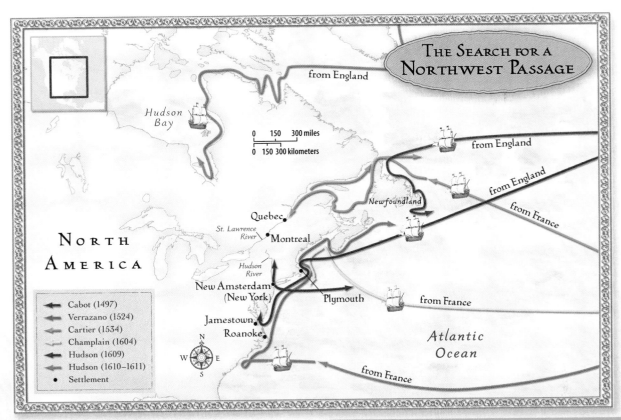

THE SEARCH FOR A
NORTHWEST PASSAGE

from England

Hudson Bay

0   150   300 miles
0   150 300 kilometers

NORTH
AMERICA

from England

from England

from France

Newfoundland

Quebec

St. Lawrence River

Montreal

Hudson River

New Amsterdam (New York)

Plymouth

from France

Jamestown

Roanoke

Atlantic Ocean

Cabot (1497)
Verrazano (1524)
Cartier (1534)
Champlain (1604)
Hudson (1609)
Hudson (1610–1611)
• Settlement

from France

N
W   E
S

Map Skill

MOVEMENT **About how many miles of coastline did Verrazano explore?**

did take over the ship. Hudson, his son, and eight loyal sailors were placed into a small boat. They were never seen again. When the *Discovery* reached England, its crew was arrested.

QUICK CHECK

Cause and Effect **What was the result of Hudson's search for the Northwest Passage?**

Check Understanding

1. **VOCABULARY** Write one sentence using both of these vocabulary terms.

   Northwest Passage
   merchant company

2. **READING SKILL Cause and Effect** Use your cause and effect chart from page 78 to write about the Northwest Passage.

Cause	→	Effect
	→	
	→	
	→	

3. **Write About It** Why do you think there were battles between Native Americans and Hudson's crew?

THE FIRST FRENCH COLONIES

Lesson 6

VOCABULARY

ally p. 83

coureurs de bois p. 84

import p. 84

export p. 84

voyageur p. 84

READING SKILL

Cause and Effect
Copy the chart below. As you read, list the causes and effects of the fur trade in New France.

Cause	→	Effect
	→	
	→	
	→	

MISSOURI COURSE LEVEL EXPECTATIONS

3a.C.1, 3a.F.2, 4.F.1, 5.A.1, 5.C.2, 5.J.1, 6.I.1, 7.B.1

Jacques Cartier on Mount Royal (Montreal)

Visual Preview

How did France's relationship with Native Americans affect colonization?

A The French traded fur with Native Americans living around French settlements.

B New France attracted fur hunters, missionaries, and explorers.

Ⓐ THE FIRST FRENCH SETTLEMENT

Even though Verazzano failed to find the Northwest Passage, France continued to look for the route. In 1534 Jacques Cartier reached a peninsula near the St. Lawrence River and claimed it for France.

After three voyages in which he failed to find the Northwest Passage, Cartier returned to France disappointed. Except for a few French companies that traded with Native Americans for furs, France paid little attention to the colony for nearly 60 years.

Founding of Quebec

Starting in 1598, France tried to establish a permanent settlement called New France. It hoped that the settlement would expand the fur trade and make money for France. These attempts failed. Then, in 1608, King Henry IV sent Samuel de Champlain to New France as its governor. Champlain established a fur trading post at Quebec.

Fur coats and hats were very popular in Europe at the time. Champlain knew that if he managed the colony well, he could make a lot of money in the fur trade. In order to strengthen the colony, he established friendly relations with several Native American groups. Soon the French, Wyandot, and Algonquin became **allies**, or political and military partners. With French firearms, these Native American groups easily defeated their longtime enemy, the Iroquois.

QUICK CHECK

Cause and Effect **Why did France want to establish a permanent settlement in New France?**

▲ Samuel de Champlain's arrival at Quebec

NEW FRANCE EXPANDS

Many young French men were eager to make money from the fur trade. They became hunters and trappers called **coureurs de bois**, or "runners of the woods." So many hunters came to New France that Europe's **imports** of furs soared. Import means to bring in goods from another country for sale or use. **Export** means to send goods to another country. French officials feared the fur imports would oversupply the market and bring the price of fur down. To control the price of fur, the French government issued permits to trappers, hoping to limit their number. Those who received permits were called **voyageurs**.

New France's Slow Growth

In the early 1600s, King Louis XIII began to expand New France. He allowed more people to settle there, but few French colonists came. One reason was that the king preferred Roman Catholics to settle the colony. French people who were not Catholic were more likely to settle in the English colonies of North America. In 1666 only 3,215 colonists lived in New France.

Louis XIII also sent Catholic missionaries to Canada. French missionaries often lived among the Native Americans as they tried to convert them. Missionaries built churches at trading centers.

The Search for a Passage Continues

Meanwhile, the French continued to search for the Northwest Passage. When Champlain returned to New France in 1610, he brought along seventeen-year-old Étienne Brûlé. The young man was eager to explore. Years earlier Champlain had searched for the Northwest Passage. This time he sent Brûlé to look for it.

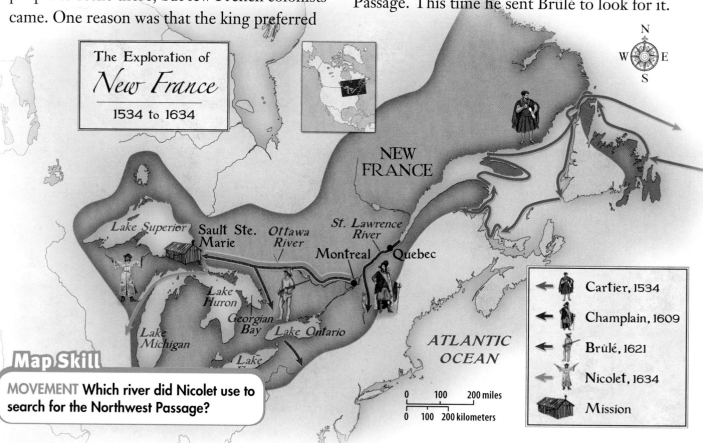

The Exploration of *New France* 1534 to 1634

NEW FRANCE

Lake Superior   Sault Ste. Marie   Ottawa River   St. Lawrence River   Montreal   Quebec

Lake Huron   Georgian Bay   Lake Ontario

Lake Michigan   Lake

ATLANTIC OCEAN

Cartier, 1534
Champlain, 1609
Brûlé, 1621
Nicolet, 1634
Mission

0   100   200 miles
0   100   200 kilometers

Map Skill

MOVEMENT **Which river did Nicolet use to search for the Northwest Passage?**

Samuel de Champlain sailing up
the St. Lawrence River in 1603

Young Brûlé was the first French explorer to see Lake Huron. He explored the western edge of Lake Huron, then turned back. During his search for the Northwest Passage, Brûlé also explored parts of Lake Ontario, Lake Erie, and Lake Superior. By the end of his career, he had explored four of the Great Lakes.

In 1617 another explorer, Jean Nicolet, continued the search for the Northwest Passage. Nicolet followed the route that Étienne Brûlé took to Lake Huron. Then he pushed on and went further than Brûlé. He became the first European to see Lake Michigan. Both Brûlé and Nicolet lived amongst Native American groups and explored the Great Lakes region.

QUICK CHECK

Cause and Effect **Why did New France fail to grow?**

Check Understanding

1. **VOCABULARY** Write about fur trappers using these vocabulary terms.

   coureurs de bois   **voyageurs**

2. **READING SKILL Cause and Effect** Use your cause and effect chart from page 82 to write about the fur trade in New France.

Cause	→	Effect
	→	
	→	
	→	

3. **Write About It** Write about why the Wyandot, Algonquin, and French became allies.

The First English Colonies

VOCABULARY

charter p. 87

cash crop p. 88

indentured servant p. 89

House of Burgesses p. 89

Pilgrim p. 90

sachem p. 92

READING SKILL

Cause and Effect

Copy the chart below. As you read, list the causes and effects of the Pilgrims settling in Plymouth.

Cause	→	Effect
	→	
	→	
	→	

MISSOURI COURSE LEVEL EXPECTATIONS

3a.C.1, 3a.F.2, 4.F.1, 5.A.1, 5.C.2, 5.J.1, 6.I.1, 7.B.1

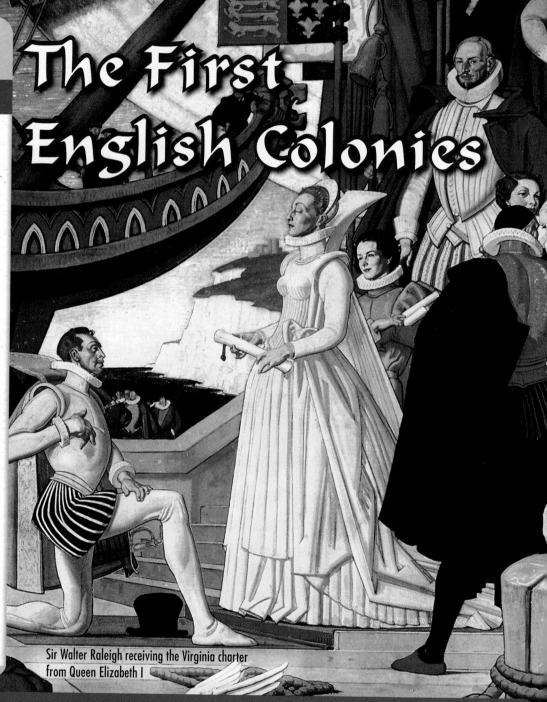

Sir Walter Raleigh receiving the Virginia charter from Queen Elizabeth I

Visual Preview

What challenges did English settlers face?

A Both attempts to settle Roanoke Island were failures.

B Colonists at Jamestown had trouble making a profit until they grew tobacco.

C Pilgrims created a plan of self-government called the Mayflower Compact.

D The Pilgrims had trouble growing food, but were helped by the Wampanoag.

A THE LOST COLONY

While Spain was getting rich from its colonies in the Americas, England's Queen Elizabeth I and her adviser, Sir Walter Raleigh, came up with a plan to make England a power in the Americas.

In 1585 Queen Elizabeth gave Sir Walter Raleigh a **charter**. A charter is an official document that grants its holder special rights. The charter said that Raleigh was supposed to start a colony for the purpose of finding gold and other riches in North America. Raleigh called the new colony Virginia. Virginia was named in honor of Queen Elizabeth I, the Virgin, or unmarried, Queen.

Raleigh's First Try

After sending explorers to find a good place for a colony, Sir Walter Raleigh decided upon what is now Roanoke, North Carolina. About 100 men were sent to Roanoke Island. Many of the colonists had little experience living off the land. They did not know what supplies they would need. Instead of planting crops, the colonists traded with several Native American groups for food. When Native American groups were not interested in the trade, some colonists stole food. As a result, fighting broke out. Meanwhile, the colonists did not find gold. After a difficult winter, the colonists returned to England.

Raleigh Tries Again

In 1587 John White and a second group of colonists settled in Virginia. Supplies ran low and White returned to England for help. He arrived just as war between England and Spain broke out, and England needed all its ships. White did not return until 1590. When he arrived, the colony was empty. No one knows what happened to the colonists.

QUICK CHECK

Cause and Effect Why were the Roanoke settlements failures?

A reconstruction of the ship that brought colonists to Roanoke Island ▶

Captain John Smith

▲ Today you can visit a model of colonial Jamestown to see how the settlers lived.

Ⓑ THE JAMESTOWN COLONY

The English decided to continue searching for gold in North America. King James I gave a charter to a merchant company called the Virginia Company. In 1607 the Virginia Company sent a group of 144 men and boys to start a new settlement. The colonists landed near a river that they named the James River. They built a new settlement there called Jamestown. It was the first permanent English settlement in North America.

Captain John Smith

Like the Roanoke colony, the Jamestown colony soon ran out of food. It survived only because of the leadership of John Smith, who proclaimed, "Those who don't work, don't eat!" Smith forced the colonists to plant crops and build homes. In 1609 Smith was injured when his gunpowder bag exploded, and he returned to England. Without him, the colonists stopped working. The winter after Smith left was called "the starving time." By the end of the winter, only 60 of the settlers were alive.

A New Crop

The Jamestown colonists discovered that Virginia had the perfect soil and climate for growing tobacco. Tobacco had been recently introduced into Europe, and the demand for it was growing.

Colonist John Rolfe harvested the first tobacco crop, which was a huge success. Tobacco became Virginia's first **cash crop**, or crop grown to be sold for profit. Soon the demand for tobacco was so great that new fields were needed. The colonists decided to take land that belonged to the Powhatan, a group of nearby Native Americans.

Growing tobacco required many field workers. To attract workers, the Virginia Company paid travel expenses from Europe for people who would work in tobacco fields. These **indentured servants** promised to pay back the travel expenses by working five to seven years. After their time of service, they received land and supplies to start farms.

Jamestown's First Government

People in England had been electing their governments for a long time. The Virginia Company, therefore, allowed colonists to establish a colonial assembly similar to the one in England. The representatives were known as burgesses. The assembly, called the **House of Burgesses**, made laws for the colony. Only white men who owned land could vote for representatives. The House of Burgesses first met July 30, 1619, making it the first elected assembly of Europeans in the Americas.

The Powhatan Fight Back

As Jamestown grew, the colonists took more and more land. This threatened the Powhatan way of life. In 1622 the Powhatan attacked English villages. Nearly 350 English settlers, about one-third of the colonists, were killed. These attacks convinced King James I to cancel the Virginia Company charter. In 1624 the colony became a royal colony under the direct control of the king.

QUICK CHECK

Cause and Effect Why was Jamestown a successful colony?

PEOPLE

The Powhatan were a strong and united group. **Pocahontas**, the daughter of the Powhatan chief, often visited Jamestown. In 1614 John Rolfe married Pocahontas. Their marriage helped keep peace between the Powhatan and the colonists. The "Peace of Pocahontas" lasted for several years.

Pocahontas

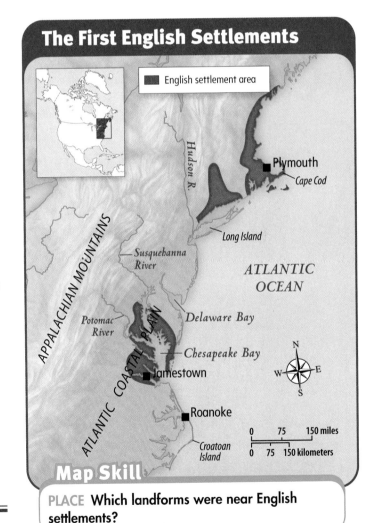

The First English Settlements

English settlement area

Hudson R.

Plymouth
Cape Cod

Long Island

APPALACHIAN MOUNTAINS

Susquehanna River

ATLANTIC OCEAN

Potomac River

ATLANTIC COASTAL PLAIN

Delaware Bay

Chesapeake Bay

Jamestown

Roanoke

Croatoan Island

0   75   150 miles
0   75   150 kilometers

Map Skill

PLACE **Which landforms were near English settlements?**

ⓒ THE PILGRIMS

By 1534 King Henry VIII had left the Roman Catholic Church and established the Church of England. In the early 1600s, some groups in England wanted to leave the Church of England. People called Separatists wanted to separate and form their own churches. This type of action was not allowed in England.

Many Separatists were threatened by the English government and tossed into jails. This led one group of Separatists, known as **Pilgrims**, to ask permission to settle in Virginia. A pilgrim is someone who travels to a place for religious reasons. The Virginia Company agreed to pay for the voyage.

The Mayflower

On September 16, 1620, the Pilgrims and other colonists boarded the *Mayflower* at Plymouth, England, and set sail for Virginia. On board were more than 100 men, women, and children. For 66 days the tiny, crowded ship crossed the Atlantic Ocean. Finally, in November someone spotted land.

The *Mayflower* had reached land, but not Virginia. The Pilgrims came ashore on Cape Cod in what is now Massachusetts. By the time they landed, it was almost winter. They decided to settle the area near where they landed. The Pilgrims called their settlement New Plymouth, which is today Plymouth, Massachusetts.

A Step Toward Self-Government

The Pilgrims took steps to establish a new colony in this place not yet claimed by England. Before they left the ship, the Pilgrims wrote a form of government for their new colony. They called their agreement the Mayflower Compact. The compact, or agreement, was an early plan of self-government by colonists in North America. Only men signed the compact.

◄ The *Mayflower* often sailed in rough seas as it crossed the Atlantic Ocean.

Life in Plymouth

The Pilgrims had a difficult time almost from the beginning. By the time they landed, it was cold, making it more difficult to build a colony. The Pilgrims did manage to build some small shelters, but many avoided the frigid cold by huddling together on the *Mayflower*.

Some of the Plymouth colonists were from cities such as London, and had never farmed. In addition, the Pilgrims were not prepared for harsh Massachusetts winters. By the end of the first winter, almost half of the 100 settlers had died from starvation and disease. If it had not been for the help of nearby Native Americans, all of the settlers might have died.

QUICK CHECK

Cause and Effect Why did many Pilgrims die during the first winter?

Cooperation and Compromise

People cooperate when they work together to make rules or laws or to solve a problem. People compromise when they give up part of something they want. By getting along and working together, everyone contributes to a solution.

Write About It Write a paragraph about a time you gave up something you wanted in order to solve a problem or settle a disagreement.

◀ These reenactors show Pilgrim life after the first difficult year.

D

Remember all those people searching for the Northwest Passage? By the time the Pilgrims arrived, disease carried by Europeans had killed many of the Native Americans in the region. One of the largest groups, the Wampanoag, had lived for centuries along the coast where the Pilgrims landed. The Massachuset, Narragansett, Pequot, and Mohegan groups also lived in the area.

Helping the Pilgrims

Massasoit was the Wampanoag **sachem**. A sachem, or leader, was the head of each group of Native Americans. One person living among the Wampanoag was a member of the Pawtuxet named Squanto. In 1615 he had been captured by English sailors and eventually learned to speak English. A sachem called Samoset learned to speak English from fishermen who visited the area. These three Native Americans helped the Pilgrims survive their first years in the region we call New England.

The Pilgrims had settled on land that was once the home of the Pawtuxet. Disease had wiped out the Pawtuxet years earlier. Squanto decided to live among the Pilgrims and farm

his Pawtuxet land. He showed the Pilgrims how to grow maize, using fish to fertilize the soil. He taught the newcomers how to trap rabbits, deer, and other wild animals. He also showed them where to fish.

Thanksgiving

By the fall of 1621, the Pilgrims had built seven houses in the Plymouth colony. With the help of Squanto, they learned to grow maize and barley. The Pilgrims celebrated their first harvest with three days of feasting. Massasoit and 90 Wampanoag came to the feast, bringing five deer. The Pilgrims added wild goose and duck.

During this time many Native American and European groups held harvest festivals to give thanks for the growth of their crops. The Spanish, French, and English colonists held thanksgiving services in America before the Pilgrims' celebration in 1621. The feast shared by the Pilgrims and Wampanoag would later be called our country's first "thanksgiving." Just as then, we still gather with friends, give thanks, and eat!

QUICK CHECK

Cause and Effect Why did the Pilgrims hold a thanksgiving feast?

▼ This recreation of Thanksgiving brought together descendants of Pilgrims and Native Americans who took part in the first Plymouth Thanksgiving.

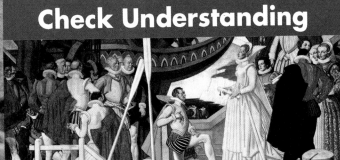

Check Understanding

1. **VOCABULARY** Write a synonym for each vocabulary word.

   charter   **sachem**   **pilgrim**

2. **READING SKILL Cause and Effect** Use your cause and effect chart from page 86 to write about the Pilgrims settling in Plymouth.

Cause	→	Effect
	→	
	→	
	→	

3. **Write About It** Write about how life changed for the Pilgrims after they met Native Americans.

Vocabulary

Number a paper from 1 to 4. Beside each number write the word from the list below that matches the description.

navigation	empire
frontier	cash crop

1. Plants grown to be sold for profit
2. A large area in which different groups of people are controlled by one ruler or government
3. The far edge of a settled area
4. Finding direction and following routes at sea

Comprehension and Critical Thinking

5. Why were Europeans willing to pay a lot for products from Asia?
6. Why did the Pilgrims seek permission to leave England?
7. Why did Columbus return to Spain in 1493 with Taíno people?
8. **Reading Skill** How did de Soto's expedition hurt Native Americans?
9. **Critical Thinking** Why was the Northwest Passage important?
10. **Critical Thinking** How was the society of New Spain different from the society in Jamestown?

Skill

Understand Latitude and Longitude

Write a complete sentence to answer each question.

11. What are the coordinates on the map for Mexico City?
12. Santa Fe is about how many degrees north of Mexico City?

Southwest United States and Mexico: Latitude and Longitude

⊛ National capital
★ State capital

40°N

Santa Fe ★
AZ NM
★ Phoenix

OK
★ Oklahoma City

TX
Austin ★

30°N

PACIFIC OCEAN

115°W

Gulf of California

20°N

MEXICO

N
W   E
S

Gulf of Mexico

Mexico City ⊛

0   250   500 miles
0   250   500 kilometers

105°W   95°W

MAP Test Preparation

Directions Read the letter written by Don Miguel Costansó from the Port of San Diego on June 28, 1769. Then answer Numbers 1 through 3.

Having recently arrived . . . many are the things to be attended to at one time: the care of our own defenses occupied . . . everyone; the rations and attendance of the sick occupies others; also the firewood and water. . . . In the new quarters we also built [a] pole stockade for our security and put up some large sheds in order to cover the provisions and equipment. . . . [I]n time of drought as now, the water of the wells which were dug by the men . . . is very salty and only in an urgent case of necessity is one able to drink it and then with danger to his health.

1 **Where was Don Miguel Costansó when he wrote this letter?**

○ San Francisco

○ San Diego

○ Portland

○ at sea

2 **Which of the following is the best description of life at the Port of San Diego?**

○ People hardly ever worked.

○ There was a large supply of food and water.

○ People worked very hard.

○ Everyone was constantly sick.

3 **What seems to be the most dangerous condition in the Port of San Diego?**

Write your answer on a separate piece of paper.

The Big Idea Activities

What happens when people from different cultures first meet?

Write About the Big Idea

FOLDABLES™
Study Organizer

Descriptive Journal Entry
Use the Unit 2 foldable to help you write a journal entry that answers the Big Idea question, "What happens when different cultures first meet?" Use the notes you wrote under each tab in the foldable. Decide whether to write your entry from "Before," "During" or "After" the cultures meet. Decide which cultures meet and when the meeting takes place. Describe the setting in your journal entry.

When different cultures meet

Before | During | After

Make a Photo Collage

Work individually to make a photo collage of the Columbian Exchange.

1. Study the examples on page 65 of food and animals that made up the Columbian Exchange.

2. Choose one example and use magazines, newspapers, or the Internet to find photos of that food or animal.

3. Make a photo collage of the ways that food or animals are used today.

When you finish your collage, present it to your class. Discuss what you have learned about the food or animal you chose.

Chocolate Today

Colonial America

EXPLORE The Big Idea

Essential Question
Why do people settle new areas?

FOLDABLES Study Organizer

Make Generalizations
Make and label a Concept Map Foldable book before you read this unit. Across the top tab write **Why People Settle New Areas.** Label the three tabs **New England Colonies, Middle Colonies,** and **Southern Colonies.** Use the Foldable to organize information as you read.

Why People Settle New Areas

| New England Colonies | Middle Colonies | Southern Colonies |

LOG ON For more about Unit 3 go to www.macmillanmh.com

English settlers came to America in search of a better life and new opportunities.

PEOPLE, PLACES, AND EVENTS

Anne Hutchinson

Metacomet

Portsmouth, Rhode Island

1638
Anne Hutchinson establishes a settlement in Rhode Island.

New England

1675
King Philip's War takes place in New England.

1625   1650   1675   1700

In 1638 **Anne Hutchinson** and her followers founded the religious settlement of **Portsmouth, Rhode Island**.

Today you can visit Founders Brook Park in Portsmouth, where Hutchinson first settled.

In 1675 **Metacomet**, also called King Philip, led Native Americans in a war against **New England** colonists.

Today you can visit the scene of a famous battle in South Deerfield, Massachusetts.

Benjamin Franklin

Andrew Bryan

Philadelphia, Pennsylvania

Savannah, Georgia

1749 | Benjamin Franklin founds the University of Pennsylvania.

1788 | Andrew Bryan founds the First African Baptist Church in Savannah, Georgia.

1725   1750   1775   1800

Benjamin Franklin founded the **University of Pennsylvania** in Philadelphia, Pennsylvania.

Today you can see statues honoring Franklin in Philadelphia.

In 1788 **Andrew Bryan**, an enslaved person, founded the **First African Baptist Church**.

Today you can see the African Baptist Church building in Savannah, Georgia.

99

NEW ENGLAND

VOCABULARY

covenant p. 102

common p. 102

tolerate p. 103

fundamental p. 103

slavery p. 104

READING SKILL

Make Generalizations
Copy the chart below. As you read, fill it in to make a generalization about Puritans.

Text Clues	What You Know	Generalization

MISSOURI COURSE LEVEL EXPECTATIONS

3a.C.1, 3a.F.2, 5.A.1, 5.C.2, 5.J.1, 6.E.1, 6.I.1, 7.A.1, 7.B.1

This saltbox house shows the style of homes in New England during the 1600s.

Visual Preview

How did differences shape New England?

A Puritans went to New England for religious freedom and governed themselves.

B Settlers who disagreed with Puritan life established new colonies.

C Wars between settlers and Native Americans broke out in New England.

(A) MASSACHUSETTS BAY COMPANY

In June 1630, 300 hungry and exhausted passengers aboard the ship Arabella *arrived in Massachusetts Bay.* Arabella *led a fleet of 11 ships with about 1,000 passengers.*

Most of the people aboard the ships entering Massachusetts Bay were Puritans. Unlike the Pilgrims, Puritans didn't want to separate from the Church of England—they wanted to change the church. King James of England and many church leaders were furious and jailed some of the Puritans. When the Puritans were freed, many decided to leave England.

In 1629 a group of wealthy Puritans obtained a charter for the Massachusetts Bay Company. This company owned land in New England.

Puritans Arrive

To avoid the hardships of the Pilgrims, the Puritans brought more supplies, including horses and a herd of cows. They also arrived during warm weather instead of the beginning of winter.

The Puritans' charter allowed them to govern themselves. They held elections at town hall meetings, but only white men who owned property could vote. John Winthrop was elected the first governor.

Winthrop wrote about building "a city upon a hill" that would show how God wanted people to live. The Puritans named their first settlement Boston. By 1640 about 20,000 colonists lived near the shores of the Charles and Mystic rivers, which help form the peninsula of Boston.

QUICK CHECK

Make Generalizations Why did Puritans come to New England?

A New England town hall meeting ▶

LIFE IN NEW ENGLAND

Religion was so important to the Puritans that every member of the community had to enter a **covenant**, or contract, with the church. In this agreement the family promised to follow the rules of the Puritan church. Those who didn't follow the rules usually were forced to leave the colony.

Village Life

In the center of each Puritan village was a grassy area called the village **common**. The nearby meeting house also served as a church. At town meetings, issues were discussed and decisions were made by a majority vote.

Puritan adults treated young people like grown-ups. Children were expected to work hard to help their families and the community. Girls spun wool, made soap, cooked, and did household jobs. Boys cut wood, cared for animals, and worked on farms.

The Puritans wanted children to read the Bible, so every village had a school. The town chose one person, usually a religious leader, to teach the children. Schooling was so important to Puritans that they established Harvard College in 1636, six years after they arrived.

A New England Village

Mill

Inn

Meeting House

Blacksmith

Stocks

Barrel maker

Common

Rebels Start New Colonies

Even though each person entered a covenant, some people still disagreed with Puritan leaders. These disagreements led to the establishment of other colonies.

One person who disagreed with Puritan leaders was Roger Williams. He believed that government should **tolerate** people with different religious views. To tolerate means to allow people to have beliefs or behaviors that are different from others. Puritans accused Williams of spreading "new and dangerous opinions" and tried to silence him. After he was forced to leave the colony, Williams moved south where he lived with the Narragansett. In 1636 he bought land from the Narragansett and founded the settlement of Providence in what later became Rhode Island. It was the first colony to allow freedom of religion.

Anne Hutchinson was another person who disagreed with Puritan leaders. She told Puritans who met in her home that people should understand the Bible in their own way. They should not let ministers tell them what to think. She said:

> He who has God's grace in his heart cannot go astray.
>
> —ANNE HUTCHINSON

Puritan leaders put her on trial and forced Hutchinson out of the Massachusetts Bay Colony in 1638. She and her followers founded the settlement of Portsmouth in Rhode Island.

Diagram Skill

What kind of work did villagers in early New England do?

Primary Sources

It is Ordered . . . that there shall be yearly two General Assemblies . . . the first shall be called the Court of Election, wherein shall be yearly chosen from time to time . . . one to be chosen as Governor . . . shall have the power to administer justice according to the Laws here established . . . .

A section from The Fundamental Orders of Connecticut

by Thomas Hooker, 1639

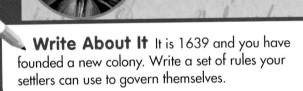

Write About It It is 1639 and you have founded a new colony. Write a set of rules your settlers can use to govern themselves.

Thomas Hooker also disagreed with Puritan beliefs. He thought that churches should be independent from one another and should choose their own leaders. In 1636 he led a group of settlers to the fertile Connecticut River valley. The rich soil was perfect for farming. There, he helped the settlers draw up a set of **fundamental**, or basic, rules to govern themselves. Read a section of *The Fundamental Orders of Connecticut* above.

QUICK CHECK

Make Generalizations What generalization can you make about Williams, Hooker, and Hutchinson?

ⓒ NATIVE AMERICAN CONFLICTS

The Wampanoag and Pequot were two of the Native American groups living in the New England area. At first the Wampanoag helped English colonists, and the two groups were peaceful neighbors. However, later colonists ignored the rights of Native Americans. As colonists settled across New England, groups such as the powerful Pequot did not want colonists to take their land.

The Pequot War

In 1637 war finally broke out. In a surprise attack, settlers surrounded a Pequot village in Mystic, Connecticut, and set fire to it. Hundreds of Pequot men, women, and children were killed as they ran from their homes. Many more were captured. Those who were captured were sold into **slavery**. Slavery is the practice of treating people as property and forcing them to work.

By 1638 the once powerful Pequot had lost hundreds of their people. The defeated Pequot gave away the rights to their land and went to live with other nearby Native American groups. After that, English settlers moved into areas of present-day New Hampshire, Vermont, and Maine.

King Philip's War

Massasoit, the Wampanoag leader who helped the Pilgrims, died in 1661. For 40 years he had kept peace with the colonists. This would soon change. English colonists continued to arrive during the 1600s. The new colonists seized land that had belonged to the Wampanoag for centuries.

▼ Settlers destroy a Pequot fort in Connecticut.

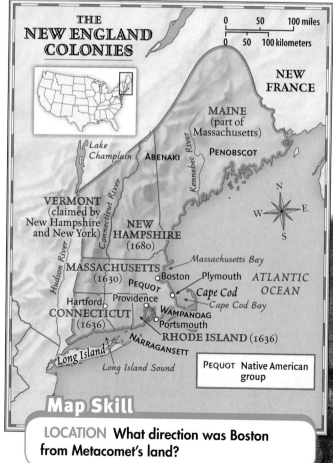

THE NEW ENGLAND COLONIES

0   50   100 miles
0   50   100 kilometers

NEW FRANCE

MAINE (part of Massachusetts)

Lake Champlain   ABENAKI   PENOBSCOT

Kennebec River

VERMONT (claimed by New Hampshire and New York)

Connecticut River

Hudson River

NEW HAMPSHIRE (1680)

N W E S

MASSACHUSETTS (1630)   Massachusetts Bay

Boston   Plymouth   ATLANTIC OCEAN

PEQUOT

Hartford   Providence   Cape Cod

CONNECTICUT (1636)   WAMPANOAG   Cape Cod Bay

Portsmouth

RHODE ISLAND (1636)

NARRAGANSETT

Long Island

Long Island Sound

PEQUOT Native American group

Map Skill

LOCATION **What direction was Boston from Metacomet's land?**

The new leader of the Wampanoag was Massasoit's son, Metacomet. Called "Philip" by the English colonial governor, Metacomet became known as "King Philip" to the colonists.

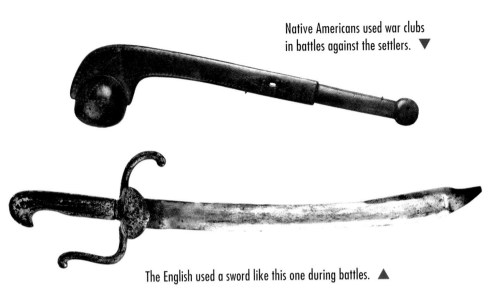

Native Americans used war clubs in battles against the settlers. ▼

Metacomet wanted to stop the English from taking more land. He sent messengers to his enemies, the Narragansett, asking for their help against the settlers. They refused, but other Native American groups across New England joined Metacomet.

The English used a sword like this one during battles. ▲

King Philip's War began in 1675 and lasted for more than a year. It was one of the bloodiest wars ever fought in North America. Metacomet's fighters attacked 52 towns and killed more than 600 colonists. Entire towns were burned. Crops were destroyed.

The colonists fought in the style of the Native Americans. They hid in the forests and launched surprise attacks. They burned the villages of the Native Americans.

Finally, in August 1676, Native American scouts helped colonists trap Metacomet in a swamp in Rhode Island. The Wampanoag leader was killed by a Native American helping the English colonists.

With King Philip's death, the war ended. About 4,000 Native Americans had been killed and many more, including Metacomet's wife and son, had been sold into slavery. Native American power in New England never recovered.

QUICK CHECK

Make Generalizations Why did colonists fight in a style like Native Americans?

Check Understanding

1. **VOCABULARY** Write a paragraph about Puritans using the word that means "agreement."

   covenant   **tolerate**

   common   **fundamental**

2. **READING SKILL Make Generalizations** Use your chart from page 100 to help you write about Puritans.

Text Clues	What You Know	Generalization

 3. **Write About It** Write about why Native Americans wanted to stop colonists from settling new areas.

The Middle Colonies

Lesson 2

VOCABULARY

patroon p. 107

proprietor p. 108

READING SKILL

Make Generalizations
Copy the chart below. As you read, fill it in to make a generalization about why the Middle Colonies had a diverse population.

Text Clues	What You Know	Generalization

MISSOURI COURSE LEVEL EXPECTATIONS

3a.C.1, 3a.F.2, 5.A.1, 5.C.2, 5.H.1, 5.J.1, 6.I.1, 7.B.1

New Amsterdam traders and merchants

Visual Preview

What factors influenced the development of the Middle Colonies?

A New Netherland was a center for trade filled with people from all over the world.

B Settlers from many different cultures came to New York and New Jersey.

C William Penn showed the world that a diverse population could live in peace.

106

A NEW NETHERLAND

In 1609 Henry Hudson claimed the land that is now New York for the Dutch. Then in 1621 the Dutch West India Company decided to set up a colony there. They called it New Netherland.

New Amsterdam, present-day Manhattan, was one of the most important settlements in New Netherland. The Dutch had bought the land from the Manahates. New Amsterdam had a great natural harbor, which made it perfect for trade. The colony's many natural resources included timber, fish, and fur-bearing animals. It soon was filled with sailors and traders from all over the world. The Dutch were tolerant of different religions and ethnic groups.

To attract new settlers, the Dutch West India Company offered land grants to **patroons** in 1629. Patroons were wealthy Dutch men who agreed to bring 50 people to the colony. However, because settlers had to clear the land themselves and share their crops with the patroons, the system did not attract many colonists.

The English Take New Netherland

In 1664 King Charles II of England gave his brother James, the Duke of York, a gift. This gift included all the land between the Connecticut and the Delaware Rivers, including New Netherland. The Duke of York arrived in the harbor of New Amsterdam with four warships. Peter Stuyvesant, the fiery governor of New Netherland, wanted to fight them. The Dutch colonists had no interest in fighting the English. New Netherland fell without firing a shot. The English renamed the colony New York, and New Amsterdam became New York City. The Duke of York gave part of New York to two friends who named it New Jersey in honor of the English island of Jersey. New York and New Jersey would become important English colonies.

QUICK CHECK

Make Generalizations What generalization can be made about the patroon system?

EVENT

Around 1637 Swedish colonists founded New Sweden along Delaware Bay. **Peter Stuyvesant** believed the land they settled belonged to the Dutch. In 1655 Stuyvesant captured New Sweden. Today it is part of New Jersey, Pennsylvania, and Delaware.

Peter Stuyvesant

Through trade, New York and New Jersey soon developed strong economies. Like New York's Hudson River, New Jersey's Delaware River became a major river for trade. The colony also had flat farmland and a mild climate. With rich soil and mild weather, agriculture kept New Jersey's economy strong.

Groups from Many Lands

Instead of being owned by the king or a company, both New York and New Jersey were owned by a man or a small group of men. They were called **proprietors**. These owners appointed the governors and ran the colonies as businesses.

To attract new settlers, proprietors offered newcomers free land. They also promised religious freedom and gave settlers a voice in their government. What was the downside? Settlers had to pay a tax. Still, a diverse population of German, Dutch, Irish, English Quaker, and Swedish settlers came to the colonies from Europe.

▼ Because farms grew so much corn, wheat, and oats, the Middle Colonies were known as the "Breadbasket of the Colonies."

Daily Life

Have you ever heard the phrase "sharing is caring?" Well, sharing is not only caring, it is also very smart. The settlers of New York and New Jersey learned new skills by sharing their knowledge. Swedes, for example, taught people how to build cabins out of logs. Scots shared farming ideas with Germans. Native Americans taught the colonists how to hunt for whales off the shores of Long Island.

The new settlers had to work hard to earn a living. Some grew corn, wheat, barley, or oats. Others worked as merchants, loggers, shipbuilders, or ironworkers.

Walking in colonial New York City, people heard different languages and tasted foods from many different countries in restaurants and homes. People also practiced many different religions. In both New York and New Jersey, Catholics, and Protestants worshipped freely. For these groups, life was better in the Middle Colonies than it had been in Europe or New England.

However, life was not better for everyone in the Middle Colonies. When the English took over New Netherland, free Africans had been working in the colony since 1626. But that came to an end in 1690. The English wrote new laws that said that even free Africans could be enslaved.

QUICK CHECK

Make Generalizations What generalization is made about religion in New York and New Jersey?

▼ A New York City street in the 1700s

Benjamin West painted *William Penn's Treaty with the Indians.*

ⓒ PENNSYLVANIA AND DELAWARE

William Penn came from a rich family that belonged to the Church of England. He left England to establish an American colony and became a member of a religious group called the Society of Friends, or Quakers.

Penn's Colony

Fortunately for Penn, King Charles II owed money to his father. After the death of Penn's father, the king paid his debt by giving William Penn a large piece of land in the Middle Colonies. Penn named the colony Pennsylvania, or "Penn's Woods," in honor of his father. He called his first settlement Philadelphia. In Greek the word means "city of brotherly love." Philadelphia soon became a center for trade along the Delaware River.

Like the Puritans, the Quakers in England had been jailed for their beliefs. Penn wanted a place where they could worship without fear.

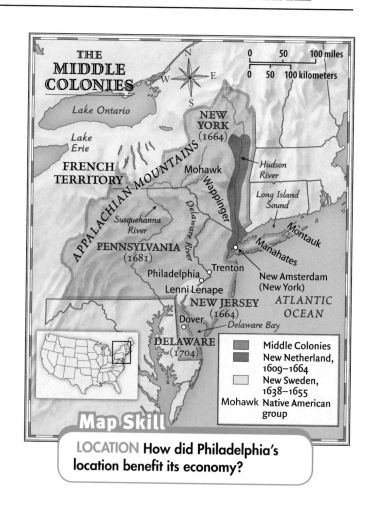

THE MIDDLE COLONIES

0   50   100 miles
0   50   100 kilometers

Lake Ontario
Lake Erie
FRENCH TERRITORY
NEW YORK (1664)
APPALACHIAN MOUNTAINS
Mohawk
Hudson River
Wappinger
Long Island Sound
Susquehanna River
Delaware River
Montauk
PENNSYLVANIA (1681)
Manahates
Philadelphia
Trenton
New Amsterdam (New York)
Lenni Lenape
NEW JERSEY (1664)
ATLANTIC OCEAN
Dover
Delaware Bay
DELAWARE (1704)

Middle Colonies
New Netherland, 1609–1664
New Sweden, 1638–1655
Mohawk Native American group

Map Skill

LOCATION **How did Philadelphia's location benefit its economy?**

William Penn

When most everyone else in the colonies took land from Native Americans, **William Penn** paid them for their land. He believed that Native Americans and colonists could live in peace.

When Penn wrote his *Frame of Government of Pennsylvania* in 1682, he included in it the right to free worship and the right to a trial by jury.

Settlers from Different Lands

Pennsylvania attracted people from a variety of religions and backgrounds. Many Germans, for example, came to Pennsylvania to escape wars in their homeland. Other German immigrants belonged to a religious group called the Mennonites. They were called "plain people" because they lived and dressed simply. German settlers in Pennsylvania are often called "Pennsylvania Dutch." The reason for this could be that the word for "German" in the German language is *Deutsch*. One German settler wrote about his voyage in 1683:

> **"**My company consisted of many sorts of people. . . . They were not only different in respect to their occupations, but were also of such different religions and behaviors that I might . . . compare the ship . . . with Noah's Ark.**"**

In addition to settlers from Germany and England, Pennsylvania attracted many Scots-Irish people. The Scots-Irish were people from Scotland who settled in Ireland in the early

1600s. They left Ireland in search of jobs and land to farm—in short, a better life.

Delaware

The southeastern part of Pennsylvania was called the Three Lower Counties. Before the English settled there, the region had been a part of New Sweden. The colonists of the Three Lower Counties wanted to make their own laws. In 1704 Penn allowed this area to elect its own assembly under the control of Pennsylvania's governor. Today this area is the state of Delaware.

QUICK CHECK

Make Generalizations **What generalization is made about the Mennonites?**

Check Understanding

1. **VOCABULARY** Write a sentence that explains the difference between the two words below.

   patroon   **proprietor**

2. **READING SKILL Make Generalizations** Use your chart from page 106 to write about why the Middle Colonies had a diverse population.

Text Clues	What You Know	Generalization

3. **Write About It** Write about why many Scots-Irish people settled in the Middle Colonies.

Lesson 3

VOCABULARY

plantation p. 114

indigo p. 114

debtor p. 115

READING SKILL

Make Generalizations
Copy the chart below. As you read, fill it in to make a generalization about the economy of the Southern Colonies.

Text Clues	What You Know	Generalization

MISSOURI COURSE LEVEL EXPECTATIONS

3a.C.1, 3a.F.2, 5.A.1, 5.C.2, 5.J.1, 6.I.1, 7.B.1

The Southern Colonies

Currier & Ives painted this Virginia plantation.

Visual Preview

How did the Southern Colonies differ from other settlements?

A Catholics and Protestants found religious freedom in Maryland.

B Carolina split into north and south, while Georgia started as a debtor colony.

C In Georgia, colonists made friends with the Creek and grew rice.

112

Ⓐ MARYLAND

If you started a colony, how would you attract settlers? Virginia advertised the benefits of settling there. These stories drew many settlers and encouraged the English to establish more colonies in the South.

George Calvert was a wealthy lord who was well-liked. But he became a Catholic in England at a time when that was illegal. Luckily, King Charles I liked Calvert, also known as Lord Baltimore, and granted him the land north of Virginia along the Chesapeake Bay. Calvert dreamed of starting a colony for Catholics, but he died before he could carry out his dream.

A Colony for Catholics

Calvert's son, Cecilius, actually founded the colony, but he stayed in England to make sure the king supported the colony. Cecilius believed Catholics and Protestants could live together in peace. Leonard Calvert, his brother, became the first governor of Maryland. Cecilius and Leonard ran Maryland like a business. Under their rule, the colony grew wealthy, with large tobacco farms dotting the shores of the bay. The city of Baltimore became a busy port.

Religion and Democracy

Conflicts between Catholics and Protestants soon arose. Lord Baltimore feared Maryland would become a

▲ George Calvert

Protestant colony. He proposed that Protestants and Catholics should have the right to worship freely. In 1649 the assembly passed the Toleration Act, allowing religious freedom for Christians. It declared that Catholics and Protestants could not threaten one another.

QUICK CHECK

Make Generalizations What generalization can you make about the Calverts?

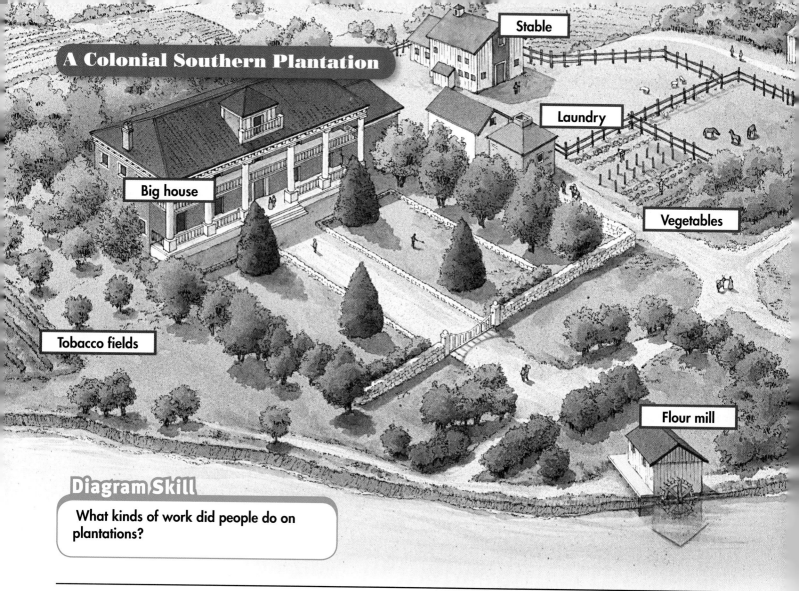

A Colonial Southern Plantation

Stable

Laundry

Vegetables

Big house

Tobacco fields

Flour mill

Diagram Skill

What kinds of work did people do on plantations?

B CAROLINA AND GEORGIA

King Charles II gave eight proprietors a charter to found Carolina in 1663. Seven years later, the first big city in the Southern Colonies, Charles Town, was founded in Carolina. Charles Town's natural harbor, warm climate, and natural resources made it a center for agriculture and trade. Wealthy colonists built **plantations** outside the city. Plantations are large farms that grow one main crop as a cash crop. Plantations in Carolina grew tobacco and rice. They also grew **indigo**, a plant used to make blue dye. Plantations were like small villages. Look at the diagram of a plantation above.

North and South Separate

Colonists who settled the land of northern Carolina grew tobacco and sold forest products such as timber and tar. The economy in northern Carolina grew slowly due to the lack of a good harbor. In southern Carolina the harbor in Charles Town allowed for easy trade. It was discovered that rice grew well in the coastal lowlands of the southern part of the colony. Rice soon became the leading cash crop. In 1729 these differences in colonial life in Carolina resulted in the colony splitting into North Carolina and South Carolina.

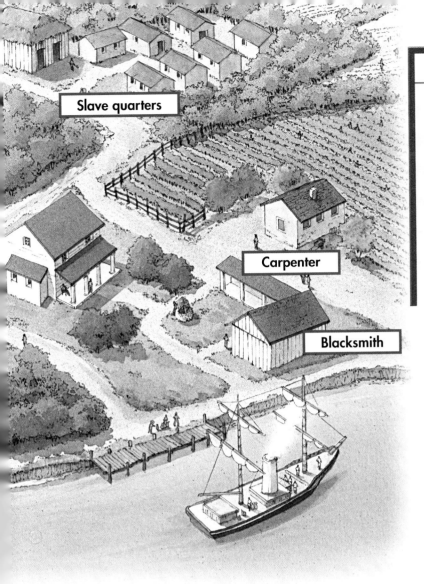

Slave quarters

Carpenter

Blacksmith

PLACES

By 1770 **Charles Town** was the fourth-largest city in the colonies. Today the city is called **Charleston** and has the fourth-largest container seaport in the United States. Its beautiful historic homes and tree-lined streets make the city a favorite among tourists.

Charleston, South Carolina

Settling Georgia

British General James Oglethorpe had a great idea. What if **debtors** could be sent to the colonies? Debtors are people who owe money but cannot repay it. At that time debtors were put in prison. Oglethorpe thought that instead of wasting away in prison, debtors could be free to live and work in Georgia. He thought slavery would not be necessary with all the debtors to do the work. Oglethorpe also thought that Georgia had the right conditions for making products such as silk that were in high demand in England. He said:

❝ The Colony of Georgia . . . shall [supply] . . . England . . . with raw Silk, Wine, Oil, Dyes, Drugs, and many other materials for manufactures. . . . ❞

Oglethorpe was a decorated general and became a member of the English Parliament in 1722. Because of his military experience, Oglethorpe received a charter to start a colony south of the Carolinas. King George II wanted a military man to run the colony because England, France, and Spain had all claimed this land south of the Carolinas. Oglethorpe would protect the Southern Colonies from the Spanish to the south and the French who had settlements to the west.

In 1732, 116 men, women, and children left London and set sail for the newest English colony in America. It was named Georgia, after King George II.

QUICK CHECK

Make Generalizations Make a generalization about why Carolina split into two colonies.

C THE CREEK HELP OGLETHORPE

Oglethorpe understood that for his new colony to succeed, he needed to have peace with the Native Americans in the area. A Creek group, the Yamacraw, lived near Yamacraw Bluff, where Oglethorpe planned to build his first settlement, Savannah. Oglethorpe obtained Yamacraw Bluff from Chief Tomochichi, the leader of the Yamacraw. Tomochichi also helped the colonists establish peaceful relations with other Creek groups.

Tomochichi remained a lifelong friend of the English colonists. In 1734 Oglethorpe invited Tomochichi to go to England and meet King George II. Tomochichi gave the king some eagle feathers as a token of peace. Before Tomochichi died in 1739, he told his people to remember the kindness of the king of England and said he hoped they would always be friendly to the colonists.

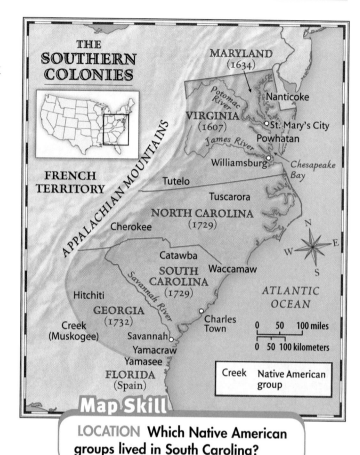

THE SOUTHERN COLONIES

FRENCH TERRITORY

APPALACHIAN MOUNTAINS

MARYLAND (1634)
Potomac River
Nanticoke
VIRGINIA (1607)
St. Mary's City
Powhatan
James River
Williamsburg
Chesapeake Bay
Tutelo
Tuscarora
NORTH CAROLINA (1729)
Cherokee
Catawba
SOUTH CAROLINA (1729)
Waccamaw
Hitchiti
Savannah River
GEORGIA (1732)
Creek (Muskogee)
Savannah
Charles Town
ATLANTIC OCEAN
Yamacraw
Yamasee
FLORIDA (Spain)

0 50 100 miles
0 50 100 kilometers

Creek | Native American group

Map Skill

LOCATION **Which Native American groups lived in South Carolina?**

Mary Musgrove also helped the Creek and the colonists become friends. Her mother came from a powerful Creek family. Her father was English. Musgrove had learned the Creek language and customs from her mother. When Oglethorpe arrived in Savannah, she became the translator for the settlers and the Creek.

James Oglethorpe's first meeting with Chief Tomochichi at the first Georgia settlement, Savannah ▶

▲ James Oglethorpe

Early Failures

Georgia got off to a difficult start. Oglethorpe had planned to raise silkworms, but the silk industry failed. Oglethorpe's plan for England's debtors also failed, because few debtors came.

Georgia Expands

While few debtors settled in Georgia, many other people did. The colony promised freedom of religion to all Protestant Christians. Colonists were also given free land to use for 10 years. This attracted settlers who were seeking a better life.

Hundreds of poor people came from Great Britain. Religious refugees from Germany and Switzerland also settled in Georgia. The colony soon had the highest percentage of non-British settlers compared to any other British colony in the Americas.

The Colony Changes

In the beginning, the colonists of Georgia grew tobacco. Later rice became the most profitable cash crop. Until 1750 Georgia was the only English colony that did not allow slavery. Oglethorpe had planned for the settlers to do all the work. However, there were not enough workers so some colonists smuggled enslaved workers into Georgia from South Carolina.

Enslaved Africans worked on the rice plantations of South Carolina. After slavery became legal in Georgia in 1750, many planters from South Carolina moved into Georgia, bringing enslaved workers with them. In the 1760s Georgians brought captives directly from Africa. By 1775 Georgia had 18,000 enslaved Africans.

QUICK CHECK

Make Generalizations What generalization can you make about the growth of slavery in Georgia?

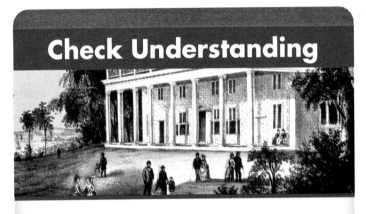

Check Understanding

1. **VOCABULARY** Write a paragraph about the Southern Colonies using two of the words below.

   plantation   **indigo**   **debtor**

2. **READING SKILL Make Generalizations**
   Use your chart from page 112 to write about the economy of the Southern Colonies.

Text Clues	What You Know	Generalization

3. **Write About It** Write about the reasons settlers came to the Southern Colonies.

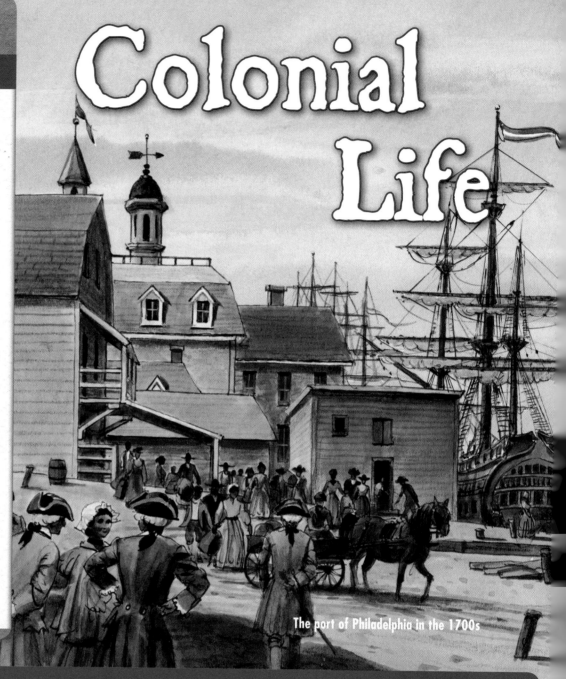

Colonial Life

The port of Philadelphia in the 1700s

VOCABULARY

slave trade p. 119

apprentice p. 120

growth rate p. 121

Great Awakening p. 121

backcountry p. 122

READING SKILL

Make Generalizations
Use the chart to make a generalization about the quality of life in colonial towns compared to life on the frontier.

Text Clues	What You Know	Generalization

MISSOURI COURSE LEVEL EXPECTATIONS

3a.C.1, 3a.F.1, 3a.F.2, 5.A.1, 5.C.2, 5.H.1, 5.J.1, 7.A.1

Visual Preview

How did economic needs affect life in the colonies?

A Many came to the colonies for a better life, while others came against their will.

B Colonists learned crafts, while the colonies grew rapidly and changed.

C As colonists settled the West, they came into conflict with Native American groups.

118

A WHY THEY CAME

Living conditions in Europe during the 1700s were miserable for many people. Some fled wars or food shortages in their homelands to settle in the English colonies. They were drawn by the promise of cheap land, economic opportunity, and religious freedom.

The dangerous journey across the Atlantic Ocean took between two and three months. It was a terrible time for those aboard a ship. The ships were crowded, damp, and filthy. Storms sank many vessels. Ships often ran out of food and water. Diseases spread quickly and killed many of the people on ships sailing to the colonies from Europe.

Enslaved Africans were crowded into the holds of slave ships.

Captives and Servants

Conditions for African captives were even more dreadful. Every part of the **slave trade**, or the business of buying and selling people, was designed to bring profits to the traders. On ships, captives were chained together and crammed into spaces where they could barely sit up. One out of seven captives died from disease, starvation, or poor treatment during the journey.

Indentured servants were people who chose to come to the colonies but could not pay their way. They contracted, or agreed, to work for a colonist usually for five to seven years to repay the price of the voyage. Indentured servants also received food, clothing, and shelter in return for their work. However, their living conditions were often harsh and their work, especially in the fields, was difficult. When their contracts ended, indentured servants often received farmland, animals, and supplies of lumber and tools.

QUICK CHECK

Make Generalizations What generalization can you make about the voyage across the Atlantic Ocean?

Most colonial families worked on farms. Men planted crops and hunted. Women did household work such as cooking, gardening, sewing, cleaning, spinning, and weaving. Children did chores such as feeding chickens, milking cows, gathering eggs, and cleaning. When they were not helping at home or studying, children played with marbles, kites, and jump ropes.

Learning a Trade

To learn a skill, a young person could become an **apprentice**. An apprentice is someone who works for a skilled person and in exchange, learns a trade or craft. After studying and practicing, an apprentice might become a silversmith, printer, or barrel maker, for example. Apprentices were not paid, but they received meals and housing while they learned their trade. At first only boys were allowed to be apprentices. After 1647 girls became apprentices in such trades as printing.

Early Communities

Colonists often combined work with play. An entire community, for example, would gather to build a house for a newly married couple. Examples of other community activities were cornhusking competitions and

A cabinetmaker teaches his young apprentice how to make a cabinet.

▲ A chest of drawers from the 1700s

quilting bees. At quilting bees neighbors sewed together pieces of cloth to make a bedspread.

The Colonies Grow and Change

Trade along the Atlantic coast led to population growth in the colonies. The population **growth rate** from 1700 to 1750 was about 450 percent. The growth rate is a year-to-year change expressed as a percentage. Philadelphia was the largest city in the colonies. By 1750 it had grown to almost 20,000 people. Benjamin Franklin did much to help the city grow. He established the first fire department and public library. Franklin also improved the city's police department and postal system.

Religion Changes

Religion also changed in the colonies during the 1700s. Growing interest in religion led to a period known as the **Great Awakening**. Preachers such as Jonathan Edwards and George Whitefield spread their message with a dramatic and emotional style. The more dramatic the sermon, the more people attended. During the Great Awakening, less formal church services taught that all people should have religious experiences.

During this time, many people changed from Puritanism to other forms of worship. For example, some Puritans became Baptists or Methodists. Some New England Baptist groups welcomed enslaved Africans at their church meetings.

QUICK CHECK

Make Generalization What generalization can you make about working in the colonies?

ⓒ LIFE ON THE FRONTIER

A Cherokee chief

In 1715 the Yamasee, with their allies the Muscogee and Choctaw, attacked the colonists, causing many settlers to flee to other colonies. The Cherokee, however, agreed to help the colonists in exchange for weapons and other goods. The Yamasee lost the war and fled to Florida. The Cherokee then became the most powerful Native American group in the Carolinas.

QUICK CHECK

Make Generalizations Why did fighting break out between the colonists and Native Americans in the backcountry?

During the 1740s, groups of settlers began to move into the area between the Appalachian Mountains and the Atlantic Coastal Plain. This area was known as the **backcountry**. Land in the backcountry cost much less money than land on the Atlantic Coastal Plain. Most of these settlers came from Ireland, Scotland, and Germany. Families in the backcountry built log cabins and cleared areas in the forests to grow corn and wheat. Life was hard, but people still managed to have fun. Like other colonists, they held dances, quilting contests, and other competitions.

The Yamasee War

Many Native Americans also lived in the backcountry. The Yamasee were originally friends of the Carolina colonists. The Yamasee complained when colonists began taking too much land and breaking their promises.

Check Understanding

1. **VOCABULARY** Write a paragraph about the colonial way of life using the words below.

   apprentice   backcountry

2. **READING SKILL Make Generalizations** Use your chart from page 118 to write about why people changed to new forms of worship during the Great Awakening.

Text Clues	What You Know	Generalization

3. **Write About It** Write about why German, Scottish, and Irish immigrants who came to the colonies in the 1700s settled in the backcountry.

Map and Globe Skills

Use a Historical Map

VOCABULARY

historical map

As you have read, colonists in New England lived along rivers and the Atlantic coast. They used these waterways for transportation. Over time, this land became too expensive for many colonists, so many people began moving inland where land was less expensive. You can see this movement of people by looking at a **historical map**. This kind of map shows where events from the past took place.

Learn It

- Look at the map title and dates to find the map topic. Most historical maps have dates.

- Look at the map key to find out the meaning of symbols or shading on the map.

Try It

- Which parts of New England were settled between 1700 and 1760?

- Which color represents land settled between 1660 and 1700?

Apply It

- As you read the rest of this unit, look for other historical maps.

- Compare the information that is given in those maps with the information that you read in each lesson.

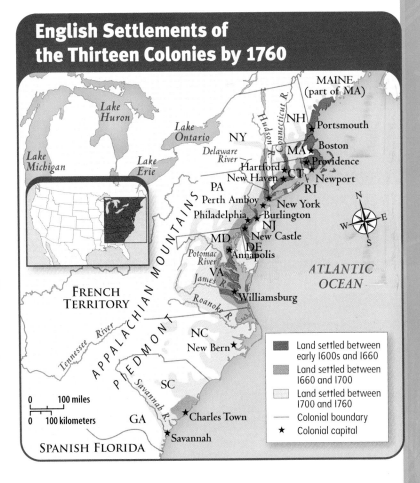

English Settlements of the Thirteen Colonies by 1760

- ■ Land settled between early 1600s and 1660
- ■ Land settled between 1660 and 1700
- □ Land settled between 1700 and 1760
- — Colonial boundary
- ★ Colonial capital

Lesson 5

VOCABULARY

slave codes p. 125

spiritual p. 127

READING SKILL

Make Generalizations
Copy the chart below. As you read, fill it in to make a generalization about why slavery was established in the thirteen colonies.

Text Clues	What You Know	Generalization

MISSOURI COURSE LEVEL EXPECTATIONS

3a.F.2, 5.C.2, 6.I.1

SLAVERY IN THE COLONIES

The first African captives arriving in Jamestown in 1619

Why did slavery develop in the English Colonies?

A The supply of enslaved workers kept growing because of new laws.

B Slavery was more common on large plantations in the South than in the North.

C Enslaved Africans led rebellions on ships and in the colonies.

124

A THE SLAVE TRADE

Slavery began when people started farming 10,000 years ago. At that time most enslaved people were those who had lost a war. Many had some legal rights. Slavery in the 1700s was different.

For a long time the English believed people who were not Christians could rightly be enslaved. If the captives converted to Christianity, then they would be set free. It didn't matter what color skin they had. But the Atlantic slave trade—the transporting of enslaved people from Africa to the Americas—changed that. Some Europeans became rich by kidnapping, transporting, and selling captive Africans. By the middle of the 1700s, more than 250,000 enslaved Africans had been brought to North America. Far more were brought to Brazil and the Caribbean Islands.

Slavery Becomes Legal

In 1641 Massachusetts became the first colony to make slavery legal. By 1751 Africans could legally be enslaved in all thirteen colonies.

Colonists believed that the use of enslaved workers was needed for the colonial economy to grow and stay strong. As a result, the demand for enslaved workers grew dramatically.

Laws called **slave codes** set rules of slavery. Some of the earliest Africans in the colonies were indentured servants. The slave codes ended that. These laws said that African captives brought to the colonies would have almost no rights.

The first slave laws said that people who were not Christians could be enslaved. Soon some Native Americans and Africans became Christians. But the demand for enslaved workers kept growing, so the colonists changed the laws. After that, any captive African could be enslaved, including Christians and children born to enslaved workers.

QUICK CHECK

Make Generalizations Why did slave codes allow Christians to become enslaved?

A slave auction

Enslaved Africans did many kinds of work, often depending on the economy of the colony where they lived. Some were skilled workers, such as carpenters, blacksmiths, cooks, and weavers. Other captive Africans worked as field hands or in the homes of slaveholders.

The Northern Colonies

In the North many enslaved Africans worked in New England's shipyards. In Rhode Island, Connecticut, and New York, enslaved workers did farm labor. Northern farms were generally small. Colonists in the North rarely owned more than one or two enslaved workers. However, many Northern colonists owned the slave ships. Before the 1770s most captive Africans were shipped to Rhode Island to be sold throughout the colonies.

New York had the largest enslaved population of the Northern colonies. In New York City, some people used enslaved workers in construction. Enslaved Africans even built the wall that gave Wall Street its name.

The Southern Colonies

Many Southern farms, on the other hand, were large and grew cash crops, especially tobacco. Both rice and tobacco required many workers to plant, tend, and harvest the crop. About one-fourth of white Southern farmers were slaveholders. Farms with a small number of captive Africans were more common than large plantations. Hundreds of enslaved people worked the fields on large plantations. In South Carolina by 1720, more than half of the colony's population was enslaved Africans.

▼ Reenactment of enslaved field work

A plantation celebration

African Culture

Despite brutal hardships, enslaved Africans carried on the culture from their homes in Africa. African words such as *banjo* and *gumbo*, for example, first came into the English language in the South.

Slave codes made it illegal for enslaved Africans to read or write. As a result, they often told traditional stories to their children and to each other. Many stories told how a clever animal, such as a fox, outsmarted a powerful person. Africans also created work songs, which they sang as they worked. **Spirituals**, the religious songs of enslaved Africans, have had a great influence on American music today. A number of spirituals are about freedom.

▲ This apprentice is learning how to make a basket.

QUICK CHECK

Make Generalizations Why was the population of enslaved people higher in the Southern Colonies than in the Northern Colonies?

Enslaved Africans had been kidnapped, forced to work for others, separated from their families, and often punished harshly. As a result, they looked for ways to fight back against the colonists. Some resisted slavery by slowing their work or by breaking or losing tools. Others escaped, hoping to find freedom in less settled areas. Some found freedom living among Native Americans and other runaway Africans in the backcountry. Some enslaved Africans who escaped hoped to find family members who had been sold away.

Slave Revolts

Enslaved Africans sometimes rebelled violently. Although rebellion was rare, it remained a constant fear among colonists. Twice within 30 years, slave rebellions alarmed the thirteen English colonies.

One of the first slave revolts was in New York City in 1712. During the revolt, about 25 Africans and 2 Native Americans launched a surprise attack. Armed with guns, hatchets, and swords, they set fire to a building and waited for a crowd to gather. Then they opened fire on the crowd killing several colonists. The colonists reacted quickly to this revolt and captured and killed most of the rebels.

The Stono Rebellion

Another revolt broke out in South Carolina in 1739. An enslaved African named Jemmy and about 20 of his followers stole guns and gunpowder from a

warehouse in Stono, South Carolina, about 15 miles from Charles Town. They killed several colonists in Stono and marched down the road with a banner that read "Liberty!" As many as 100 enslaved workers joined them.

Captives who revolted at sea were often killed by the ship's crew. ▼

The group hoped to reach St. Augustine, a Spanish colony, where they had been promised freedom. However, a mob of plantation owners from South Carolina attacked them, killing about 40 of the rebels.

QUICK CHECK

Summarize In what ways did enslaved Africans resist slavery?

▲ This reproduction shows the living conditions of enslaved workers.

Check Understanding

1. **VOCABULARY** Write two sentences about slavery in the English colonies using these vocabulary terms.

   slave code   **spiritual**

2. **READING SKILL Make Generalizations** Use your chart from page 124 to write about slavery in the colonies.

Text Clues	What You Know	Generalization

3. **Write About It** Why were Africans brought to the Americas in the 1700s?

Lesson 6

VOCABULARY

triangular trade p. 132

Middle Passage p. 133

industry p. 134

READING SKILL

Make Generalizations
Copy the chart below. As you read, use it to make a generalization about English trade laws.

Text Clues	What You Know	Generalization

MISSOURI COURSE LEVEL EXPECTATIONS

3a.F.2, 5.A.1, 5.C.2, 5.J.1, 6.I.1, 7.A.1, 7.B.1

Colonial Economies

A reenactment of coopers making colonial style barrels

Visual Preview

What influenced the development of colonial economies?

A Colonists ignored laws that England passed to regulate Colonial trade.

B Ships on the triangular trade routes moved cargo and enslaved Africans.

C Each colony developed an economy based on the resources of its region.

COLONIAL TRADE

Between 1651 and 1764, England passed trade laws to control what and how the colonists could trade. The laws also controlled what colonists could make. To earn a profit, many colonists ignored the laws and turned to smuggling.

England wanted the colonists to buy their manufactured goods. For this reason, England made it illegal for the colonies to manufacture goods that competed with English goods. For example, it was illegal for the colonists to make hats, nails, and horseshoes. English trade laws, called the Navigation Acts, listed goods that the colonies could sell only to England or its colonies. These included farm products such as sugar, tobacco, lumber, cotton, wool, and indigo.

English Trade Laws

The English charged the colonists high shipping costs. England used the raw materials from the colonies to make manufactured goods and exported them to other countries for huge profits.

In 1663 a new trade law said everything the colonies imported had to first be shipped to England and taxed. This made money for England, but raised the price of imports in the colonies. Colonists claimed England was destroying their economy. Some colonists began to smuggle, or secretly import, goods. They also traded in foreign ports and allowed ships from other countries into their ports. Luckily for colonists, England was far away, so it was difficult for the English government to make sure laws were being followed.

QUICK CHECK

Make Generalizations What happened after England imposed taxes on trade goods?

▼ The busy port of Boston in the 1600s

B WORLD TRADE

In 1675 King Charles II formed a committee to oversee colonial trade. This committee was formed to make sure the colonists were following trade laws. Its members soon learned that Boston Harbor was crowded with Dutch ships and ships from other countries. The colonists were unlawfully trading with Europe, the Caribbean, and Africa. Many colonists in Massachusetts were upset by English trade laws. They did not want to follow laws they thought were harmful to the colony. New England's shipbuilding industry and economy grew as a result of this illegal trade with other countries. As one historian said:

" . . . selfishness of the English [trade laws] was digging a [wedge] between the mother country and the colonists. **"**

Triangular Trade

Ships on the **triangular trade** routes sold products and picked up cargo at each stop. This came to be known as the triangular trade because the routes formed triangles on the map. The triangular trade made many merchants rich, especially in the New England Colonies. Using their wealth, merchants in Northern cities began trading with the Southern Colonies, exchanging Northern fish, rum, and grain for Southern rice, tobacco, and indigo. The illustration on this page shows how the colonial trade routes formed triangles.

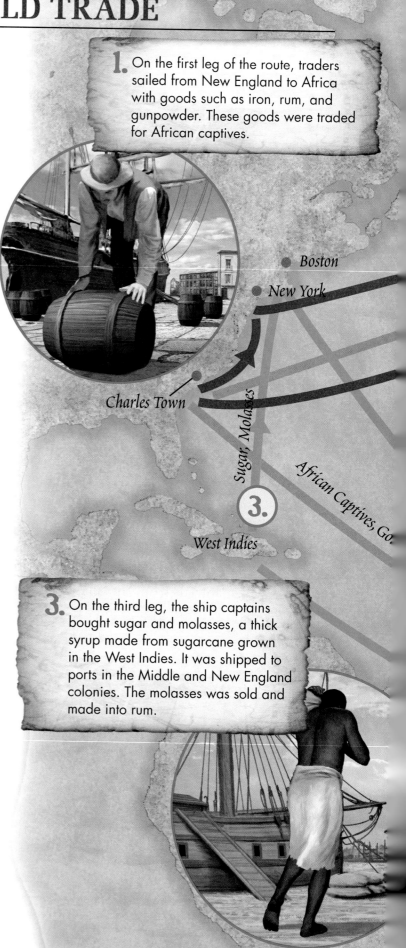

1. On the first leg of the route, traders sailed from New England to Africa with goods such as iron, rum, and gunpowder. These goods were traded for African captives.

Boston

New York

Charles Town

Sugar, Molasses

African Captives, Go.

3.

West Indies

3. On the third leg, the ship captains bought sugar and molasses, a thick syrup made from sugarcane grown in the West Indies. It was shipped to ports in the Middle and New England colonies. The molasses was sold and made into rum.

QUICK CHECK

Make Generalizations **Why did shipowners keep their ships filled with cargo on every leg of the voyage?**

The Triangular Trade

England
London

Lumber, Cod, Furs

Tobacco, Rice, Indigo

Manufactured Goods

Guns, Cloth

Africa

Rum, Iron

1.

2. African Captives

2. On the second leg of the route, the traders took the African captives to the West Indies. This part of the route was called the **Middle Passage**, because it was the middle part of the three-sided trade. In the West Indies, the Africans were sold into slavery.

ⒸREGIONAL ECONOMIES

Now that you have read about the triangular trade, let's find out what each region produced and exported. Each region's economy was based on its resources, industries, and the hard work of its people.

New England

Most of New England's soil was too rocky for farming. Many farmers there grew fruits and vegetables for themselves, but not enough to export. New Englanders needed other ways to earn a living. The forests provided lumber for the shipbuilding **industry**. An industry is all the businesses that make one kind of product or provide one kind of service. Wood was cheap in New England, where there was a good supply of trees. Logs were cut and tossed into rivers where they floated to towns and shipyards.

Soon Boston's shipbuilding industry competed with English shipbuilders. New Englanders also made excellent fishing boats, and fishing became a profitable industry. Cod was New England's "cash crop."

The Middle Colonies

Farmers in the Middle Colonies could supply just about everything needed for a picnic. They grew wheat for bread and raised dairy cattle for cheese. Farmers shipped these products to New York City and Philadelphia. From there they were exported to other countries. These port cities also became centers of business. Printers, shoemakers, cabinetmakers, and other craftworkers opened shops there.

DataGraphic
Major Colonial Exports

Most colonists made their living by farming. Each region grew different crops. Study the map and graph. Then answer the questions.

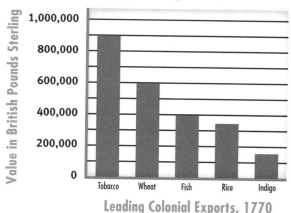

Major Exports, 1770

Leading Colonial Exports, 1770

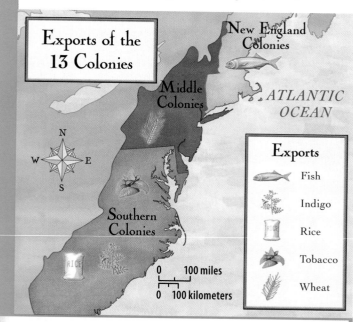

Exports of the 13 Colonies

Exports
Fish
Indigo
Rice
Tobacco
Wheat

Think About Exports

1. What was New England's major export?

2. Which region's exports had the most value?

▲ Colonial general stores sold many of the manufactured goods people needed.

The Southern Colonies

The hot, humid climate and good soil of the Southern Colonies were well suited to growing crops. Tobacco and rice made many plantation owners wealthy in the Southern Colonies. At first these products were shipped only to England. Later they were shipped all over the world. Another crop grown in the Southern Colonies was indigo, a plant used to make blue dye. English merchants needed the blue dye from indigo for their huge cloth-making businesses. The tobacco, rice, and indigo trades brought great wealth to the Southern Colonies.

QUICK CHECK

Make Generalizations **Why did each region have a different economy?**

Check Understanding

1. **VOCABULARY** Draw a poster of triangular trade using the vocabulary terms below.

   **triangular trade   industry
   Middle Passage**

2. **READING SKILL Make Generalizations**
   Use your chart from page 130 to help you write a paragraph about colonial trade with England.

Text Clues	What You Know	Generalization

3. **Write About It** Write about why some colonists in New England settled in areas with heavy forests.

VOCABULARY

assembly p. 137

legislation p. 137

READING SKILL

Make Generalizations
Copy the chart below. As you read, fill it in to make a generalization about the power of colonial assemblies.

Text Clues	What You Know	Generalization

MISSOURI COURSE LEVEL EXPECTATIONS

3a.F.2, 5.A.1, 5.C.2, 7.A.1

COLONIAL GOVERNMENTS

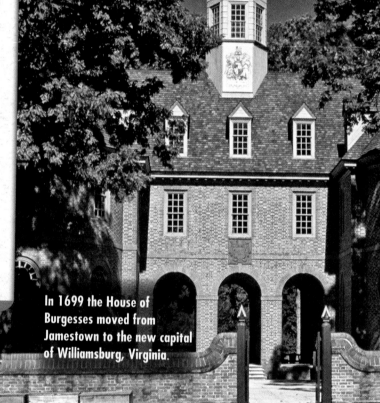

In 1699 the House of Burgesses moved from Jamestown to the new capital of Williamsburg, Virginia.

Visual Preview

How did values shape colonial governments?

A Charters allowed colonies to make their own laws and assemblies.

B Governors battled strong assemblies, which represented the people.

C The Zenger trial and Phyllis Wheatley's poems were calls for freedom.

136

A SELF-GOVERNMENT

The colonists made many laws that were new ideas at the time. Colonists demanded rights that the English thought were almost rebellious! With laws protecting freedom of speech, colonists were building a system of government that represented the people.

An **assembly**, or lawmaking body, was guaranteed in the charters of most colonies. English kings allowed the colonies to make their own laws, but these laws had to be approved by England's government.

Colonial Assemblies

Sometimes assemblies made laws that protected and expanded people's rights and freedoms. Remember the Toleration Act in Maryland? Later, England would try to take some of these rights away.

The colonists felt independent from England, which was thousands of miles away. Colonial assemblies gathered to make laws for their colonies. This **legislation**, or making of laws, was a first step on the road to self-government.

Colonial governments weren't perfect. It fact, they were unfair to many groups. Women, indentured servants, enslaved Africans, and Native Americans could not vote or hold office. At first only white men who owned land could vote. Later a small number of men who did not own land were elected to assemblies. In some colonies, these voters also had to belong to a certain church.

QUICK CHECK

Make Generalizations Why were colonists on the road to self-government?

▼ A reenactment of the House of Burgesses during a recess

England allowed assemblies to control a colony's taxes and spending. This gave assemblies a great deal of power—the kind of power they held onto with a tight grip.

Powerful Assemblies

Colonists expected assemblies to represent their views rather than the views of the English rulers. Colonists saw themselves as English citizens who had the right to make their own decisions. The Virginia Charter stated that its colonists would have the same freedoms as people born in England.

Colonial governors constantly fought with their assemblies. Governors were usually appointed either by the king or by the colony's proprietor. Unlike the other colonies, Connecticut and Rhode Island elected their own governors. The governor's job was to represent the interests of the king or proprietor. The assembly's job was to represent the people of the colony. The governor could reject any law passed by a colonial assembly. The assemblies could stop paying the governor's expenses until their laws were approved. Withholding money wasn't the best way to solve a problem, but it helped assemblies protect their power.

Local Government

How did colonial towns solve their problems? In New England and some Middle Colonies, male colonists held town meetings. At these meetings, colonists sometimes had heated debates about local issues, elected local officials, and made laws. Most Southern

Colonies had county governments. Usually the governor appointed county officials. This gave more power to governors in the South.

Local courts settled disputes between individuals or answered questions about the law. Judges supervised colonial courts. The governor and the assembly selected colonists to serve as judges.

Natural Rights

John Locke believed that people were naturally good. He was an English thinker who believed that all people have "natural rights." Among these rights were life, freedom, and the right to own property. Locke wrote that the main duty of government was to protect these rights. When a government failed to protect these rights, Locke thought people could overthrow, or change, that government. Most colonists understood what Locke meant by life and property rights. But people disagreed about the meaning of the word *freedom*.

QUICK CHECK

Make Generalizations Generalize Locke's belief about what people should do if a government fails to protect their natural rights.

◄ A lawbreaker might have to spend days in the public pillory. This form of public embarrassment was a punishment for minor crimes, such as swearing. More serious crimes, such as robbery, could be punished by whipping or even hanging.

Does freedom include printing something bad about someone, even if it is true? John Peter Zenger came from Germany and started a newspaper in New York City called *The New York Weekly Journal*. In the newspaper, Zenger published articles about the governor of New York, William Cosby. Cosby took Zenger to court, saying that Zenger's articles had insulted him. Zenger's lawyer, Andrew Hamilton, told the jury that Zenger had the right to print the truth. Read a section from Hamilton's address on this page.

Hamilton's words meant that people had the freedom to write or speak the truth. The jury agreed and found Zenger not guilty. The Zenger trial helped establish the idea that newspaper publishers could not be punished for printing the truth. Later, freedom of the press became part of the U.S. Constitution.

Primary Sources

"The question before the court and you . . . is the best cause. It is the cause of liberty. . . . [E]very man who prefers freedom to a life of slavery will bless and honor you. . . . [We] have laid a noble foundation for securing to ourselves, our **posterity**, and our neighbors . . . the liberty both of exposing and opposing **arbitrary** power (in these parts of the world, at least) by speaking and writing the truth. . . ."

A section from Address to the Jury by Andrew Hamilton August 14, 1735

posterity	future generations
arbitrary	not limited

▼ **Andrew Hamilton defending John Peter Zenger during his trial.**

Write About It Write about how freedom of speech can expose dishonesty in elected officials.

Phillis Wheatley

Some enslaved Africans also wrote about freedom. Phillis Wheatley published her first poem at age 13. Wheatley believed enslaved Africans had natural rights. In one of her poems, Phillis Wheatley urged colonists to fight for freedom:

"No longer shalt [you fear] the iron chain . . . meant t'enslave the land."

George Washington praised Wheatley's writing. While growing up, her life had been difficult. At age seven Wheatley was kidnapped from Africa and enslaved. Then she was purchased in Boston by John Wheatley, but her life was different from most enslaved Africans. John's wife, Susannah Wheatley, taught Phillis to read and write English and other languages. By the time she was 13 years old, she was writing poetry. In 1773, at age 20, Phillis Wheatley published a book of poems and was freed from slavery.

QUICK CHECK

Make Generalizations How was Phillis Wheatley's life different from most enslaved Africans?

John Peter Zenger

Check Understanding

1. **VOCABULARY** Write one sentence using both of these vocabulary words.

   assembly   **legislation**

2. **READING SKILL Make Generalizations** Use your chart from page 136 to help you write about colonial assemblies.

Text Clues	What You Know	Generalization

3. **EXPLORE The Big Idea Write About It** How did the Virginia Charter encourage settlement?

Unit 3   Review and Assess

Vocabulary

Number a paper from 1 to 4. Beside each number write the word from the list below that matches the description.

apprentice   **slave codes**

industry   **assembly**

1. Businesses that provide one kind of product or service

2. Rules that controlled the lives of enslaved Africans

3. A lawmaking body

4. A person who works for a skilled person to learn a craft or trade

Comprehension and Critical Thinking

5. How did the economy of the Southern Colonies contribute to the growth of slavery?

6. **Reading Skill** Why did some Puritans leave Massachusetts Bay Colony to start other colonies?

7. **Critical Thinking** Why did William Penn want freedom of religion in Pennsylvania?

8. **Critical Thinking** Why did England allow colonies to have assemblies?

Skill

Use Historical Maps

Write a complete sentence to answer each question.

9. Which main groups settled in Pennsylvania?

10. Which main group settled in Northwestern Maryland?

Main Immigrant Groups in 1760

- African
- Dutch
- English
- German
- Scotch-Irish
- No main group
- — Colony boundary

0   50   100 miles
0   50   100 kilometers

N W E S

MA

CT

NEW YORK

New York •

PA

Philadelphia •

NEW JERSEY

Baltimore •

DELAWARE

MARYLAND

VIRGINIA

ATLANTIC OCEAN

MAP Test Preparation

Directions   Read the passage. Then answer Numbers 1 through 3.

"The question before the court and you . . . is the best cause. It is the cause of liberty . . . [and] every man who prefers freedom to a life of slavery will bless and honor you. . . . [We] have laid a noble foundation for securing to ourselves, our posterity, and our neighbors . . . the liberty both of exposing and opposing arbitrary power (in these parts of the world, at least) by speaking and writing the truth. . . ."

—A section from the Address to the Jury by Andrew Hamilton August 14, 1735

1   **Which of the following words could replace the word posterity in the passage above?**

- ○ government officials
- ○ farmland
- ○ future generations
- ○ writing

2   **Based on the information from this passage, to whom is Hamilton speaking?**

- ○ a judge
- ○ lawyers
- ○ a jury
- ○ a court reporter

3   **What does Hamilton think will expose and oppose "arbitrary power"?**

Write your answer on a separate piece of paper.

Activities

Why do people settle new areas?

Write About the Big Idea

Study Organizer

Descriptive Journal Entry
Use the Unit 3 Foldable to help you
write a descriptive journal entry
that answers the Big Idea question,
Why do people settle new areas?
Use the notes you wrote under
each tab for details to support each
main idea. Be sure to describe the
region and why people settled in that area.

Why People Settle New Areas

| New England Colonies | Middle Colonies | Southern Colonies |

Make a Bar Graph

With a partner, make two bar graphs showing the
population growth of the Thirteen Colonies from
1700 to 1760 and the projected population of the
United States from 2000 to 2060.

1. Use these figures to make your colonial
bar graph.

1700	250,900		1740	905,600
1720	466,200		1760	1,593,600

2. Use these figures to make your U.S. bar graph.

2000	275 million		2040	370 million
2020	323 million		2060	432 million

When you have finished your bar graphs, take turns
presenting each graph to the class. Compare and
contrast the rate of population growth.

The Struggle for North America

EXPLORE The Big Idea

Essential Question
Why do people take risks?

FOLDABLES Study Organizer

Main Idea and Details

Make and label a Concept map before you read this unit. Write the word **Risks** at the top. Label the three tabs **French, British,** and **American**. Use the Foldable to organize information.

Risks

French | British | American

LOG ON For more about Unit 4 go to
www.macmillanmh.com

British General Braddock was fatally wounded during the French and Indian War.

PEOPLE, PLACES, AND EVENTS

Robert Cavelier, Sieur de La Salle

Jean Baptiste Le Moyne, Sieur de Bienville

Mississippi River

1682
La Salle claims Mississippi River for France

New Orleans

1718
Bienville founds New Orleans

1675   1700   1725

La Salle led French explorers down the **Mississippi River** by canoe in search of a water route across North America.

Today the Mississippi River is one of the world's most important waterways.

Bienville believed it was important for the French to build cities in Louisiana. He founded **New Orleans**.

Today you can visit cities founded by the French, including New Orleans and Baton Rouge.

Thomas Jefferson

George Washington

Philadelphia

1776

Jefferson writes
the Declaration of
Independence

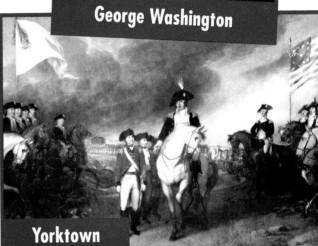

Yorktown

1781

British surrender to
George Washington
at Yorktown, Virginia

1750   1775   1800

Thomas Jefferson wrote the Declaration of Independence at the Graff House in **Philadelphia**.

Today you can tour the rebuilt Graff House in Philadelphia.

The British surrendered to **George Washington** at **Yorktown**.

Today you can see the battlefield where the fighting of the American Revolution ended.

The French in Louisiana

VOCABULARY

tributary p. 149

territory p. 149

READING SKILL

Main Idea and Details
Copy the chart below.
Use it to fill in the main
idea and details about the
French exploration of the
Mississippi River valley.

Main Idea	Details

**MISSOURI COURSE
LEVEL EXPECTATIONS**

5.A.1, 5.C.2, 5.J.1, 6.I.1, 7.A.1,
7.B.1

French explorers paddled canoes from
the Great Lakes to the mouth of the
Mississippi River.

**Visual
Preview**

How did France's control of the Mississippi River affect settlement?

A La Salle claimed
new territory for
France and named it
Louisiana.

B French settlers
built settlements
at Biloxi Bay and New
Orleans.

148

Ⓐ LA SALLE CLAIMS LOUISIANA

In 1670 New France consisted of only a few fur trading posts in Canada. This would change after 1673, when two French explorers reached a mighty river flowing south. Native Americans called it the Mississippi—"Father of Waters."

The first French colonists to explore the Mississippi River were Jacques Marquette, a missionary, and Louis Jolliet, a fur trader. In 1673 they traveled by canoe as far as the Arkansas River, a **tributary** of the Mississippi, before turning back. A tributary is a river or stream that flows into a larger river.

La Salle's Expedition

As word of the enormous river spread across New France, other explorers saw an opportunity to gain wealth. In 1682 Robert de La Salle led an expedition down the Mississippi River. His followers built a fort at what is today Memphis, Tennessee. Then they continued, paddling to the mouth of the river on the Gulf of Mexico. There La Salle claimed the Mississippi River and its tributaries for France. He named the **territory** Louisiana. A territory is an area of land controlled by another country.

Plan for Settlement

Excited by his discovery, La Salle sailed to France to gather support for a new colony. Two years later, he returned with several hundred men. The plan was to sail west across the Gulf of Mexico and build a settlement at the mouth of the Mississippi River. From there, La Salle planned to travel farther west and take control of silver mines in New Spain.

La Salle's plan excited his followers, but it ended in failure. A poor navigator, he sailed 400 miles past the mouth of the river, landing in present-day Texas. Many of La Salle's men died from disease and starvation. Still others were killed by Native Americans. In the end, the few men who survived revolted against La Salle. He was killed by his own men.

QUICK CHECK

Main Idea and Details What happened on La Salle's second expedition to the mouth of the Mississippi River?

EVENT

On April 9, 1682, Robert de La Salle **claimed the Louisiana Territory** for France. He named the territory for the French king, Louis XIV.

Louisiana Territory claimed

By 1690 France had claimed much of what is now the central United States and Canada. At that time only a few thousand settlers lived in New France. Almost no Europeans had settled in the Louisiana Territory.

The French realized that they were in danger of losing Louisiana to England or to Spain, whose explorers had reached the area. King Louis XIV of France decided to strengthen French control of the region.

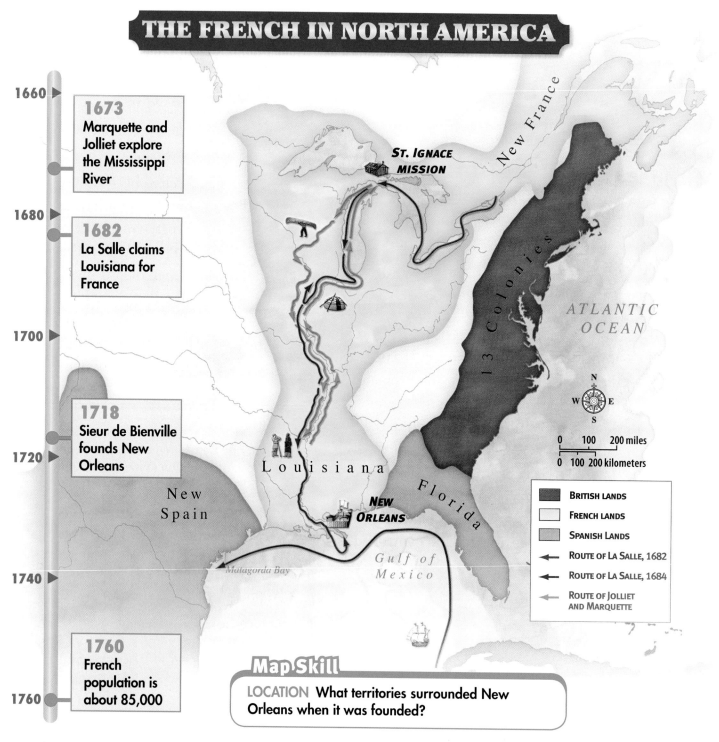

THE FRENCH IN NORTH AMERICA

1660

1673
Marquette and Jolliet explore the Mississippi River

1680

1682
La Salle claims Louisiana for France

1700

1718
Sieur de Bienville founds New Orleans

1720

1740

1760
French population is about 85,000

1760

St. Ignace Mission

New France

13 Colonies

ATLANTIC OCEAN

Louisiana

New Spain

Florida

New Orleans

Gulf of Mexico

Matagorda Bay

N W E S

0   100   200 miles
0   100 200 kilometers

BRITISH LANDS
FRENCH LANDS
SPANISH LANDS
ROUTE OF LA SALLE, 1682
ROUTE OF LA SALLE, 1684
ROUTE OF JOLLIET AND MARQUETTE

Map Skill

LOCATION **What territories surrounded New Orleans when it was founded?**

The city of New Orleans was settled about 100 miles north of the mouth of the Mississippi River.

First Settlements

In 1698 the French king appointed Pierre Le Moyne, Sieur d'Iberville as the first governor of Louisiana. D'Iberville agreed with the king—France needed to control the Mississippi River. To do that, France needed a larger population in the area. D'Iberville feared the English would take over and wrote:

❝If France does not seize this most beautiful part of America and set up a colony . . . ❞

New Orleans

After d'Iberville died in 1706, his brother Jean-Baptiste Le Moyne, Sieur de Bienville became governor of Louisiana. In 1718 he founded New Orleans about 100 miles north of the mouth of the Mississippi River. The settlement drew many settlers to Louisiana.

New Orleans became the largest French settlement in Louisiana. Unlike settlers of New France, who worked mainly in the fur trade, colonists in Louisiana built plantations. Planters brought in enslaved Africans to raise indigo, rice, and tobacco.

Slow Growth

By 1740 France claimed an area from Canada down the Mississippi River to the Gulf of Mexico. By 1760 the French had 85,000 settlers, compared to 2 million in the English colonies. However, French control of the area prevented the English from moving west.

QUICK CHECK

Main Idea and Details In what ways were settlers in Louisiana different from settlers in New France?

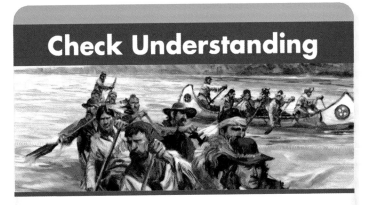

Check Understanding

1. **VOCABULARY** Write two sentences about Louisiana that use these vocabulary words.

   tributary   territory

2. **READING SKILL Main Idea and Details.** Use the chart from page 148 to explain how New Orleans was founded.

Main Idea	Details

 3. **Write About It** What made La Salle take the risk of sailing from France around Florida to the mouth of the Mississippi River?

The French and Indian War

Lesson 2

VOCABULARY

French and Indian War p. 153

Treaty of Paris p. 154

Proclamation of 1763 p. 154

READING SKILL

Main Idea and Details
Copy the chart. Use it to list the main idea and details about the French and Indian War.

Main Idea	Details

MISSOURI COURSE LEVEL EXPECTATIONS

3a.D.1, 3a.F.2, 5.A.1, 5.C.2, 5.J.1, 6.I.1, 7.B.1

French officers meet leaders of the Wyandot, also called the Huron.

Visual Preview

How did the French and Indian War change the colonies?

A English settlers moved to land claimed by France.

B Great Britain's victory united English colonists for the first time as Americans.

152

A — WAR IN NORTH AMERICA

In 1707 the king of England united England and Scotland and named the new country Great Britain. Its people were now known as "British." British settlers fought the French over land in North America.

Disagreements between France and Great Britain arose when English colonists settled on land claimed by France in the Ohio River Valley. The settlers were farmers. The French trappers feared that the newcomers would cut down forests, which would hurt their fur trade. The dispute over land led to the **French and Indian War**. In this war, the French and their Native American allies, the Wyandot, fought the British.

Washington's Victory

In 1754 the lieutenant governor of Virginia sent a young officer, George Washington, to Fort Duquesne, located in present-day Pittsburgh, Pennsylvania. Washington's men defeated a force of French soldiers near the fort. It was the first battle of the French and Indian War. But Washington did not capture the fort.

Loss for Great Britain

In 1755 British General Edward Braddock led British troops against Fort Duquesne. Washington was one of his officers. This time the British were defeated. Nearly 900 British troops were killed or wounded by the French and Wyandot. Braddock was killed.

Washington later wrote:

> **"**I luckily escaped . . . though I had four bullets through my coat, and two horses shot out under me.**"**

The Turning Point

News of the French victory caused panic among the British colonists. They asked British leader William Pitt to spend more money in the war. In November 1758, with Pitt's support, the British captured Fort Duquesne. They renamed it Fort Pitt. What city still bears his name?

QUICK CHECK

Main Idea and Details. Why did French trappers want to keep British settlers out of the Ohio River Valley?

▼ British and French troops also fought in Canada during the French and Indian War.

After the victory at Fort Duquesne, the British decided to drive the French out of Canada. In June 1759 British forces attacked Quebec, which is located on steep cliffs above the St. Lawrence River. To carry out this surprise attack, British troops silently climbed narrow paths up the cliffs at night.

The French awoke to find the British at the gates of the city. The siege lasted for months. Finally, on September 13, the French surrendered Quebec. One year later, the British seized Montreal, and the French were forced from Canada.

The Proclamation of 1763

War between Great Britain and France in Canada ended with the fall of Montreal. But battles between the two countries continued in Europe until 1763, when France was defeated. The two countries signed the **Treaty of Paris**, ending the French and Indian War. After the treaty was signed, Great Britain claimed all of France's colonies in North America.

After the war, the French could no longer help the Native Americans. On the other hand, Great Britain could not afford to use troops to protect settlers in the Ohio Valley. As a result, Great Britain issued the **Proclamation of 1763**. This official announcement set aside land west of the Appalachian Mountains for Native American groups.

North America, 1763

Hudson Bay

Great Lakes

St. Lawrence River

THE THIRTEEN COLONIES

LOUISIANA

PACIFIC OCEAN

NEW SPAIN

Rio Grande

Mississippi

ATLANTIC OCEAN

FLORIDA

Gulf of Mexico

West Indies

Caribbean Sea

N W E S

- British lands
- French lands
- Spanish lands
- Russian lands
- Disputed or unclaimed lands by Europeans
- Proclamation Line of 1763

0   500   1,000 miles
0   500   1,000 kilometers

Map Skill

LOCATION Why was land under Spanish control called Louisiana?

Pontiac

Although the British claimed former French lands, they did not have firm control of them. In 1763 Ottawa Chief Pontiac united Native Americans in the Ohio River valley to drive out the British. He called the British:

> Those who will do you nothing but harm.

▼ British troops climbed the steep cliffs below Quebec and attacked French troops in the city.

Pontiac's fighters captured and burned several British settlements in the area but were defeated by the British army in 1763.

Results of the War

The British victory in the French and Indian War united the colonists. They had joined together to fight a powerful enemy. They had discovered strong leaders such as Washington. Soon a new, independent spirit developed among the "Americans," as they called themselves. Victory in the French and Indian War set the stage for the American Revolution.

QUICK CHECK

Main Idea and Details What was the purpose of the Proclamation of 1763?

Check Understanding

1. **VOCABULARY** Make a time line of the French and Indian War. Use the terms below.

   French and Indian War   **Treaty of Paris**

   Proclamation of 1763

2. **READING SKILL Main Idea and Details** Use the graphic organizer to help write two paragraphs about the French and Indian War.

Main Idea	Details

3. **Write About It** Explain the risks that British settlers took when they moved to the Ohio River Valley.

155

VOCABULARY

Stamp Act p. 157

boycott p. 157

repeal p. 157

delegates p. 159

READING SKILL

Main Idea and Details
Copy the chart below. Use it to fill out the main idea and details of the colonial protests against Great Britain.

Main Idea	Details

MISSOURI COURSE LEVEL EXPECTATIONS

3a.D.1, 5.C.2, 6.I.1

COLONISTS PROTEST BRITISH RULE

Colonists burned printed documents and British stamps to protest the Stamp Act.

Visual Preview

What caused the colonists to unite against Great Britain?

A The colonists protested the taxes British leaders raised to pay war debts.

B British troops came to Boston and other cities to stop protests.

156

A NEW TAXES

*An angry crowd marched down the narrow streets of Boston
protesting the newly passed Stamp Act.
Why were they so angry about stamps?*

The French and Indian War was very costly for the British government. In 1763 King George III and British leaders agreed that taxes should be raised to pay the war debts. But British citizens were already paying high taxes. So British leaders decided to raise taxes on the colonists.

◄ A British stamp used on printed documents

The Stamp Act

In 1765 the British government passed the **Stamp Act**. Under this act, colonists had to buy stamps and place them on all printed documents, including letters, wills, newspapers, and even playing cards.

Many colonists said the British could not tax them without their consent, or agreement. One colonist who led the fight against the Stamp Act was Samuel Adams of Massachusetts. He sent protest letters to newspapers. In one letter he wrote:

> **❝** If our trade may be taxed, why not our lands? Why not . . . everything we possess or use? **❞**

Colonists Organize

When the Stamp Act went into effect on November 1, angry colonists staged a **boycott**. To boycott means to refuse to buy goods or services from a person, group, or country. Most colonists refused to use the stamps. To protest the Stamp Act, Adams and other colonists formed a group they called the Sons of Liberty.

In 1766 Parliament voted to **repeal**, or end, the Stamp Act. However, in 1767 Parliament passed the Townshend Acts. They taxed factory-made goods such as paper, glass, and paint.

Again, the colonists boycotted the newly taxed items. They also boycotted any colonial merchant who sold or used taxed goods. British leaders feared that the boycotts could lead to violence. They sent troops to the city of Boston, whose citizens had caused the most trouble.

QUICK CHECK

Main Idea and Details **How did British leaders raise taxes on the colonies?**

▲ Silversmith Paul Revere made this engraving of the Boston Massacre.

Engrav'd Printed & Sold by PAUL REVERE BOSTON

Ⓑ PROTEST IN BOSTON

No city in the colonies caused more problems for the British than Boston, Massachusetts. It was the location of two key events that led to the Revolution.

The Boston Massacre

On March 6, 1770, colonists gathered at the Boston Customs House, where taxes on goods from Great Britain were paid. The group included Crispus Attucks, a person who had escaped from slavery. Historians are uncertain exactly what happened next.

It seems that a member of the crowd insulted a British soldier, who knocked the boy down. Other colonists threw snowballs at the guard. British soldiers fired into the crowd, killing five colonists, including Attucks. This event became known as the Boston Massacre.

The Boston Tea Party

The British government repealed the Townshend Acts, but it passed the Tea Act in 1773. This act was passed to help the British East India Company. Parliament allowed the British East India Company to sell tea in the colonies without paying import taxes. Instead a tax was placed on colonists who bought tea. The tax was low, but colonists were angered that another law had been passed without their consent or approval.

In November 1773 three British East India Company ships entered Boston Harbor. Colonists refused to allow the ships to unload. The governor of Massachusetts, Thomas Hutchinson, ordered the ships to stay in the harbor until the tea was sold.

On the night of December 16, 1773, about 50 Sons of Liberty, some disguised as Mohawk Indians, boarded the ships. They broke open the tea chests and emptied them into the harbor. Similar attacks took place in Annapolis, Maryland, and New York city. However, this event became known as the Boston Tea Party.

The British Parliament responded by closing Boston Harbor until the colonists paid for the tea. Town meetings were banned. More British soldiers were sent to the colonies. Colonists called Parliament's actions "The Intolerable Acts." Intolerable means unbearable. The Intolerable Acts united the colonies against Great Britain. **Delegates** from the colonies met in Philadelphia to discuss the problem. Delegates are people who are chosen to represent other people. The delegates formed the First Continental Congress to decide what action to take against Great Britain.

QUICK CHECK

Main Idea and Details Why did the Intolerable Acts cause problems between the colonies and Great Britain?

▼ Colonists disguised as Mohawk Indians threw British tea into Boston Harbor.

Check Understanding

1. **VOCABULARY** Write three sentences using two of the words below.

Stamp Act	**repeal**
boycott	**delegate**

2. **READING SKILL Main Idea and Details** Use the chart from page 156 to write a paragraph about disagreements over taxes that led to protests in the colonies.

Main Idea	Details

EXPLORE The Big Idea 3. **Write About It** Why were colonists willing to take risks by protesting British laws?

VOCABULARY

militia p. 161

ammunition p. 163

READING SKILL

Main Idea and Details
Copy the chart below. Use it to fill in the main idea and details of the first battles of the Revolution.

Main Idea	Details

MISSOURI COURSE LEVEL EXPECTATIONS

3a.D.1, 5.A.1, 5.C.2, 5.J.1, 6.I.1, 7.B.1

THE REVOLUTION BEGINS

Minutemen fought off an attack by British soldiers at the Old North Bridge in Concord, Massachusetts.

What caused the American Revolution?

A The first shots were fired at Lexington and Concord.

B Colonists took over Fort Ticonderoga but lost at the Battle of Bunker Hill.

C By 1776 the British left Boston, but most colonists felt independent.

A LEXINGTON AND CONCORD

By 1775 colonists had stored weapons in Lexington and Concord, near Boston. Two well-known supporters of independence, Samuel Adams and John Hancock, were also in Lexington.

On April 18, 1775, British general Thomas Gage sent about 700 soldiers from Boston. They had orders to seize the weapons and arrest Samuel Adams and John Hancock.

Paul Revere, a Boston silversmith, set off for Lexington to warn of the British approach. A second rider, William Dawes, took a different route. A third rider, Dr. Samuel Prescott, also joined them.

By the time the British reached Lexington, Adams and Hancock had fled. Captain John Parker waited with colonial **militia**, called minutemen. Militia are volunteer soldiers who fight only in an emergency.

The First Shots

No one knows who fired first, but many shots rang out. Eight militia members were killed. British troops continued toward Concord, about ten miles away.

When the British soldiers arrived, many minutemen were waiting. They stopped the British there. As the British retreated to Boston, minutemen continued shooting along the way. More than 90 British soldiers were killed.

QUICK CHECK

Main Idea and Details What did British troops do on April 18, 1775?

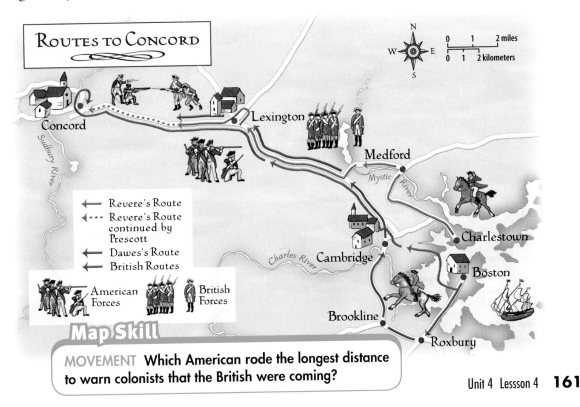

ROUTES TO CONCORD

- ← Revere's Route
- ◄···· Revere's Route continued by Prescott
- ← Dawes's Route
- ← British Routes
- American Forces
- British Forces

Concord · Lexington · Medford · Charlestown · Cambridge · Boston · Brookline · Roxbury · Sudbury River · Mystic River · Charles River

N / W / E / S — 0 1 2 miles — 0 1 2 kilometers

Map Skill
MOVEMENT Which American rode the longest distance to warn colonists that the British were coming?

This famous painting shows colonists fighting British soldiers at the Battle of Bunker Hill.

B EARLY BATTLES

Three weeks after the battles took place in Massachusetts, a young New Englander named Benedict Arnold led a militia force toward Fort Ticonderoga. This was a British fort on Lake Champlain in New York. News traveled slowly in the 1700s. Therefore, the British at Fort Ticonderoga did not know about the events at Lexington and Concord.

Ethan Allen

Arnold planned to capture the cannons at Fort Ticonderoga and take them to the colonial army camped near Boston. His force joined those of another New Englander— Ethan Allen. Allen's troops, the Green Mountain Boys, were militia from the area that is now Vermont.

Early on May 10, 1775, Allen's men sneaked into Fort Ticonderoga. They surprised the guards, capturing the fort without firing a shot.

The Battle of Bunker Hill

In June, back in Boston, British general Thomas Gage decided to take control of the hills around Boston. That way, American cannons could not fire down into the city. But colonists learned of the plan. The colonial militia, led by Colonel William Prescott and General Israel Putnam, were ordered to defend Bunker Hill in Charlestown across the Charles River from Boston. Instead, they decided to defend Breed's Hill, which was closer to the river. The colonists worked all night to build earthen walls for protection.

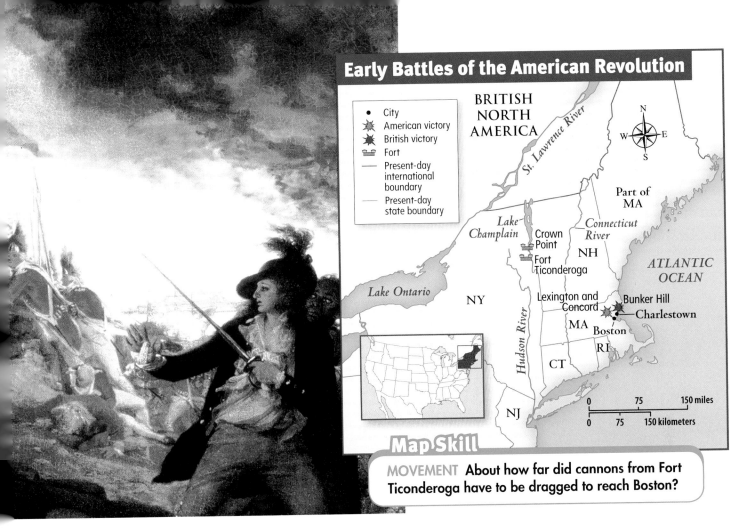

Early Battles of the American Revolution

- • City
- American victory
- British victory
- Fort
- — Present-day international boundary
- — Present-day state boundary

BRITISH NORTH AMERICA

St. Lawrence River

Lake Champlain

Crown Point

Fort Ticonderoga

Lake Ontario

NY

Hudson River

NH

Connecticut River

Part of MA

ATLANTIC OCEAN

Lexington and Concord

Bunker Hill
Charlestown

MA
Boston

RI

CT

NJ

0   75   150 miles
0   75   150 kilometers

Map Skill

MOVEMENT **About how far did cannons from Fort Ticonderoga have to be dragged to reach Boston?**

The Battle Begins

On June 17, British soldiers led by Major John Pitcairn crossed the Charles River in boats. They marched up Breed's Hill toward the earthen walls where colonists waited. The Americans did not have much **ammunition**, or musket balls and gunpowder. Officers told them not to waste ammunition by firing at soldiers too far away. Historians say that either Prescott or Putnam said:

❝Don't shoot until you see the whites of their eyes.❞

A British Victory

Twice the British charged up the hill. Both times they were turned back by American fire. Finally the Americans ran out of powder and musket balls. Peter Brown, an American soldier, described the third advance by the British troops:

❝When the enemy came in, [I] jumped over the wall and ran . . . [musket] balls flew like hail stones and cannon[s] roared like thunder. . . .❞

The British won what was later called the Battle of Bunker Hill. More than 400 colonists were killed or wounded, but the victory was costly for the British. More than 1,000 British soldiers were killed or wounded. The British commander, Major Pitcairn, was one of many British officers killed that day.

QUICK CHECK

Main Idea and Details. What happened at the Battle of Bunker Hill?

C NEW YEAR BRINGS HOPE

Word of the high cost of British victories spread beyond Massachusetts. Many colonists came to believe that by working together, the colonies could win their freedom. As 1776 began, hopes were high that the Revolution would be short and successful.

The British Leave Boston

Many colonists even found hope in the defeat at Bunker Hill. The British had won, but the Americans had fought hard. Abigail Adams had watched the battle from a hill near her house. She wrote to her husband, John:

> **"The spirits of the people are very good. The loss of Charlestown affects them no more than a drop in the bucket. . . ."**

Colonial soldiers led by General Henry Knox dragged cannons from Fort Ticonderoga to Boston.

In January 1776 cannons dragged from Fort Ticonderoga and Crown Point by colonial soldiers finally reached Boston. Soon, cannon fire poured into British camps in the city. In March, the British sailed out of Boston.

Some Seek Compromise

As American colonists heard about these battles they had to make a choice. Should they join the rebels or remain loyal to Britain? Most colonists wanted to end what they saw as British bullying. But not all colonists wanted to completely cut ties with Great Britain. They hoped that the British government would compromise. Some of these colonists worked to help the British government. Others feared that they might lose their property during the fighting. Still others, called Loyalists, simply did not want to separate from Great Britain. They thought that taxes and restrictions were not good reasons for rebellion.

No Turning Back

Most colonists understood that a compromise would not be reached. They knew that once British soldiers were killed, the British government would not back down. But the events around Boston made colonists see themselves in a new way. They were no longer British citizens living in British colonies. They were citizens of a new country that was fighting to free itself from British rule. Patrick Henry declared this at the First Continental Congress:

"I am not a Virginian but an American."

QUICK CHECK

Main Idea and Details **Why did some colonists want to compromise with Great Britain?**

▼ Cannons like this were dragged from Fort Ticonderoga to Boston.

Check Understanding

1. **VOCABULARY** Write one sentence using both vocabulary words below.

   militia   **ammunition**

2. **READING SKILL Main Idea and Details** Use the chart from page 160 to write a paragraph explaining why colonists saw hope in the defeat at Bunker Hill.

Main Idea	Details

 3. **Write About It** In what ways did the events of 1775 and 1776 show colonists the risks they were taking by fighting the British?

VOCABULARY

Continental Army p. 167

Declaration of Independence p. 168

READING SKILL

Main Idea and Details
Copy the chart below. Use it to fill in the main idea and details of the Declaration of Independence.

Main Idea	Details

MISSOURI COURSE LEVEL EXPECTATIONS

1.A.1, 3a.D.1, 5.C.2, 6.I.1

The Declaration of Independence

Delegates to the Second Continental Congress signed the Declaration of Independence in 1776.

Visual Preview

Why is the Second Continental Congress important?

A The Congress sent a peace petition to Great Britain that King George III rejected.

B The Congress approved the Declaration of Independence.

A PEACE PLANS FAIL

On May 10, 1775, about a month after the battles at Lexington and Concord, colonial delegates met in Philadelphia at the Second Continental Congress.

John Hancock, a Boston merchant who had escaped from Lexington, was elected president of the Second Continental Congress. Hancock soon learned that the delegates did not all have the same goals for the Congress.

Delegates Disagree

Samuel Adams and John Adams, from Massachusetts, and Richard Henry Lee and Thomas Jefferson, of Virginia, wanted independence from Great Britain. John Dickinson of Pennsylvania and others hoped the colonies could remain British subjects but could govern themselves.

In July 1775 the Congress sent what they called the "Olive Branch Petition" to King George III. An olive branch is a symbol of peace. The petition asked the king to repeal his governing policies for the colonies. The petition angered the king. He refused to even read it. Instead he ordered more troops to be sent to the colonies. When word of the king's response reached the Congress, most delegates agreed that independence was their only choice.

A Continental Army

By late 1775, the Congress faced the task of raising an army and naming a commander. Most fighting had taken place in the North. This led John Adams to say that a Southern commander would help unite the regions. He nominated George Washington from Virginia as the leader of the

King George III ▶

Continental Army, the name given to the colonial force. Washington had served as an officer in the French and Indian War, and colonial soldiers trusted him.

Congress sent Representatives to France, the Netherlands, and Spain to seek financial support. These countries wanted to help the Americans fight Great Britain, their longtime enemy. However, Great Britain was the strongest country in Europe. No country would risk sending money or supplies until the Continental Army proved it could defeat the British.

QUICK CHECK

Main Idea and Details How did George Washington become the leader of the Continental Army?

In June 1776 a committee was appointed by Congress to write a **Declaration of Independence**, a document stating that the colonies were independent from Great Britain. The committee members were John Adams of Massachusetts, Benjamin Franklin of Pennsylvania, Robert Livingston of New York, Roger Sherman of Connecticut, and Thomas Jefferson of Virginia. The members of the committee decided that Jefferson should write the first draft.

Writing Begins

Jefferson worked on a draft for two weeks. Then Franklin and Adams made some changes and presented the draft to the Congress on June 28. Throughout the hot summer days of early July, delegates discussed the final wording of the Declaration. Adams later said he was delighted with Jefferson's "high tone," yet he later wrote:

> **"There were other expressions . . . which I thought too much like scolding."**

Jefferson included a list of crimes that he accused the king of committing. Other delegates wanted to remove parts of this section before sending it to the king.

Jefferson had also attacked the slave trade. Representatives from the Southern colonies, whose economy depended on slavery, removed words attacking slavery and the slave trade.

General Washington had the Declaration of Independence read to his soldiers.

The power of Jefferson's words inspired the delegates. But the final statement of his document made the most important point:

"The good people of these colonies, solemnly publish and declare, that these United Colonies are, and of right ought to be free and independent states."

Approval and Signing

At last the delegates were satisfied. They passed the final version of the Declaration of Independence on July 4, 1776. John Hancock, as president, signed it first. He said that he wrote his name large enough for the king to read without his glasses. Americans still celebrate this date as "Independence Day."

Soon copies of the Declaration were sent throughout the colonies. On July 19 Congress ordered a special copy of the Declaration to be written on parchment, a sheepskin paper used for important documents. Its new title was "The Unanimous Declaration of the Thirteen United States of America." It was the first time the name of the new country was used in an official document.

On August 2, the other delegates added their signatures under Hancock's, which was the largest. Eventually, 56 delegates signed the document. Every person who signed it became an enemy of the king and could be hanged. Declaring independence was a great risk.

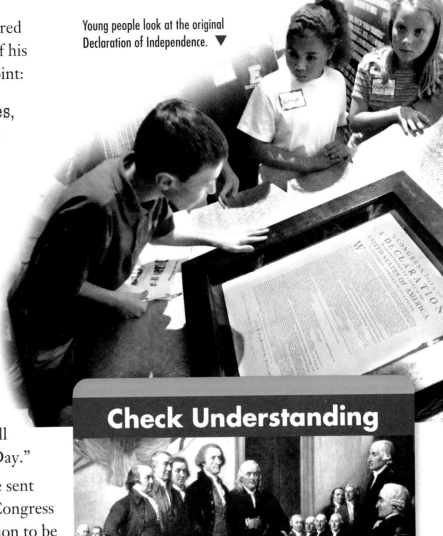
Young people look at the original Declaration of Independence. ▼

QUICK CHECK

Main Idea and Details What was the purpose of the Declaration of Independence?

Check Understanding

1. **VOCABULARY** Write a sentence explaining how the Second Continental Congress is connected to each vocabulary term.
   Continental army
   Declaration of Independence

2. **READING SKILL Main Idea and Details** Use the chart from page 166 to explain how the Declaration of Independence was written.

Main Idea	Details

3. **Write About It** Why did King George's rejection of the Olive Branch Petition cause the colonists to risk their lives for independence?

Fighting the War

VOCABULARY

Patriot p. 171

mercenary p. 172

Loyalist p. 172

profiteering p. 176

inflation p. 176

READING SKILL

Main Idea and Details
Copy the chart below. Use it to fill in the main idea and details about the ways colonists supported the war.

Main Idea	Details

MISSOURI COURSE LEVEL EXPECTATIONS

3a.D.1, 5.A.1, 5.C.2, 5.J.1, 6.I.1, 7.A.1, 7.B.1

Soldiers from Germany, called Hessians, fought for the British.

Visual Preview

Why did the war present challenges?

A Americans were eager to fight, but they lost many early battles.

B The British did not recognize the Americans' strengths or their own weaknesses.

C Americans had to support the Revolution on and off the battlefield.

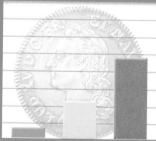

D Americans faced serious economic problems during the Revolution.

READY FOR WAR?

By late August 1776, American soldiers under General Washington were eager to fight in the Revolution. But they were up against a powerful enemy—their home country, Great Britain.

The American soldiers and other Americans who supported the Revolution called themselves **Patriots**. Patriots are people who love their country. In the Revolution the Patriots were willing to fight to gain freedom from Great Britain. Yet few Patriot soldiers had ever fought on a battlefield. And they were about to fight the most powerful fighting force in the world—the British army.

Early Defeat

One of the earliest battles took place on Long Island, New York, on August 27, 1776. Here the 10,000-man American army faced 20,000 British soldiers.

The Patriots were badly beaten. In the following weeks, they lost several other battles around New York City. By October 1776 the British controlled New York City.

The British then chased Washington's army across the Hudson River. The Americans retreated across New Jersey. Many Patriots, including officers, began to question Washington's leadership.

QUICK CHECK

Main Idea and Details What happened to American soldiers in the early years of the Revolution?

Although they lacked training and supplies, Patriot soldiers often held off experienced British soldiers.

British soldiers

Patriot soldier

Patriot soldiers were eager to fight. But at first they were no match for the British army. Many British military leaders believed the war would end quickly. Instead, it lasted five years. The British had not counted on the Americans' strengths. And they did not recognize their own weaknesses.

BRITISH ARMY

Strengths

▶ **Army** The British had more than 60,000 soldiers in the American colonies. They included many **mercenaries**, professional soldiers from other countries. Most were Hessians from Germany.

▶ **Training** British soldiers were well-trained fighters who joined the army for life.

▶ **Equipment** Each soldier carried a gun called a musket tipped with a sharp bayonet.

▶ **Support** British soldiers were helped by **Loyalists**, colonists who supported Great Britain.

Weaknesses

▶ **Army** Soldiers and military supplies sent from Great Britain to the American colonies had to be shipped across the Atlantic Ocean.

▶ **Training** British soldiers trained to fight on open battlefields. But Patriots fired from hidden positions.

▶ **Equipment** The red uniform coats made British soldiers easy targets.

▶ **Support** Some British did not support the war because it raised the taxes they paid.

The British did not understand that the Patriots were willing to suffer a great deal to gain their freedom. Many Americans—those in the army and those at home—gave everything they had to win their independence.

QUICK CHECK

Main Idea and Details **What was the difference in training between Patriot soldiers and British soldiers?**

AMERICAN ARMY

Strengths

▶ **Army** Patriots fought to protect their homes, families, and a new nation.

▶ **Training** Patriots attacked by surprise, firing from well-protected spots. They used the tactics they learned during the French and Indian War.

▶ **Equipment** Many Patriot soldiers used Kentucky long rifles, which were more accurate than muskets.

▶ **Support** Citizens supported the army by making musket balls or blankets. Farmers gave food to soldiers.

Weaknesses

▶ **Army** General Washington never had more than 17,000 soldiers at any time in the war.

▶ **Training** Soldiers signed up for six months. That was not long enough to train to fight on open battlefields.

▶ **Equipment** Lack of uniforms, especially shoes, was a constant problem.

▶ **Support** Some Americans hid supplies or sold food to the army at high prices.

SUPPORTING THE WAR

Americans supported the Revolution in many ways. Some raised money for the army or loaned money to the new government. Robert Morris, a wealthy merchant, loaned the new government $10,000—a huge amount then—to buy gunpowder, food, and supplies. Other Americans made weapons or ran businesses left behind by men who joined the army.

Support at Home

American women helped the fight for freedom in many ways. Some traveled to military camps. There they cooked meals or cared for sick and wounded soldiers.

Women also became carpenters, blacksmiths, and shipbuilders. Others took charge of family farms or shops when their husbands, fathers, or sons went to war.

Some women gave hope to Americans through writing. Mercy Otis Warren wrote a history of the American Revolution. Phillis Wheatley wrote poems about freedom.

Abigail Adams, the wife of John Adams, supported the Revolution from her home near Boston. You can read part of her letter about the Declaration of Independence below.

◀ Molly Pitcher loads a cannon.

Primary Sources

Last Thursday . . . I went . . . to Kings Street to hear the proclamation for independence read. . . . When Col(onel) Crafts read . . . great attention was given to every word. As soon as he ended . . . every face appeared joyful.

A section from a letter by Abigail Adams, July 21, 1776, Boston

Write About It It is 1776. Write a letter to a friend in another town describing the scene when the Declaration of Independence is read in your town square.

▲ This painting shows black soldiers from the First Rhode Island Regiment at the Battle of Newport.

Support in the Field

Several women helped on the battlefields. Sybil Luddington was called "the female Paul Revere" when she warned colonists of a British attack on Danbury, Connecticut. Deborah Sampson disguised herself as a man to join the army. Mary Ludwig Hays McCauley—we know her as "Molly Pitcher"—carried water to thirsty soldiers during battle. When her husband was wounded during the Battle of Monmouth, New Jersey, she took his place at the cannon.

African Americans were also encouraged to join the war. At this time, most African Americans in the colonies were enslaved and could not serve as soldiers at the beginning of the war. There were some free African American colonists who joined the American army. The words "all men are created equal" from the Declaration of Independence gave them hope that victory might create a new nation that treated all people equally.

About 5,000 African American colonists served with the Continental army. Rhode Island's African American soldiers formed their own unit in 1777, called the First Rhode Island Regiment. In 1781, the soldiers of the First Rhode Island Regiment fought in the final battle of the Revolution, a victory over the British at Yorktown, Virginia.

QUICK CHECK

Main Idea and Details How did the Revolution change the roles of colonial women?

Ⓓ WARTIME SHORTAGES

Paper Dollars Equaling One-Dollar Coin, 1777–1781

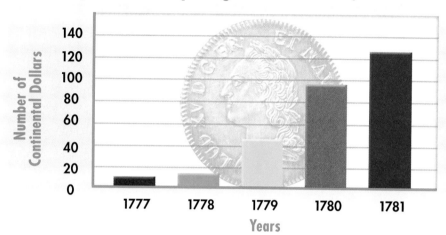

Chart Skill

In 1779 about how many Continental dollars would you need to buy an item worth a one-dollar coin?

Patriot soldiers faced many shortages during the war. However, most Americans also lacked food and clothing. Items such as cloth, kettles, and tools were made in British factories—and all trade was cut off when the fighting began.

Unfair Practices

Americans themselves caused other shortages. Hoarding, or hiding away goods, such as flour, molasses, and manufactured items was a serious problem. Hoarding made these products hard to get—which raised their price. Some farmers and merchants became wealthy by **profiteering**, or charging high prices, for goods they hoarded.

Printing Money

Profiteering also hurt the government. Forced to pay high prices for supplies, Congress printed more paper money called "Continentals." However, the treasury did not have enough gold to back up their value. The drop in the value of Continentals led to **inflation**. Inflation is a large and rapid rise in prices. People at the time described something that was useless as "not worth a Continental."

QUICK CHECK

Main Idea and Details How did profiteering hurt Americans?

Check Understanding

1. **VOCABULARY** Use two words below in a sentence about economic problems.

   Patriot   profiteering

   mercenary   inflation

   Loyalist

2. **READING SKILL Main Idea and Details** Use the chart from page 170 to explain the strengths and weaknesses of each side.

Main Idea	Details

3. **Write About It** Why were Patriots willing to risk fighting the powerful British army?

Map and Globe Skills

Use a Battle Map

VOCABULARY

battle map

One way to study historical battles is to look at a **battle map**. A battle map shows important places, actions, and troop movements during a battle. The map on this page explains an early battle of the American Revolution, the Battle of Bunker Hill, which took place in June 1775.

Learn It

- Look at the map key, or legend. It tells the meaning of the symbols on the map. On this map, the red-coated figures show British troops. The blue-coated figures show American troops. Arrows show the directions troops moved. Bursts show where the actual fighting took place.

- Look for a scale to find out how far troops traveled. Look at the compass to tell you in which direction they moved.

Try It

- What direction is Bunker Hill from Breed's Hill?

- On what hill did most of the fighting take place?

- How far did British troops have to travel by water and land to fight the Americans?

Apply It

- What information can you get from a battle map that is not in the text?

- Write one sentence that tells what you have learned about the Battle of Bunker Hill from the map.

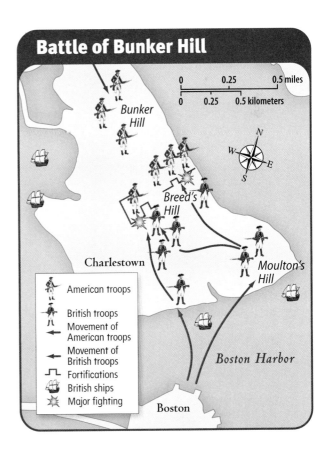

Battle of Bunker Hill

0   0.25   0.5 miles
0   0.25   0.5 kilometers

Bunker Hill

Breed's Hill

Charlestown

Moulton's Hill

Boston Harbor

Boston

American troops
British troops
Movement of American troops
Movement of British troops
Fortifications
British ships
Major fighting

AMERICAN VICTORIES

Lesson 7

VOCABULARY

desert p. 179

Treaty of Alliance p. 181

READING SKILL

Main Idea and Details
Copy the chart below. Fill in the main idea and details of events that happened between 1776 and 1778.

Main Idea	Details

MISSOURI COURSE LEVEL EXPECTATIONS

3a.D.1, 5.A.1, 5.C.2, 5.J.1, 6.I.1, 7.B.1

Washington won victories in New Jersey in 1776 and early 1777.

Visual Preview

How did Patriots influence the war?

A In 1776 the Patriots won an important battle at Trenton, New Jersey.

B The Patriot victory at Saratoga, New York, in 1777 was a turning point.

C Americans faced a hard winter and won victories outside the colonies and at sea.

Ⓐ MAJOR PATRIOT VICTORY

*The final weeks of 1776 were dark days for the Patriots.
General Washington's army had lost battles around New York City.
Now British troops chased the Patriots
across New Jersey into Pennsylvania.*

Writer Thomas Paine was among the Patriot soldiers escaping to Pennsylvania. In a pamphlet titled *The Crisis*, he described those dark days with these words:

These are the times that try men's souls.

Washington led the Patriots across the icy Delaware River. ▲

Victory in New Jersey

By December 25, many Patriot soldiers had left the army. Some chose to **desert**, or run away. Many who remained had no shoes or supplies. Without a victory to give Americans hope, Washington believed the Revolution would fail. So, he came up with a bold new plan.

Washington decided to cross the Delaware River from Pennsylvania and attack the Hessian soldiers in Trenton, New Jersey, on Christmas night. An icy storm blew in on December 25 and the Patriots finally reached New Jersey at

4 A.M. Washington's plan worked. At Trenton, the surprised Hessians quickly surrendered. Washington lost only two men in the battle—both froze to death.

On January 3, 1777, the Patriots defeated the British at Princeton, New Jersey, and captured badly needed supplies from the British. Now Patriot soldiers had food, weapons, shoes—and hope.

QUICK CHECK

Main Idea and Details Why did George Washington come up with a bold plan?

BATTLE OF SARATOGA

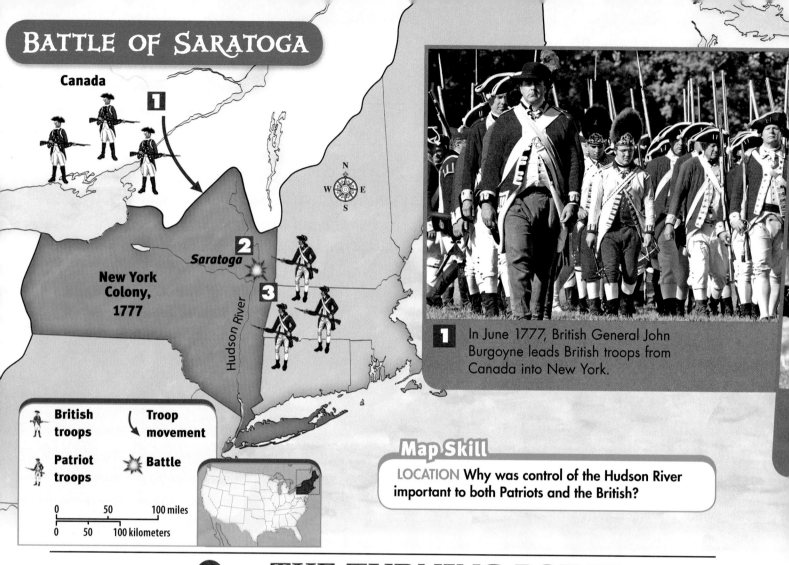

Canada

1

Saratoga

2

3

New York Colony, 1777

Hudson River

| British troops | Troop movement |
| Patriot troops | Battle |

0   50   100 miles

0   50   100 kilometers

1 In June 1777, British General John Burgoyne leads British troops from Canada into New York.

Map Skill

LOCATION **Why was control of the Hudson River important to both Patriots and the British?**

B THE TURNING POINT

A turning point is an event that causes an important change. For the Patriots, the Battle of Saratoga became a turning point in the Revolutionary War.

Victory at Saratoga

In June 1777, British General John Burgoyne led several thousand soldiers from Canada into New York. He believed another British force would march north. A Patriot force under General Horatio Gates would then be trapped between them.

At first, Burgoyne's army drove Gates and the Patriots south. But the British supply wagons got stuck on forest roads. The Patriots

had time to gather more troops and decided to stand and fight at Saratoga, New York. Burgoyne reached Saratoga on September 16. By then, Gates had three times more soldiers than the British general. The Patriots had also built dirt walls at Bemis Heights, near Saratoga.

On September 19, British and Patriot troops battled at Freeman's Farm, near Saratoga. The British won control of the farm. But they lost more soldiers than the Patriots. Low on troops, Burgoyne needed help—but no army marched north. Finally, he could wait no longer. On October 7, British soldiers battled Patriot soldiers at Bemis Heights. The British

2 In September 1777, British and Patriot troops battle at Freeman's Farm outside Saratoga. The British take control of the farm but suffer heavy losses.

3 In October 1777, British General Burgoyne orders an attack on Bemis Heights near Saratoga and is defeated.

had no chance to win. Burgoyne surrendered on October 17, 1777. The British defeat at Saratoga changed the outcome of the war.

Help from Europe

When news of the Patriot victory reached Paris, France, it convinced the French that the Americans could win independence from Great Britain. As a result, the French and American governments signed a **Treaty of Alliance**, or an agreement to work together. Several months later, French troops, warships, and supplies began the journey across the Atlantic Ocean.

Other Europeans who supported the Patriots also came to America to join the fight. Thaddeus Kosciuszko, an engineer educated in Poland, arrived to help build forts. One young French citizen who arrived to help the Patriots was 19-year-old Marquis de Lafayette. When Lafayette met George Washington, the two became close friends.

QUICK CHECK

Main Idea and Details Why did France agree to help the United States fight Great Britain?

PEOPLE

The dirt walls at Bemis Heights in Saratoga were designed by **Thaddeus Kosciuszko**, an engineer educated in Poland. He came to America to join the Patriots and later designed the fort at West Point, New York.

Thaddeus Kosciuszko

VALLEY FORGE AND BEYOND

The victory at Saratoga did not help the Patriots right away. In the winter of 1777 to 1778, Washington's troops faced bitter cold as they huddled around campfires at Valley Forge, Pennsylvania.

Hunger and Disease

For the first two months of that winter, soldiers lived in ragged tents. Few had shoes or blankets, and they shared coats and gloves. Food was in short supply too. At Valley Forge the main food was "fire cakes," a paste of flour and water roasted on a stick over campfires. Weak from cold and hunger, soldiers became sick. Diseases spread quickly because soldiers lived close together. At least 2,500 died from illnesses such as typhoid, influenza, and smallpox.

During that cold winter, a military instructor named Baron Friedrich von Steuben arrived from the German kingdom of Prussia. He saw that the American army needed strict training. Von Steuben taught the Patriots to march in rows and fight together instead of separately. By June 1778, the American army had become a well-trained fighting force able to defeat the British on open battlefields.

Fighting Outside the Colonies

Not all important Revolutionary battles were fought in the 13 Colonies. Key battles took place in the British territories west of the Appalachian Mountains—and even off the coast of Great Britain.

General Washington and his tired soldiers march into Valley Forge. Many soldiers deserted because of the terrible conditions.

George Washington

In February 1779, George Rogers Clark and his men marched for days across swampland. After marching for a month, the Americans attacked and defeated the British at Fort Sackville near present-day Vincennes, Indiana.

The greatest hero of the American navy was John Paul Jones. On September 23, 1779, his ship, the *Bonhomme Richard*, defeated the British warship *Serapis* off the coast of Great Britain. Today, John Paul Jones is known as the "Father of the American Navy."

QUICK CHECK

Main Idea and Details How did training at Valley Forge help the Patriot army?

Check Understanding

1. **VOCABULARY** Use each vocabulary term below in a sentence.

   desert   **Treaty of Alliance**

2. **READING SKILL Main Idea and Details** Use the chart from page 178 to write about the winter at Valley Forge.

Main Idea	Details

 3. **Write About It** Why did Burgoyne risk an attack on Bemis Heights?

183

The War Ends

Lesson 8

VOCABULARY

blockade p. 187

Treaty of Paris 1783 p. 187

READING SKILL

Main Idea and Details

Copy the chart below. Use it to fill in the main idea and details about the help that France provided in the American Revolution.

Main Idea	Details

MISSOURI COURSE LEVEL EXPECTATIONS

1.A.1, 3a.D.1, 3a.F.2, 5.A.1, 5.C.2, 5.J.1, 6.I.1, 7.B.1

Re-enactors march in uniforms like those worn in the Revolution.

Visual Preview

How did the Revolution affect life in America?

A Spain helped the Patriots as the war moved to the South.

B The British surrendered at Yorktown, Virginia, in 1781.

C Loyalists, Native Americans, and enslaved Africans faced new challenges.

A THE WAR MOVES SOUTH

By 1779 the British hoped to win the war in a region with a large Loyalist population—the Southern colonies. Controlling the wealthy Southern colonies became the main goal of British leaders.

The British plan to keep control of the South did not begin well. In 1779 the Americans gained support from Spain, a French ally. The Spanish government loaned money to the Patriots. In addition, Bernardo de Gálvez, the governor of Spain's Louisiana Territory, closed the port at New Orleans to Great Britain and opened it to American ships.

Meanwhile, George Washington appointed General Nathanael Greene to lead Patriot forces in the South. However, the Patriots continued to face problems. Congress had little money to pay troops, and supplies were low. Between 1778 and 1781, the British army won battles at Savannah, Georgia, and at Charles Town and Camden in South Carolina.

Costly Victory

For a time, it seemed that the British would remain in control of the South. But their victories were costly. In 1780 General Charles Cornwallis took command of the British army in the South. Cornwallis pursued the American army north through the Carolinas. The two armies finally met in March 1781 at Guilford Court House, North Carolina.

British General Lord Cornwallis

The British won the battle, but Cornwallis lost one-fourth of his soldiers. However, he claimed a British victory because Greene's forces left the battlefield. When one British leader learned of the many troops lost, he said:

❝Another such victory would destroy the British army.❞

QUICK CHECK

Main Idea and Details **What took place between 1779 and 1781 in the Revolution?**

THE BATTLE OF YORKTOWN

THE BATTLE
OF
YORKTOWN
1781

0   5   10 miles
0   5   10 kilometers

Chesapeake
Bay

York River

Williamsburg

Yorktown

James River

N
W   E
S

ATLANTIC
OCEAN

→ American troops
— British troops
→ French troops
⛵ British ships
⛵ French ships

Map Skill

MOVEMENT **From which direction did American and French troops approach Yorktown?**

In the summer of 1781, both armies needed a vitory to win the war. General Cornwallis led 7,000 British soldiers to Yorktown, Virginia. Cornwallis stationed his troops in Yorktown to help fortify the area. They would wait there for the ships from British headquarters in New York City to bring supplies. But stopping at Yorktown was a decision that would cause Great Britain to lose the war. General Cornwallis did not guess that the Patriots and the French would learn of his plans.

British troops were outnumbered and could not hold off attacks by American and French forces.

Lafayette's Plan

Not far from Yorktown, Marquis de Lafayette commanded a small Patriot army. His troops were no match for Cornwallis. However, Lafayette had one advantage. One of Cornwallis's servants, James Armistead, was a spy for Lafayette. Armistead passed on information that the British were waiting for supplies from New York. Lafayette sent this information to the French navy. French warships off the Atlantic coast set up a **blockade** of British ships. A blockade is an action that prevents the passage of people or supplies. The French ships kept British troops and supplies from reaching Cornwallis.

At the same time, Washington's army and a large French force joined Lafayette. Cornwallis discovered too late that his army was surrounded by a French and Patriot army of more than 16,000 men.

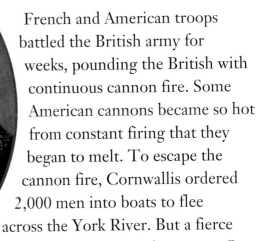

Marquis de Lafayette

French and American troops battled the British army for weeks, pounding the British with continuous cannon fire. Some American cannons became so hot from constant firing that they began to melt. To escape the cannon fire, Cornwallis ordered 2,000 men into boats to flee across the York River. But a fierce storm blew in, stopping the escape. On October 17, 1781, Cornwallis sent a runner to surrender to Washington.

The Revolution Ends

Soon after the surrender, the British government began peace talks with France, Spain, and the Americans in Paris, France. **The Treaty of Paris 1783** ended the American Revolution. Under the agreement Great Britain recognized American independence. The Mississippi River became the new nation's western border. The treaty also opened the Mississippi River to ships from France, Spain, Britain, and the United States.

The American Revolution was over. The 13 colonies were now known as the United States. In his farewell orders to the Continental army, Washington wrote that the determination of the troops:

> **❝**through almost every possible suffering and discouragement for the space of eight long years, was little short of a standing miracle.**❞**

QUICK CHECK

Main Idea and Details How did Cornwallis's decision to stop at Yorktown lead to Great Britain's defeat?

C THE RESULTS OF THE WAR

Several years after the Revolution, John Adams was asked about the war. He said that there had been two revolutions. One was the war itself. The other was:

> **"in the minds and hearts of the people."**

The United States had won independence. But not all the hearts and minds of the people had been changed.

Loyalists Leave

When the war ended, about 60,000 Loyalists remained in the United States. Many of these people had been wealthy merchants before the war. Some had been forced to give up their homes and property during the fighting. After the war, many Loyalists moved to Canada, which remained a British colony. Other Loyalists remained in the United States and tried to fit in with the new society. Many former Loyalists decided to move to the Western frontier.

Native Americans Lose Lands

During the Revolutionary War most Native Americans, including Joseph Brant who led several Native American groups, sided with the British. This was because Great Britain had protected Native American lands west of the Appalachians from American settlement.

◄ This illustration of Patriot soldiers returning from the American Revolution appeared in a magazine for young people in 1906.

Native Americans had fought to protect their own homelands, but many Americans saw them as enemies. As a result, settlers felt no guilt about taking land from people who had fought with the British.

Slavery Continues

In the Declaration of Independence, the phrase "all men are created equal" led some people to believe that slavery might end. The new American government, however, needed the support of Southern plantation owners who depended on the labor of enslaved Africans. As a result, slavery continued in the new nation.

QUICK CHECK

Main Idea and Details What were the results of the American Revolution?

Check Understanding

1. **VOCABULARY** Write one sentence using both terms below.

   blockade **Treaty of Paris 1783**

2. **READING SKILL Main Idea and Details** Use the chart from page 184 to write a paragraph about France's role at the Battle of Yorktown.

Main Idea	Details

3. **Write About It** Make a list of the reasons people in the following groups risked their lives in the war: Patriots, Loyalists, British soldiers, African Americans, and Native Americans.

Vocabulary

Number a paper from 1 to 4. Match each description below with the correct term.

mercenary   **Treaty of Paris 1783**

patriot   **boycott**

1. Someone who loves his or her country

2. The agreement that ended the American Revolution

3. To refuse to buy goods or services from a person, group or country.

4. Someone who is paid to fight for another country

Comprehension and Critical Thinking

5. How did women in the colonies help fight for independence during the Revolutionary War?

6. **Reading Skill** How did colonists protest against British laws and regulations?

7. **Critical Thinking** How did African Americans feel that the struggle for independence would help them?

8. **Critical Thinking** How did the victory at Yorktown affect Loyalists and Native Americans?

Skill

Use a Battle Map

Look at map on the right. Write a complete sentence to answer each question.

9. What body of water was the scene of major fighting?

10. Based on the map, what do you think was one major difference in the fortifications of the British and the Americans?

Battle of Saratoga

Major fighting
Headquarters
Building
Fortification
British troops
American troops

Freeman's Farm
Burgoyne's Headquarters
To Saratoga
Mill Creek
Hudson River
BEMIS HEIGHTS
Gates's Headquarters
To Albany

0   0.25   0.5 miles
0 0.25 0.5 kilometers

MAP Test Preparation

Directions   Read the passage. Then answer Numbers 1 through 3.

Thomas Jefferson worked on writing the Declaration of Independence for two weeks. When he was satisfied, he read it to Benjamin Franklin and John Adams. They made a few changes and then presented it to the Continental Congress on June 28.

On July 1, 1776, the Continental Congress began discussing the Declaration of Independence. Three days later, it was approved. Church bells rang across Philadelphia to tell people the good news. The Declaration was then copied on paper made of sheepskin. On August 2, John Hancock was first to sign—in large letters. Today a person's signature is sometimes called a "John Hancock".

1 **According to the passage, how long did it take Congress to approve the Declaration of Independence?**

- ○ two weeks
- ○ three days
- ○ six days
- ○ one month

2 **Why would a person most likely read this passage?**

- ○ learn about Philadelphia
- ○ discover new uses for sheepskin
- ○ learn about the Declaration of Independence
- ○ understand the duties of Congress

3 **Why do some people refer to a signature as a "John Hancock"?**

Write your answer on a separate piece of paper.

The Big Idea Activities

Why do people take risks?

Write About the Big Idea

Expository Essay
Use the Unit 4 foldable to help you write an essay that answers the Big Idea question, *Why do people take risks?* Be sure to begin your essay with an introduction. Use the notes you wrote under each tab in the foldable for details to support each main idea. End with a concluding paragraph that answers the question.

FOLDABLES™
Study Organizer

Risks

French   British   American

Make a Leadership Yearbook

Work in small groups to make a yearbook of leaders that you have read about in Unit 4. Each group should choose a different leader. Here's how to make your yearbook page.

1. Have one person find or draw a picture of the leader's face or a picture of that person in action.

2. Have one person write down the years the leader lived and important events in his or her life. Use a quote if possible.

3. Work as a group to list at least three leadership qualities of the person you have chosen.

When each group has finished its page, join all of the pages together to make a book. Decide as a class what picture or words should appear on the cover.

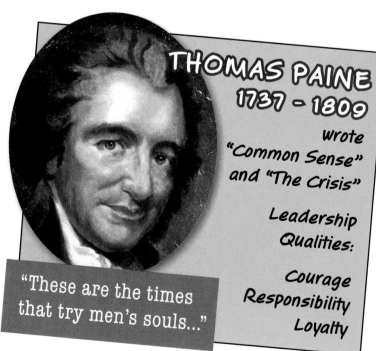

THOMAS PAINE
1737 – 1809

wrote "Common Sense" and "The Crisis"

Leadership Qualities:

Courage
Responsibility
Loyalty

"These are the times that try men's souls..."

The New Nation

Unit 5

EXPLORE The Big Idea

Essential Question
What causes a society to grow?

FOLDABLES™ Study Organizer

Draw Conclusions
Make and label a Four-tab envelope Foldable before you read Unit 5. Label the four tabs: **New Lands, Population Changes, New Inventions,** and **New Methods of Transportation.** Use the Foldable to organize information as you read.

LOG ON
For more about Unit 5 go to
www.macmillanmh.com

PEOPLE, PLACES, AND EVENTS

James Madison

Tecumseh

Philadelphia

1787
James Madison helps to create the United States Constitution.

Indiana Territory

1811
Tecumseh's forces are defeated at the Battle of Tippecanoe.

1780   1795   1810

In 1787 **James Madison** helped to create the United States **Constitution**, our nation's plan for government.

Today you can see the U.S. Constitution on display in Washington, D.C.

In 1811 Native Americans, led by **Tecumseh**, were defeated at the **Battle of Tippecanoe**.

Today in Ohio a play is performed every summer that tells the story of Tecumseh's life.

Davy Crockett

Andrew Jackson

San Antonio

1836

Davy Crockett is killed at the Alamo, fighting for the independence of Texas.

Georgia

1838

Andrew Jackson forces Native Americans west on the Trail of Tears.

1825

1840

1855

In 1836 famous pioneer **Davy Crockett** was killed at the Battle of the Alamo.

Today you can visit the **Alamo** mission in San Antonio, Texas.

In 1838 President **Andrew Jackson** forced Native Americans to leave their homes and follow the **Trail of Tears** to the west.

Today you can take a car trip along parts of the trail.

195

Lesson 1

VOCABULARY

Articles of
    Confederation p. 197

arsenal p. 198

legislature p. 200

READING SKILL

Draw Conclusions
Copy the chart below. Use
it to draw conclusions
about the need for a new
plan for government.

Text Clues	Conclusion

**MISSOURI COURSE
LEVEL EXPECTATIONS**

1.A.2, 1.A.3, 5.A.1, 5.C.2, 5.J.1,
6.I.1, 7.B.1

Planning a New Government

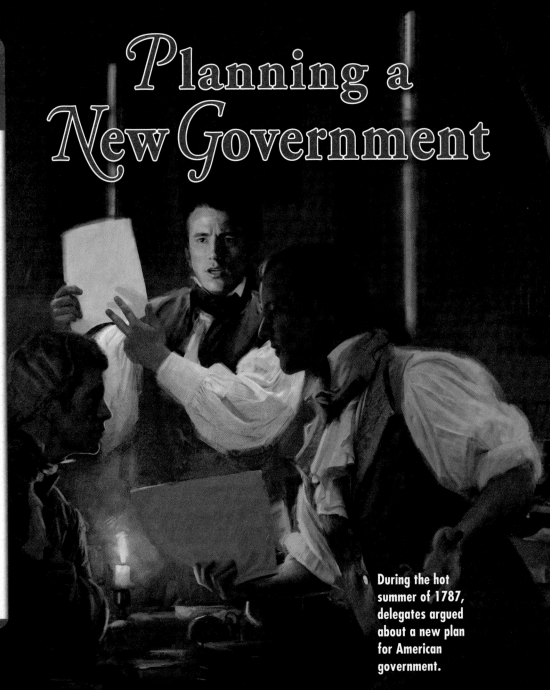

During the hot
summer of 1787,
delegates argued
about a new plan
for American
government.

Visual Preview

What problems did the government face after the Revolution?

A Many Americans
believed that the
Articles of Confederation
were a failure.

B Shays's Rebellion
showed the
weakness of the Articles
of Confederation.

C The delegates at
the Convention
disagreed about the way
to share power.

D After months of
debate and many
compromises, delegates
signed the Constitution.

Ⓐ THE ARTICLES OF CONFEDERATION

Every government needs a plan. In 1777 the Second Continental Congress approved the **Articles of Confederation**—*the first plan of government for the United States.*

At first, the Articles of Confederation met the needs of the young nation. But its weaknesses soon became obvious.

No Central Government

Under the Articles of Confederation, each state was independent. Each state printed its own money and passed its own trade laws. Money changed value between states. Merchants were uncertain which trade laws to follow.

Under the Articles of Confederation, the national government could not collect taxes. It had to ask the states for money. Congress needed money to pay off its large debts. The government also could not pay lawmakers. Even worse, it couldn't pay soldiers who had served in the Revolution.

Plan for Settlement

Overall, the articles didn't work. One law passed by Congress *did* work. The Ordinance of 1787 (also called the Northwest Ordinance) was a plan for land north of the Ohio River and east of the Mississippi River. This region was known as the Northwest Territory. The Ordinance stated that an area became a territory when its population reached 5,000. It could apply for statehood when the population reached 60,000. The states of Ohio, Indiana, Illinois, Michigan, and Wisconsin were settled this way. The Northwest Ordinance also pushed Native Americans off their land. As a result, battles between settlers and Native Americans soon broke out.

QUICK CHECK

Draw Conclusions Why did settlers and Native Americans battle in the Northwest Territories?

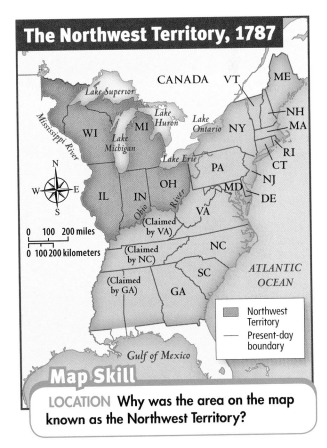

The Northwest Territory, 1787

CANADA
Lake Superior
Lake Huron
Lake Ontario
Lake Michigan
Mississippi River
Lake Erie
VT
ME
NH
MA
NY
RI
CT
WI
MI
PA
NJ
OH
MD
DE
IL
IN
Ohio River
VA
(Claimed by VA)
(Claimed by NC)
NC
(Claimed by GA)
SC
GA
ATLANTIC OCEAN
Gulf of Mexico

N W E S

0   100   200 miles
0 100 200 kilometers

☐ Northwest Territory
— Present-day boundary

Map Skill

LOCATION Why was the area on the map known as the Northwest Territory?

REBELLION IN MASSACHUSETTS

In 1786 the weaknesses of the Articles of Confederation led to violence in western Massachusetts. To raise money to pay state debts, Massachusetts lawmakers raised taxes on property. Lawmakers also said that people had to pay their taxes in gold or silver. The state's paper currency had little value—and there was no national currency.

Most farmers in western Massachusetts were in debt. When the legislature refused to accept paper money, hundreds of farmers were unable to pay their taxes. Those who could not pay often lost their farms. Many landed in jail.

Farmers Fight Back

To many farmers, Massachusetts lawmakers were no better than the British Parliament. Many farmers had fought the British, and had been paid in worthless paper money. Daniel Shays, a farmer who was once a Patriot officer, urged others to rebel. Shays led his men, called Regulators, across western Massachusetts. They closed courthouses and broke into jails to free debtors. News of what became known as Shays's Rebellion spread quickly.

Massachusetts leaders asked Congress to send regular army troops to capture Shays. The government had no power to raise money to pay troops. Instead, the state's governor and wealthy lawmakers paid for a private militia force with their own money.

In January 1787, more than 1,000 farmers attacked a state **arsenal**—a storage place for weapons—in Springfield, Massachusetts. There they were met by the private militia, which had better weapons, including a cannon. Cannon fire killed four rebels and wounded twenty. Many rebel farmers were captured, and some were sentenced to death. Shays finally fled to New York.

▼ Regulators blocked courthouses during Shays's Rebellion.

▼ Paper money was the only money most farmers had to pay their taxes.

The Meaning of Shays's Rebellion

Shays's Rebellion showed Americans, both rich and poor, that the Articles of Confederation had failed. Wealthy Americans wanted a national government strong enough to protect their property. Farmers wanted a government with the power to issue paper money that had value.

James Madison, whom you will soon read about, called for a meeting to decide on a new plan for government. Madison believed that unless the plan for government was changed, trouble would continue. The United States needed a plan that joined the states together under a central government that had power to pass laws for all Americans. He wrote:

> **The rebellion in Massachusetts is a warning.**

QUICK CHECK

Draw Conclusions **Why did Madison call Shays's Rebellion a "warning"?**

Shays's "Regulators" attacked an arsenal in Springfield, Massachusetts. A private militia hired by business owners defeated Shays's men.

MEETING IN PHILADELPHIA

How would you like to spend the summer shut inside a room? Delegates who created the plan for our nation's government did this when they met in Philadelphia on May 25, 1787. The delegates remained in hot rooms for almost four months. This meeting was called the Constitutional Convention.

A Difficult Task

Some delegates, such as Benjamin Franklin and George Washington, were well known. The most important delegate, however, stood 5 feet 4 inches tall and weighed 100 pounds—James Madison from Virginia. Madison believed that the Articles of Confederation had failed. He also knew that creating a new plan for government would be difficult. He wrote:

"In framing a government . . . the great difficulty lies in this: you must first enable the government to control the governed, and in the next place, oblige [force] it to control itself."

Two Different Plans

Today, we often think of the President as the most important person in government. But in 1787, the **legislature** was the most important part of government. A legislature is an elected body of people that make the laws. Madison's plan, the Virginia Plan, created a national legislature with two "houses." One house would be elected by citizens. In those days, only white men with property were allowed to

Delegates met in this room to argue about the new plan for government. James Madison later wrote, "Every word of the Constitution decides a question between power and liberty."

vote. The members of the second house would be chosen by the members of the first house. The number of members in the first house was based on a state's population. This meant that the largest states had the most representatives.

James Madison is called the "Father of the Constitution."

It is no surprise that delegates from small states disliked Madison's plan. Under the Articles of Confederation all states had equal power. William Paterson, a delegate from New Jersey, offered his New Jersey Plan—a legislature with only one house in which each state would have one vote.

Delegates argued for weeks during the heat of summer. Madison continued to support the Virginia Plan. He believed that it was more important to reach an agreement that satisfied everyone. He led the discussions that tried to find a way for states to share power.

QUICK CHECK

Draw Conclusions Why did Madison believe that creating a new plan for government would be difficult?

D ⓓ IMPORTANT COMPROMISES

After months of disagreement, Roger Sherman, a delegate from the small state of Connecticut, introduced a plan that solved the biggest problem facing the convention.

States Share Power

Under Sherman's plan, the legislature would have a House of Representatives, with the number of representatives based on a state's population. That pleased large states. In the Senate, each state would have two Senators. That pleased small states.

Under Sherman's plan, representatives would serve two years and be elected directly by the people. Senators would serve six-year terms and be chosen by state legislatures. A law would pass only when both houses approved it. Sherman's plan became known as the Great Compromise. Years later, laws changed to allow the people to elect Senators directly.

The Issue of Slavery

Almost half the delegates at the convention owned enslaved workers. These delegates wanted the workers to count as part of the population. Many delegates disagreed—thinking that would give too much power to states with enslaved people. So delegates reached the Three-Fifths Compromise. Every five enslaved people counted as three free people.

A Plan for Voting

Delegates wanted the United States to have a President. If Congress made the choice, as Madison suggested, the President would serve lawmakers rather than the American people. Instead, the delegates created the

The Constitutional Convention was held in Independence Hall in Philadelphia. ▼

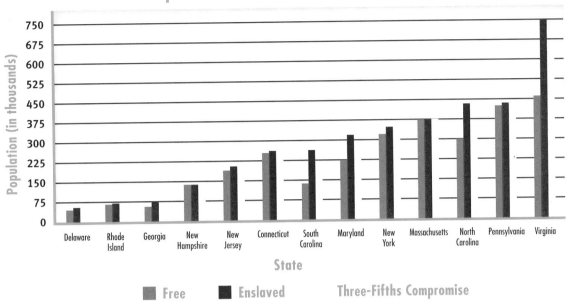

Population of the 13 States, 1790

Population (in thousands)

| 750 | 675 | 600 | 525 | 450 | 375 | 300 | 225 | 150 | 75 | 0 |

States: Delaware, Rhode Island, Georgia, New Hampshire, New Jersey, Connecticut, South Carolina, Maryland, New York, Massachusetts, North Carolina, Pennsylvania, Virginia

State

■ Free   ■ Enslaved   Three-Fifths Compromise

Electoral College. In the Electoral College, the number of electoral votes for each state was based on the number of its Congressional representatives. The electoral votes would then be cast for the candidate chosen by the people in their states.

The Signing

Finally, after nearly four months, the 39 delegates signed the Constitution on September 17, 1787. It had been a struggle to reach an agreement. In the end, with Madison leading the way, they created the United States Constitution. Today, James Madison is known as the "Father of the Constitution."

QUICK CHECK

Draw Conclusions Why is James Madison called the "Father of the Constitution"?

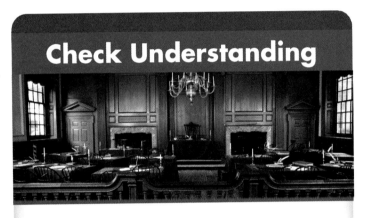

Check Understanding

1. **VOCABULARY** Describe the problems of the early government using these terms.
   Articles of Confederation
   legislature

2. **READING SKILL Draw Conclusions** Use the chart from page 196 to explain why delegates opposed Madison's idea for electing the President.

Text Clues	Conclusion

3. **Write About It** Explain how the Constitution helped large and small states grow together as a nation.

◀ Roger Sherman of Connecticut offered a plan for sharing power between large and small states.

Lesson 2

VOCABULARY

federal system p. 205

Supreme Court p. 205

ratify p. 208

bill of rights p. 208

amendment p. 209

READING SKILL

Draw Conclusions

Copy the chart below. Use it to draw conclusions about the United States Constitution.

Text Clues	Conclusion

MISSOURI COURSE LEVEL EXPECTATIONS

5.A.1, 5.C.2, 5.J.1, 6.I.1, 7.A.1, 7.B.1

United States Constitution

The ratification of the United States Constitution was celebrated with a parade in New York City.

HAMILTON

Visual Preview

Why is the Constitution a powerful document?

A State and national governments share power under the Constitution.

B The Constitution has a system of checks and balances for sharing power.

C Anti-federalists wanted a bill of rights before they would ratify the Constitution.

D Advisors worked with George Washington, the first President.

A POWER OF GOVERNMENT

The first three words of the United States Constitution explain a great deal about the government of the United States. These words are: "We the People . . ."

The delegates to the Constitutional Convention agreed that both state and national governments should share powers. This is known as a **federal system**. Under a federal system, national and state governments both make laws and collect taxes. State governments, however, control local matters, such as police services and public education.

After the Preamble, which you can read on this page, the Constitution is divided into separate parts called articles. The first three articles explain how the United States government is organized.

Article 1 establishes a legislature, called Congress, made up of a Senate and a House of Representatives. This branch has the power to make laws. Article 2 creates the office of the President, the leader of the Executive Branch, to enforce the laws. Article 3 establishes a Supreme Court. The **Supreme Court** is the highest court in the United States. It has the power to decide whether any laws work against the Constitution.

Primary Sources

We the People of the United States, in Order to form a more perfect Union, establish Justice, insure **domestic Tranquility**, provide for the common Defense, promote the general Welfare, and secure the Blessings of Liberty to ourselves and our **Posterity,** do **ordain** and establish this constitution for the United States of America.

> **Preamble to the Constitution of the United States approved by the states in 1788**

domestic tranquility   peace within the country
posterity   future generations
ordain   make legal

QUICK CHECK

Draw Conclusions Why did delegates want state and national governments to share power?

Write About It Rewrite the Preamble after "We the People" in your own words.

Checks and Balances

1 **LEGISLATIVE BRANCH** Congress (elected)
• Passes laws • Approves spending and taxes
• Can override vetoes

2 **EXECUTIVE BRANCH** President (elected)
• Enforces laws • Commander-in-Chief of military • Signs or vetoes laws

---

B BALANCE OF POWER

Many delegates to the Constitutional Convention had fought in the American Revolution to free the colonies from King George III and the British Parliament. They wanted to make certain that no branch of the United States government could become as powerful as the king or British lawmakers. That is why they created a system of government under the Constitution that gave each branch the power to check, or stop, the work of another branch.

Checks and Balances

The system of keeping one branch from gaining too much power is known as checks and balances. In the legislative branch, there are checks between the two houses. Congress can pass legislation only if both the House of Representatives and the Senate pass exactly the same measure.

There are checks between branches as well. For a measure to become law, the President must sign it. The President is also allowed to

3 **JUDICIAL BRANCH** Supreme Court and federal courts (appointed) • Decides Constitutional questions about laws

Write About It In your opinion, which branch is the most important part of government? Explain.

veto, or reject, a law. Congress can override, or cancel, the President's veto with a two-thirds vote in each house.

In the judicial branch, the Supreme Court has the power to declare a law unconstitutional. This power, known as judicial review, was first used in the case of *Marbury* v. *Madison* in 1803.

The powers of the three branches of government are also balanced. Under the Constitution, no branch can take the powers given to another branch. The President cannot decide whether laws are constitutional.

Congress cannot enforce laws. The Supreme Court cannot make laws. Some delegates complained that the new Constitution created too strong a plan for government. But James Madison defended the system of checks and balances. He wrote:

> **❝**If men were angels, no government would be necessary.**❞**

QUICK CHECK

Draw Conclusions **Why did delegates believe that power should be shared among the three branches?**

C STEPS TO APPROVAL

At least nine of the thirteen states had to **ratify**, or officially approve, the Constitution. Supporters of the Constitution called themselves Federalists. Those opposing the Constitution, the Anti-federalists, wanted a more limited plan for federal government, such as that created by the Articles of Confederation.

Debate Over the Constitution

Federalists took steps to explain the advantages of the new Constitution. Their explanations appeared in a series of 85 newspaper essays written by Alexander Hamilton, James Madison, and John Jay. These essays are now known as *The Federalist Papers*.

Anti-federalists also spoke out. In Virginia, George Mason, who had been a delegate at the Philadelphia convention, wrote:

"There is no declaration of any kind, for preserving the liberty of the press, or the trial by jury . . . . "

Mason and many others agreed that the Constitution needed a **bill of rights**. This was a statement of the liberties guaranteed by the government to the people. Many state constitutions already had a bill of rights. For that reason, Madison and Hamilton argued that a bill of rights was not necessary in the United States Constitution.

Ratification

In June 1788 the Constitution officially became the law of the United States when New Hampshire became the ninth state to ratify it. Two of the largest states, Virginia and New York, had strong groups of Anti-

❧ Bill of Rights ❧

First Ten Amendments

First	People have freedom of religion, freedom of speech, freedom of the press; the right to assemble peacefully; the right to complain about government		**Sixth**	Guarantees the right to trial by jury and a lawyer in criminal cases
Second	People have the right to own and use firearms		**Seventh**	Guarantees the right to trial by jury in civil cases
Third	Prevents the government from forcing people to house soldiers during peacetime		**Eighth**	Prohibits high bail, fines, and cruel or unusual punishment
Fourth	People cannot be searched or have property taken without reason		**Ninth**	The rights of the people are not limited to those in the Constitution
Fifth	Protects people who are accused of crimes		**Tenth**	Powers not given to the federal government belong to the states or to the people

federalists who fought against ratification. They demanded that the Constitution spell out clearly the rights of the people. A nation that had won independence from a king would never approve a plan that did not guarantee their liberties, said the Anti-federalists. Federalists such as Virginia's Madison and New York's Hamilton believed that without ratification by large states, the Constitution, and the federal government, would be weak.

Adding the Bill of Rights

To win ratification of the large states, Madison agreed to submit a bill of rights to Congress for approval. He promised Anti-federalists that he would work to get the bill of rights approved if they voted to ratify the Constitution. Madison kept his promise. In June 1789 he asked the House of Representatives to add a bill of rights to the Constitution. Changes to the Constitution are known as **amendments**. One of the first acts of the first Congress was to pass the ten amendments known as the Bill of Rights. By 1790 all of the original 13 states had ratified the Constitution.

Changing the Constitution

Since 1790 the Constitution has had 17 other amendments added to it. To become part of the Constitution, an amendment must be approved by two-thirds of the House and Senate and then by three-fourths of the states. An amendment can also be considered if two-thirds of the states ask Congress to meet in a special session.

QUICK CHECK

Draw Conclusions Why did Anti-federalists want a bill of rights?

Tourists look at the original Constitution in Washington, D.C.

D THE FIRST PRESIDENT

Many men and women had given their lives for liberty. Many others had done the hard work of creating a new plan of government. When it came time to elect the first President, however, there was only one choice. He had been called "The Father of the Country" by many. For once, all Americans agreed that the new nation under the new Constitution should be led by one man: George Washington.

President's Advisers

To help the President run the Executive Branch of the government, Congress created the departments of treasury, state, and war. An official called a secretary headed each office. The Secretary of the Treasury, Alexander Hamilton, formed a plan for the economy. The Secretary of State, Thomas Jefferson, handled affairs with other countries. The Secretary of War, Henry Knox, took charge of the country's defense. These advisers became known as the President's cabinet. Washington chose John Jay as the first Chief Justice, or head judge, of the U.S. Supreme Court.

George Washington took the oath of office as the first President in New York City.

In 1797 Washington returned to Mount Vernon, his plantation in Virginia, after serving two terms as President. He died two years later. Henry Lee, a representative from Virginia, expressed the feelings of many Americans when he said Washington was:

"first in war, first in peace, and first in the hearts of his countrymen."

Benjamin Banneker

Black Heritage USA 15c

◄ Benjamin Banneker laid out the streets of Washington, D.C.

A New Capital

- In 1790 government leaders decided that the capital would be moved to land along the Potomac River. Maryland and Virginia both gave land to form a new area called the District of Columbia.

- President Washington appointed Benjamin Banneker to lay out the streets of the new capital. Banneker was one of the first African Americans to work for the federal government.

QUICK CHECK

Draw Conclusions **Why did Lee say Washington was first in the hearts of his countrymen?**

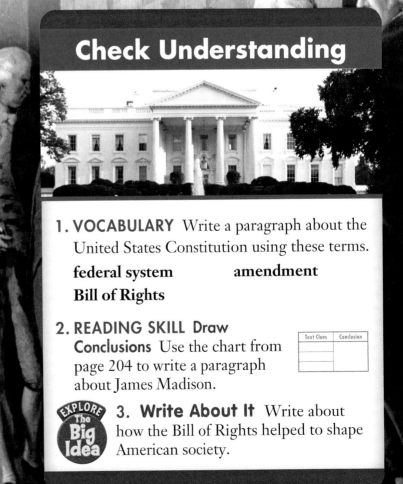

Check Understanding

1. **VOCABULARY** Write a paragraph about the United States Constitution using these terms.

   federal system   **amendment**

   Bill of Rights

2. **READING SKILL** Draw Conclusions Use the chart from page 204 to write a paragraph about James Madison.

Text Clues	Conclusion

3. **EXPLORE The Big Idea** **Write About It** Write about how the Bill of Rights helped to shape American society.

Lesson 3

VOCABULARY

pioneer p. 213

impressment p. 215

READING SKILL

Draw Conclusions

Copy the chart below. As you read, use it to draw a conclusion about the Corps of Discovery.

Text Clues	Conclusion

MISSOURI COURSE LEVEL EXPECTATIONS

5.A.1, 5.C.2, 5.J.1, 7.B.1

THE LOUISIANA PURCHASE

Lewis and Clark explored the Missouri River and western lands.

Visual Preview

How did the expansion of the United States affect North America?

A During Jefferson's term, Congress bought the Louisiana Territory.

B Lewis and Clark's team explored the Louisiana Territory, and Jefferson avoided war.

A OPENING THE WEST

By a crackling fire, John Findley told his old friend Daniel Boone about an incredible place of huge buffalo herds, deer at every salt lick, and rich farmland. He had seen Kentucky from the Ohio River. Now he needed an overland route that a wagon could pass through.

Daniel Boone and John Findley found a passage through the Appalachian Mountains that they called the Cumberland Gap. Working with other men, Boone carved a road wide enough for wagons that was called the Wilderness Road. It became the main route for Americans going west in the late 1700s.

The first people to enter a region are called **pioneers**. White settlers called themselves pioneers. The area west of the Appalachians had been home to Native Americans for centuries. In the 1790s, Native American groups joined together to drive white settlers off their lands.

President Washington sent the army to Ohio three times to protect settlers. In 1794 American soldiers defeated Native Americans at the Battle of Fallen Timbers in Ohio. The next year, some Native American leaders there accepted the Treaty of Greenville. Other leaders refused to sign the treaty. They did not want to lose their lands. Trouble between settlers and Native Americans continued into the 1800s.

French Louisiana

In the South, the French port city of New Orleans had become important to the growing trade of the western territories along the Mississippi River. In 1803 American representatives in France offered to buy New Orleans for $10 million. At the same time, the French needed to pay for a war against Great Britain. To the surprise of Americans, the French offered to sell the entire Louisiana Territory for $15 million. Congress agreed to the price. The purchase nearly doubled the size of the United States.

QUICK CHECK

Draw Conclusions How do you think Native Americans who refused to sign the Treaty of Greenville felt about pioneers?

EVENT

In the **election of 1800,** Thomas Jefferson led a new party called the Democratic-Republicans to a hard-fought victory. The election led to a case in which the Supreme Court claimed the right to decide whether laws were constitutional.

Election of 1800

B THE LOUISIANA TERRITORY

The United States got a tremendous bargain—almost 525 million acres of land for about 3 cents an acre. But few Americans knew anything about this huge territory. Some believed that woolly mammoths roamed the land and that the Native Americans spoke Welsh. Others believed the Northwest Passage lay within the territory.

Lewis and Clark

President Jefferson chose Meriwether Lewis, his secretary, to lead what is called the Corps of Discovery. In June 1803, Lewis offered to share command with his army officer friend, William Clark. He was the younger brother of George Rogers Clark, the Revolutionary War hero.

The expedition set out to map the course of the Missouri River and find a land route to the Pacific Ocean. Jefferson also wanted information about the land, its resources, and the Native Americans who lived in the region. It was a journey that would take them thousands of miles. They would see lands, rivers, and people that no white American had seen before.

In May 1804, the Corps of Discovery headed west from St. Louis on the Missouri River. William Clark relied on a compass to measure land distances, directions, and

◀ Meriwether Lewis (left) and William Clark (right)

The Journeys of Lewis and Clark
1804 to 1806

Map Skill

LOCATION **Which river led Lewis and Clark to the Pacific Ocean?**

landforms. Other instruments used to survey and map the land were a quadrant, sextant, and chronometer.

In 1805 the group was joined by a Shoshone woman named Sacagawea, who served as a guide and interpreter. Sacagawea traveled with the expedition to the Pacific Ocean and back. Lewis and Clark traveled 8,000 miles, mostly on Native American trails, following Native American maps, and led by Native American guides. They returned to St. Louis in 1806.

Jefferson's Foreign Policy

During Jefferson's term in office, France and Great Britain were at war. The United States did not take sides in this war. Americans continued to trade with both countries. This enraged both the British and the French. Warships from both countries stopped American merchant ships at sea and took their goods. The British also forced American sailors to serve on British ships. This practice, called **impressment**, enraged Americans.

To protect American ships and lives, an angry Congress passed the Embargo Act in 1807. The act closed all American ports. No ships could trade in American waters. This law was a bad idea. It was passed to hurt Great Britain and France. Instead, it hurt American shipping and weakened the nation's economy. In spite of efforts to avoid conflict, relations with France and Great Britain grew worse. The United States was at the edge of war.

QUICK CHECK

Draw Conclusions Why would closing American ports weaken the nation's economy?

▼ Sacagawea guided Lewis and Clark during their exploration of the Louisiana Territory.

Check Understanding

1. **VOCABULARY** Draw a picture illustrating one of these vocabulary words.

   pioneer   **impressment**

2. **READING SKILL Draw Conclusions** Use your chart from page 212 to help you write about the Corps of Discovery.

Text Clues	Conclusion

3. **Write About It** Write a paragraph about the ways the Louisiana Purchase helped the United States to grow.

The War of 1812

Lesson 4

VOCABULARY

War Hawks p. 217

Era of Good Feelings p. 219

Adams-Onís Treaty p. 219

Monroe Doctrine p. 220

READING SKILL

Draw Conclusions

Copy the chart below. As you read, use it to draw conclusions about the War of 1812.

Text Clues	Conclusion

MISSOURI COURSE LEVEL EXPECTATIONS

5.A.1, 5.C.2, 5.J.1, 6.I.1, 7.A.1, 7.B.1

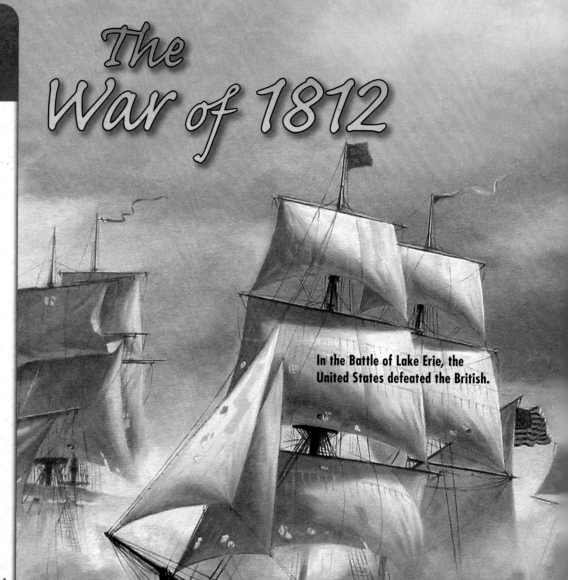

In the Battle of Lake Erie, the United States defeated the British.

Visual Preview

How did the War of 1812 affect Americans?

A Americans disagreed about going to war with Great Britain.

B The end of the War of 1812 united Americans and expanded the country.

C The Monroe Doctrine stopped the colonization of the Americas after the war.

A WAR WITH GREAT BRITAIN

*When the War of 1812 began, Great Britain had been fighting with France for nearly 20 years. U.S. "**War Hawks**" believed that they could conquer Canada and take control of the whole continent.*

Many **War Hawks** were settlers from areas west of the Appalachian Mountains. To fight the settlers, the Shawnee chief Tecumseh united several Western groups. In 1811 Tecumseh's forces were defeated by troops led by General William Henry Harrison at the Battle of Tippecanoe in present-day Indiana.

"Mr. Madison's War"

The War Hawks complained that the British had helped the Native Americans in the West. The War Hawks also felt the United States should fight to protect American sailors from impressment in the British navy. In June 1812 Congress, led by lawmakers who were War Hawks, declared war on Great Britain. President James Madison signed the declaration.

Not all Americans supported the war. New England merchants depended on trade with Great Britain. They wanted to settle problems peacefully. When war broke out, New Englanders called the war "Mr. Madison's War."

QUICK CHECK
Draw Conclusions Why did War Hawks want war with Great Britain?

Citizenship

Mobilizing Groups

Tecumseh formed a confederacy to stop Americans from taking more land from Native Americans. Mobilizing groups is one way to organize people. Movements have been used throughout history to call attention to unfair treatment and bring change. The American Indian Movement fought to improve the lives of thousands of Native Americans living on reservations. Is there a movement you want to join?

Write About It Write about a way a group could bring change in your community.

VICTORIES AND DEFEATS

The American navy won important victories early in the war. In 1812 the U.S.S. *Constitution* defeated the British ship *Guerrière*. When British cannonballs bounced off the thick oak sides of the *Constitution*, the ship earned the nickname "Old Ironsides."

In 1813 ships under American Oliver Hazard Perry won the Battle of Lake Erie. Perry's victory forced the British to retreat into Canada. American troops then invaded Canada. They captured supplies in York, present-day Toronto, and burned the town.

The Burning of Washington, D.C.

In 1814 the British sent thousands of well-trained soldiers to invade the United States and attack Washington, D.C. The British wanted to punish the Americans for invading Canada and destroying York.

When the British soldiers landed in Maryland, the local militia fled. British troops then marched into Washington, D.C. British officers walked through the White House with muddy boots and ate dinner in President Madison's dining room. By then, the Madisons had fled. Soon, the White House, the Capitol building, and other government buildings were in flames.

As Washington lay in ashes, the British sailed up the Chesapeake Bay to attack Baltimore, Maryland. The city was protected by Fort McHenry. British warships stopped about two miles from the fort. From that distance, the warship fired rockets at the fort. These were 32-pound metal tubes filled with gunpowder, whose tips exploded when they hit a target.

▼ The American defense of Baltimore's Fort McHenry inspired Francis Scott Key to write "The Star-Spangled Banner" in 1814.

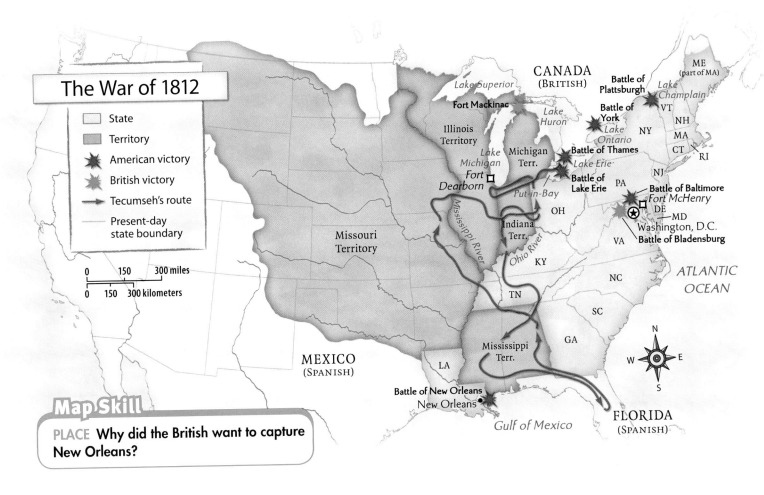

The War of 1812

Legend:
- State
- Territory
- ★ American victory
- ★ British victory
- → Tecumseh's route
- Present-day state boundary

0   150   300 miles
0   150   300 kilometers

Map labels: CANADA (BRITISH), Lake Superior, Fort Mackinac, Lake Huron, Illinois Territory, Lake Michigan, Fort Dearborn, Michigan Terr., Lake Ontario, Battle of York, Battle of Thames, Lake Erie, Put-in-Bay, Battle of Lake Erie, OH, Indiana Terr., Ohio River, Mississippi River, Missouri Territory, KY, TN, Mississippi Terr., LA, MEXICO (SPANISH), Battle of New Orleans, New Orleans, Gulf of Mexico, FLORIDA (SPANISH), Battle of Plattsburgh, Lake Champlain, ME (part of MA), VT, NH, NY, MA, CT, RI, NJ, PA, Battle of Baltimore, Fort McHenry, DE, MD, Washington, D.C., Battle of Bladensburg, VA, NC, SC, GA, ATLANTIC OCEAN

Map Skill

PLACE **Why did the British want to capture New Orleans?**

The British attack on Fort McHenry began on September 13. For 25 hours, the fort was bombarded by more than 1,500 cannonballs and rockets. Francis Scott Key, an American prisoner on a British ship, watched the night sky light up with "the rockets' red glare." The next morning, Key saw that the American flag still flew over Fort McHenry. Key expressed his feelings in "The Star-Spangled Banner," a poem that later became our national anthem.

The War Ends

In December 1814, the Treaty of Ghent ended the War of 1812. Neither side won the war, but they agreed to stop fighting. News of the treaty traveled slowly. In January 1815, Americans led by Andrew Jackson crushed the British at the Battle of New Orleans. Although the treaty had been signed before this battle, Jackson became a national hero. The end of the War of 1812 created a feeling of unity among Americans. Newspapers named this period the **Era of Good Feelings**.

The United States Grows

Still a popular general, Andrew Jackson led his troops into the Spanish colony of Florida in 1818. He claimed that he was chasing Native Americans who had attacked Georgia settlements. Spain did not want to fight with Jackson or the Americans. Under the **Adams-Onís Treaty** of 1819, Spain sold Florida to the United States. In return, the United States gave up its claim to Texas west of the Sabine River.

QUICK CHECK

Draw Conclusions **Why did the British army burn Washington, D.C.?**

President James Monroe talking to his Cabinet members about the Monroe Doctrine

Ⓒ THE MONROE DOCTRINE

By 1822 Spain was losing control of its colonies in the Americas. Argentina, Chile, Colombia, Mexico, and Peru had become independent countries. To prevent European countries from regaining colonies in Latin America, President James Monroe issued the **Monroe Doctrine** in 1823. It stated that the United States would not allow European powers to establish new colonies in the Americas. In return, the United States would not interfere with existing colonies in the Americas or European affairs. The doctrine's authors saw it as a way for the United States to oppose colonial powers. Americans would later use it to expand the United States. For example, Spanish Puerto Rico became a U.S. territory in 1898.

QUICK CHECK

Draw Conclusions **Why did the United States want to prevent new European colonies in the Americas?**

Check Understanding

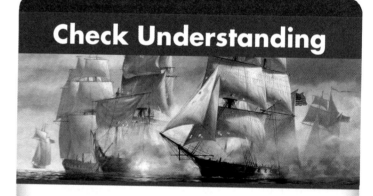

1. **VOCABULARY** Write an essay describing the relationship between Spain and the United States. Use these vocabulary terms.

   Adams-Onís Treaty   **Monroe Doctrine**

2. **READING SKILL Draw Conclusions** Use your chart from page 216 to write about the War of 1812.

Text Clues	Conclusion

 3. **Write About It** Write about how Andrew Jackson's actions in 1818 helped the United States grow.

Map and Globe Skills

Compare Maps at Different Scales

VOCABULARY

map scale
small-scale map
large-scale map

All maps are drawn to scale. A **map scale** uses a unit of measurement, such as an inch, to show distance on Earth. A map scale explains the size of the area on a map.

A **small-scale map**, such as Map A, shows a large area, but cannot include many details. A **large-scale map**, such as Map B, shows a smaller area with more details.

Learn It

- If you want to find out where many battles occurred during the War of 1812, use a small-scale map, or Map A. It has a scale of 300 miles. It shows a large area.

- If you want to know about the Battle of Baltimore, you would need the large-scale map, or Map B. It has a scale of 2 miles and shows more details, such as ships and troop locations.

- Compare the scales of both maps.

Try It

- Which map would you use to plan a route from one state to another?

- Which map would you use to make a detailed plan of the attack on Baltimore?

Apply It

- Compare a map of the United States with a map of your state.

- Compare the map scales. Is the state map a large-scale or a small-scale map?

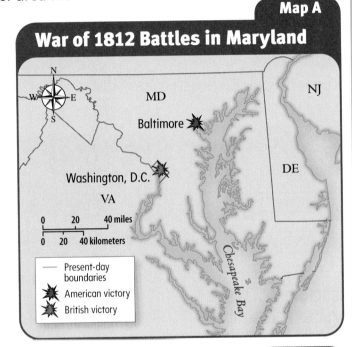

Map A

War of 1812 Battles in Maryland

Map B

The Battle of Baltimore, 1814

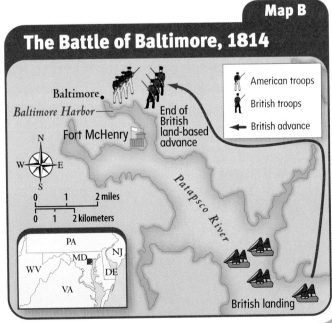

Lesson 5

VOCABULARY

Industrial Revolution p. 223

cotton gin p. 223

interchangeable part p. 223

reaper p. 224

steam engine p. 224

READING SKILL

Draw Conclusions
Copy the chart below. As you read, draw a conclusion about the Industrial Revolution.

Text Clues	Conclusion

MISSOURI COURSE LEVEL EXPECTATIONS

5.A.1, 5.C.2, 5.J.1, 6.I.1, 7.B.1

The Industrial Revolution

Textile mills in the 1830s often employed women and young children.

Visual Preview

How did the Industrial Revolution change people's lives?

A The cotton gin helped build the cotton textile industry in the United States.

B Technology impacted the way people farmed, traveled and transported goods.

Ⓐ INDUSTRY BOOMS

Until the early 1800s, most families made the items they needed, such as tools and clothes, by hand. Then came a period of rapid invention, when machines began to do the work people once did.

This period of invention was called the **Industrial Revolution**. It was a time when new machines and new ideas changed the way people worked, traveled, and lived.

The Cotton Gin

In 1793 Eli Whitney built a **cotton gin** to remove seeds from cotton. The gin, which is short for "engine," could clean more cotton in a few minutes than a whole team of workers could clean by hand in a day. The cotton gin made cotton the most important cash crop in the South.

Textile Mills

With more cotton coming from the South, textile mills grew in the North. A textile mill is a factory where workers turn cotton into cloth. In the early 1800s, mills were built near rivers because the machines were powered by water.

In 1813 Francis Cabot Lowell built a power loom at a mill in Waltham, Massachusetts. All stages of cloth-making happened in that one place. Lowell's business partners later built several textile mills, as well as a town, called Lowell, for the workers. By 1850 Lowell had more than 10,000 workers. Many were young women who left home to work in Lowell. They worked 12-hour days, six days a week, and lived on the grounds of the mill.

Whitney's Next Innovation

In 1801 Eli Whitney had another important idea—**interchangeable parts**. Interchangeable parts are pieces made in the same or standard sizes, so they would fit any specific product. A barrel for one rifle would fit another rifle of the same type, for example. With Whitney's idea, guns, tools, and other products could be made faster and at a lower cost.

QUICK CHECK

Draw Conclusions How did mill towns change the lives of women in the 1800s?

PLACES

Today you can visit **Lowell National Historic Park** to see the birthplace of the American Industrial Revolution. Trolleys tour the park's cotton mills and living quarters.

Lowell, Massachusetts

B CHANGES IN FARMING AND TRAVEL

Farming became much easier during the Industrial Revolution with the invention of the mechanical plow and the **reaper**. A reaper is a machine with sharp blades to cut grain. With better machines, fewer farmers were needed to raise food. As a result, many people in farming areas moved to cities to work in factories and mills.

The Steam Engine

Transportation improved quickly after the invention of the **steam engine**. Steam engines produced more power than a team of horses, and they could pull heavier loads. In 1807 Robert Fulton designed a boat powered by a steam engine. His steamboat traveled 150 miles in 32 hours. Boats without steam engines took 4 days to make the same trip.

The Erie Canal

In 1817 DeWitt Clinton, the governor of New York, began building a 363-mile canal, or human-made waterway. At that time, most canals were only a few miles long. The Erie Canal would connect Lake Erie to the Hudson River. It used a system of locks to raise and lower the water level, as shown below.

Even though people didn't believe the canal would work, construction began. Immigrants did most of the digging. The Erie Canal opened in 1825 and quickly became a success. New York City soon became the country's largest and most important port. For a few years, the Erie Canal was important to the U.S. economy. Then a new steam-powered invention made canals less important.

The Erie Canal

DIAGRAM SKILL

Is the canal boat going to higher or lower water? How can you tell?

upper lock gate

canal

barge

lower lock gate

tow path

◀ *Tom Thumb* racing a horse-drawn carriage

The Iron Horse

People had traveled by railroad for years, but on early railroads, horses pulled coaches over iron rails. In 1814 British inventor George Stephenson built the first train powered by a steam engine. The new trains were nicknamed "iron horses."

In 1830 Peter Cooper, an American merchant, built a small locomotive that he named *Tom Thumb*. At first, few people believed the locomotive could move without horses. A Baltimore stagecoach company challenged Cooper and his locomotive to a race against a horse-drawn carriage. The train lost that race, but trains won in the end. Railroads soon became the main form of transportation in the United States.

QUICK CHECK

Drawing Conclusions How did the invention of the steam engine improve transportation?

Check Understanding

1. **VOCABULARY** Write a short story about the growth of industry in the early 1800s. Use at least two of these terms.

   cotton gin   **steam engine**
   interchangeable part   **reaper**

2. **READING SKILL Draw Conclusions** Use your chart from page 222 to write about the Industrial Revolution.

Text Clues	Conclusion

3. **Write About It** Write a paragraph explaining how the Erie Canal helped New York City.

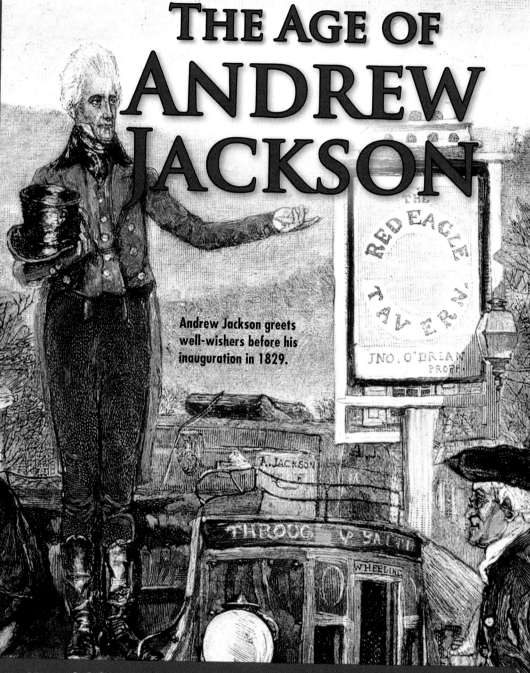

Lesson 6

VOCABULARY

Union p. 227

Trail of Tears p. 229

manifest destiny p. 229

wagon train p. 229

discrimination p. 231

READING SKILL

Draw Conclusions

Copy the chart below. As you read, use it to draw a conclusion about the Indian Removal Act.

Text Clues	Conclusion

MISSOURI COURSE LEVEL EXPECTATIONS

3a.F.1, 3a.F.2, 5.A.1, 5.C.2, 5.H.1, 5.J.1, 6.I.1, 7.A.1, 7.B.1

THE AGE OF ANDREW JACKSON

Andrew Jackson greets well-wishers before his inauguration in 1829.

Visual Preview

How did freedom change for people?

A President Jackson promised to protect the rights of average Americans.

B Native Americans were forced from their lands as settlers expanded west.

C Immigration from Europe and Asia increased, which helped cities to grow.

A A MAN OF THE PEOPLE

*In 1824 new U.S. laws allowed all white men 21 or older—
not just wealthy landowners—to vote. This wave of new voters
helped elect a new President, a "common man" who would become
one of the most controversial Presidents in history.*

Andrew Jackson was born in a frontier settlement in the Carolinas. Because of his background, many settlers saw Jackson as someone who shared their values.

Jackson as President

Jackson promised to protect the rights of the Americans who elected him— farmers, frontier settlers, and working people. Under Jackson's leadership, the office of President grew more powerful than it had ever been. Jackson's opponents protested that he was trying to take powers away from Congress.

Trouble in South Carolina

States also protested Jackson's actions. South Carolina lawmakers threatened to leave the **Union** if their state was forced to collect a new federal tax on imported goods. "Union" is the term used for states joined together as one group.

Jackson sent troops and warships to South Carolina to force the state to collect

the tax. The crisis passed when the tax was collected. People then accused Jackson of acting more like a king than a President.

QUICK CHECK

Draw Conclusions Why was Jackson popular with settlers but unpopular with state lawmakers?

This political cartoon shows Andrew Jackson as a powerful king who tramples on the Constitution. ▶

Throughout the 1800s, thousands of people moved west. Many people went west to start new lives, find open land, or become wealthy. Others were driven out of their homes and forced to move far away.

Conflict with Native Americans

In the early 1800s, many Native Americans in the Southeast lived peacefully with their white neighbors. Their right to their homeland had been guaranteed by treaties signed with the United States government.

Jackson and some of his supporters believed that Native Americans should leave their lands and allow settlers to live there. Congress passed the Indian Removal Act in 1831. This act forced Native Americans to move to what Congress called the Indian Territory, which is now the state of Oklahoma.

Primary Sources

[In] May 1838 . . . I saw helpless Cherokee arrested and dragged from their homes . . . I saw them loaded like cattle or sheep into six hundred and forty-five wagons and starting toward the west . . . many of the children rose to their feet and waved their little hands good-by to their mountain homes, knowing they were leaving them forever.

A section from *Story of the Trail of Tears* by John G. Burnett, published in 1890

Write About It Write a journal entry in which you describe your thoughts about the removal of Native Americans.

▼ In the Cherokee language, the Trail of Tears is called *Nunna daul Isunyi*—"the Trail Where We Cried." About 4,000 people died along the way. Some who refused to leave their homes were forced into slavery.

Native Americans protested in court. Jackson refused to follow a court ruling allowing Native Americans to remain on their homelands.

In 1838 the United States army forced the Cherokee people to march 800 miles west to the Indian Territory. This journey became known as the **Trail of Tears**. The primary source on page 228 describes what one soldier saw on the Trail of Tears.

Oregon Fever

In the 1840s, Americans became inspired by the idea of **manifest destiny**. This was a belief that the United States had a right to expand its borders and claim new lands. Families began catching "Oregon Fever"—the desire to get a fresh start in the West.

The 2,000-mile journey took six months. Most settlers joined **wagon trains**, a large group of wagons pulled by oxen. Wagon trains

offered protection against attacks by Native Americans. People helped one another when wagons broke down. They worked together to cross rivers and make their way through steep mountain passes. Sometimes, Native Americans helped the wagon trains cross difficult regions.

Mormons Settle Utah

Some people were forced to move west because of their religious beliefs. The Church of Jesus Christ of Latter-Day Saints, or the Mormon Church, was founded in New York. The Mormons were forced west in the 1840s. In 1847 the first Mormons arrived at the Great Salt Lake and settled what is now Salt Lake City, Utah.

QUICK CHECK

Draw Conclusions Why did people travel west together in wagon trains?

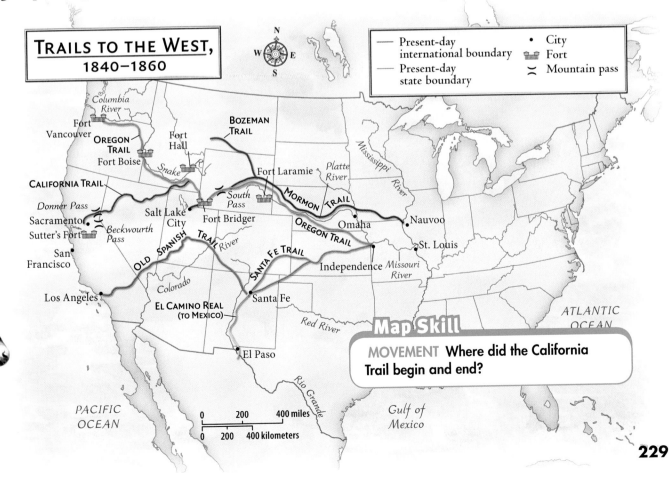

TRAILS TO THE WEST, 1840–1860

Legend:
— Present-day international boundary
— Present-day state boundary
• City
Fort
≍ Mountain pass

Columbia River
Fort Vancouver
OREGON TRAIL
Fort Hall
Fort Boise
Snake
CALIFORNIA TRAIL
Donner Pass
Sacramento
Beckwourth Pass
Sutter's Fort
San Francisco
Salt Lake City
South Pass
Fort Bridger
MORMON TRAIL
OREGON TRAIL
Omaha
BOZEMAN TRAIL
Fort Laramie
Platte River
Mississippi River
Nauvoo
St. Louis
OLD SPANISH TRAIL
SANTA FE TRAIL
River
Independence
Missouri River
Los Angeles
Colorado
Santa Fe
Red River
EL CAMINO REAL (TO MEXICO)
El Paso
Rio Grande
ATLANTIC OCEAN
PACIFIC OCEAN
Gulf of Mexico

0 200 400 miles
0 200 400 kilometers

Map Skill

MOVEMENT **Where did the California Trail begin and end?**

THE CHANGING POPULATION

Between 1845 and 1860, more immigrants came to the United States than ever before. Many people from Europe and Asia came to find work or to seek fortunes. The Irish left Ireland, their homeland, for a different reason.

The Great Hunger

Starting in 1846, potatoes—Ireland's main food crop for the common people—began to rot because of a plant disease. Irish farmers grew other crops, but the British government forced farmers to send that food to Great Britain. As a result, about 2.5 million people starved to death. The Irish people called this time "The Great Hunger." Between 1846 and 1861, more than one million Irish immigrants came to the United States.

Citizenship

Working for the Common Good

When the United States created the public school system, it was working for the common good. American public schools took on the job of integrating non-English speaking immigrants into American life. Immigrant children were taught civic responsibility, respect for the flag, and even the proper use of the toothbrush.

▶ **Write About It** Write about new ways the government can work for the common good.

Irish immigrants arriving in New York City in 1847

Free African Americans

By 1850 more than 430,000 free African Americans lived in the United States, mainly in cities where they had found work. Although slavery was illegal in most Northern states, free African Americans still faced **discrimination**. Discrimination is the unfair treatment of people, often based on their race. African Americans did not have equal legal or voting rights to whites. There were places they were not allowed to go.

Cities Grow

In 1820 about 700,000 people lived in all of the cities in the United States. By today's standards, the cities were small.

Port cities like New York grew after the Industrial Revolution because of increased trade. Other active port cities included Boston, Baltimore, Charleston, and New Orleans, which all became major cities.

Almost all immigrants entered the nation through these ports. Some immigrants moved west, but many remained in the cities. By 1840 the population of the nation's cities had risen to about 1.8 million people.

America was growing rapidly within its borders. Meanwhile, in Texas, events were about to change those borders as well.

QUICK CHECK

Draw Conclusions Why were millions of people forced to leave Ireland between 1846 and 1861?

Check Understanding

1. **VOCABULARY** Write a sentence for each vocabulary term.

   manifest destiny   **discrimination**

   wagon train

2. **READING SKILL Draw Conclusions** Use your chart from page 226 to help you write an essay describing the Indian Removal Act.

Text Clues	Conclusion

3. **Write About It** Write about the reasons for the growth of American cities in the 1800s.

Texas and the War with Mexico

VOCABULARY

Treaty of Guadalupe Hidalgo p. 235

Gold Rush p. 236

READING SKILL

Draw Conclusions

Copy the chart below. As you read, use it to draw a conclusion about the War with Mexico.

Text Clues	Conclusion

MISSOURI COURSE LEVEL EXPECTATIONS

3a.F.1, 5.A.1, 5.C.2, 5.J.1, 6.I.1, 7.B.1

Mexican soldiers under Santa Anna defeated Texans at the Battle of the Alamo.

Visual Preview

How did conflicts with Mexico change the United States?

A Americans who settled Texas won independence from Mexico in 1836.

B In 1848 the United States won a huge area of land in the War with Mexico.

C The discovery of gold brought thousands of people to California at war's end.

Ⓐ TROUBLE IN TEXAS

*In 1821 Mexico won independence from Spain.
At that time, Mexico's northern areas included present-day
Texas, New Mexico, and California.*

During those years, few people lived in this huge area. To keep the area under Mexican control, Mexico's government offered land and Mexican citizenship to Americans who settled in Texas.

Americans Settle in Texas

Moses Austin and his son Stephen received almost 18,000 acres in what is present-day Texas. They sold this land to other settlers, bringing in about 300 families. By 1835 about 25,000 Americans lived in this area. Many of these Americans did not want to live in Mexico. They complained about Mexican laws. They also wanted slavery, which was illegal in Mexico, to be legal.

In December 1835 a force of 500 Texans attacked the town of San Antonio. Within days, they took control of the Alamo, a Spanish mission that had been made into a fort.

On March 6, 1836, General Antonio López de Santa Anna, the leader of Mexico, recaptured the Alamo after an almost two-week battle. All of the Americans were killed, but the Texans fought back again. A month later, General Sam Houston surprised a larger Mexican force at San Jacinto near present-day

Houston. The Texans charged, yelling, "Remember the Alamo!" The Texans defeated Santa Ana in less than 20 minutes.

QUICK CHECK

Draw Conclusions How did a plan to offer land in Texas to American settlers hurt Mexico?

▲ Stephen Austin

▲ Antonio López de Santa Anna

THE WAR WITH MEXICO

After the victory at the Battle of San Jacinto, Texans voted to join the United States. They adopted a constitution and made slavery legal. The U.S. Congress felt that allowing Texas to join the Union might lead to war with Mexico. Instead, Texas became an independent country—the Republic of Texas. It was also known as the Lone Star Republic.

Beginning the War

In 1845 President James Polk offered to buy the Mexican territories of California and New Mexico for $30 million. When Mexico refused, Polk ordered General Zachary Taylor to march through Texas to the Rio Grande. Fighting broke out with Mexican soldiers there in April 1846. President Polk asked the

James K. Polk ▶

American soldiers invaded Churubusco, Mexico, in 1847.

U.S. Congress for a declaration of war against Mexico, and Congress agreed.

The War Ends

Fighting continued until 1847, when U.S. troops captured Mexico City. The Mexican government signed the **Treaty of Guadalupe Hidalgo** in February 1848. Under this treaty, Mexico sold Texas to the United States for $15 million. The treaty also included land that would become the states of California, Nevada, and Utah as well as parts of Arizona, New Mexico, Colorado, and Wyoming. About 13,000 Americans died during the war, mainly from disease. Thousands more Mexicans died defending their homeland.

QUICK CHECK

Draw Conclusions How did the War with Mexico help the United States grow?

Land Acquired from Mexico, 1845–1853

WYOMING
NEVADA
UTAH
COLORADO
KANSAS
CALIFORNIA
Colorado River
Arkansas River
NEW MEXICO
ARIZONA
PACIFIC OCEAN
TEXAS
Rio Grande
MEXICO

- Annexed in 1845
- Mexican land awarded to the U.S. under the Treaty of Guadalupe Hidalgo, 1848
- Gadsden Purchase, 1853
- Present-day boundary

0   150   300 miles
0   150   300 kilometers

N W E S

Map Skill

LOCATION Which states' borders were expanded in 1853?

235

Thousands of "forty-niners" like this man went to California to find gold. Very few struck it rich.

Gold miner

Gold nuggets and pan

(C) THE CALIFORNIA GOLD RUSH

In January 1848, James Marshall saw something glittering in the American River outside the town of Sacramento, California. It was gold. Marshall tried to keep the discovery a secret, but the news spread. Over the next year, thousands of miners came to search for gold in the area. Prospecting, or exploring for gold, required only a few tools and the willingness to work hard. It was difficult work, and few people struck it rich.

"Gold Fever"

The idea of sudden wealth drew thousands of people to California. So many people came that the event became known as the **Gold Rush**. By May 1849, more than 10,000 wagons had crossed the continent to reach California. In that year alone, more than 80,000 people arrived in California from around the world. Because these people came to California in 1849, they became known as "forty-niners."

▲ Miners often searched for gold in rivers using pans to separate the gold from pebbles and sand.

The Thirty-First State

By 1850 there were enough people in California to apply for statehood. Settlers wanted courts, land and water laws, mail delivery, and other government services. On September 9, 1850, President Millard Fillmore signed a law that made California the thirty-first state to enter the Union.

QUICK CHECK

Draw Conclusions Why did the growth of California's population create a desire for statehood?

Check Understanding

1. **VOCABULARY** Write a paragraph using the vocabulary terms to explain how California became a state.

   Treaty of Guadalupe Hidalgo
   Gold Rush

2. **READING SKILL Draw Conclusions** Use your chart from page 232 to help you write about the War with Mexico.

Text Clues	Conclusion

 3. **Write About It** Write about how the desire to grow wealthy caused a huge increase in California's population.

Unit 5   Review and Assess

Vocabulary

Number a paper from 1 to 4. Beside each number, write the word below that matches the description.

bill of rights   **Trail of Tears**

pioneers   **manifest destiny**

1. The belief that the United States was meant to expand its borders

2. A formal statement of rights and liberties guaranteed to the people by a state

3. The people who are the first to enter a new land or region

4. The forced march of Native Americans to Indian Territory

Comprehension and Critical Thinking

5. Why did the U.S. Congress pass the Embargo Act?

6. **Reading Skill** Why did U.S. farmers, settlers, and working-class people support Andrew Jackson?

7. **Critical Thinking** How did the Great Compromise affect the way states were represented?

8. **Critical Thinking** What effect did the Industrial Revolution have on farming?

Skill

Compare Maps at Different Scales

Write a complete sentence to answer each question.

9. What is the difference between a large-scale and a small-scale map?

10. Compare the map on the right with the map on page 219. Which map is an example of a small-scale map? How do you know?

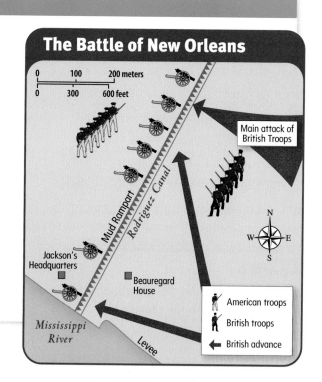

The Battle of New Orleans

0   100   200 meters
0   300   600 feet

Main attack of British Troops

Mud Rampart

Rodriguez Canal

Jackson's Headquarters

Beauregard House

N W E S

Mississippi River

Levee

American troops
British troops
British advance

MAP Test Preparation

Directions Read the passage. Then answer Numbers 1 through 3.

Eli Whitney created the cotton gin, making the production of cotton easier and more efficient. Now, the world uses cotton more than any other fiber. It is the leading cash crop in America. The production of each year's crop—just on the farming side—involves more than four billion dollars worth of supplies.

Combined, business revenue created by cotton is estimated at more than 122 billion dollars. We are surrounded by cotton. We dry our dishes with cotton towels and we sleep on soft cotton sheets. Cotton has hundreds of uses, including clothing, household items, and industrial products.

1 **What is the main idea of this passage?**

○ Cotton is an important crop for the U.S. economy.

○ Farming cotton is expensive.

○ Cotton is soft.

○ Farming cotton is hard work.

2 **What word could replace *revenue* in the passage above?**

○ supply

○ sales

○ expenses

○ demand

3 **What word is in this passage is used to describe cotton? What other adjectives could you use?**

Write your answer on a separate piece of paper.

The Big Idea Activities

What causes a society to grow?

Write About the Big Idea

Expository Essay
Use the Unit 5 Foldable to help you write an expository essay that answers the Big Idea question, "*What causes a society to grow?*" Begin with an introduction. Choose one item from each tab that you think made the biggest contribution to society's growth. Write a paragraph that explains why you have drawn that conclusion. End with a paragraph naming the single most important reason for society's growth.

FOLDABLES™
Study Organizer

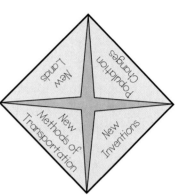

The Constitution: What's Most Important?

Now that you have read about the Constitution, decide which part of the important document means the most to you. Write a speech as if you are one of these sections of the Constitution:

Preamble

Article I (Legislative Branch)

Article II (Executive Branch)

Article III (Judicial Branch)

Bill of Rights

Complete these sentences

I am _____ the most important part of the Constitution.

My job is to _____.

Without me, _____.

When you have finished giving your speeches, hold a class election to decide the most important part of the Constitution.

EXPLORE
The Big Idea

Essential Question
What are some things people are willing to fight for?

FOLDABLES™
Study Organizer

Fact and Opinion
Make and label a Two-tab Foldable before you read this unit. Across the top, write **Things people fight for.** Label the two tabs **North** and **South.** Use the Foldable to organize information as you read.

Things people fight for

North   South

LOG ON

Find out more about the Civil War at www.macmillanmh.com

During the Civil War, many soldiers from the North and the South died on the battlefields.

Slavery AND Emancipation

PEOPLE, PLACES, AND EVENTS

Jermain Loguen

New York

1859
Jermain Loguen is a station master on the Underground Railroad.

Clara Barton

Maryland

1862
Clara Barton cares for wounded Union soldiers at the Battle of Antietam.

1855

1860

By 1859 **Jermain Loguen** had helped more than 1,500 enslaved people escape to freedom.

Today you can see the property in **Syracuse, New York**, where Loguen hid people who escaped slavery.

In 1862 **Clara Barton** helped care for Union soldiers wounded at the **Battle of Antietam.**

Today you can the visit the Antietam National Battlefield in Maryland.

LOG ON

For more about People, Places, and Events, visit
www.macmillanmh.com

Ulysses S. Grant

Robert E. Lee

Mississippi

1863
Union soldiers under Grant take Vicksburg, Mississippi.

Virginia

1865
General Robert E. Lee surrenders at Appomattox Court House.

1865

1870

In July 1863, Union troops under General **Ulysses S. Grant** defeated Confederate forces at **Vicksburg** on the Mississippi River.

Today you can tour the Vicksburg National Military Park in Mississippi.

In 1865 Confederate General **Robert E. Lee** surrendered to Union General Ulysses S. Grant at **Appomattox Court House**, Virginia.

Today you can travel to the McLean House where Lee and Grant met.

Lesson 1

VOCABULARY

slave state p. 246

free state p. 246

Missouri Compromise p. 246

tariff p. 247

READING SKILL

Fact and Opinion
Copy the chart below. As you read, fill in facts about the North and South.

Fact	Opinion

MISSOURI COURSE LEVEL EXPECTATIONS

3a.l.1, 5.A.1, 5.J.1, 6.l.1, 7.A.1, 7.B.1, 7.C.1

KING COTTON
AND THE
SPREAD OF
SLAVERY

Cotton was the most important cash crop in the Southern economy during the 1800s.

Visual Preview

How did the South affect the nation's economy and politics?

A Cotton, raised by enslaved workers, controlled the Southern economy.

B The issues of slavery and the economy divided the North and South.

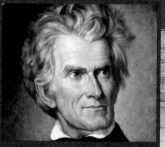

C Congress passed taxes on imported goods, which angered Southern leaders.

244

A COTTON RULES THE SOUTH

The hot climate and moist soil of the South were perfect for growing cotton. In the 1800s it became the most important cash crop in the South. By the 1830s Southerners called their crop "King Cotton."

Plantation owners used enslaved Africans to work in cotton fields. Many owners grew wealthy from selling cotton harvested by enslaved workers. It was sold mainly to Great Britain, where factories made the cotton into cloth.

Cotton plants weakened the soil. Planters needed more land, so they moved west. Cotton fields spread across Tennessee, Alabama, Mississippi, and, eventually, across the Mississippi River to Arkansas and Texas.

▲ The cotton gin removed the seeds from cotton bolls.

Enslaved Population Grows

The growth of cotton as a cash crop and the movement to the west created a need for more enslaved workers. In 1806 Congress passed a law that said no enslaved people could be brought into the United States after 1808. This law did not bring an end to slavery. The population of enslaved people continued to grow because the children of enslaved people were also enslaved. In addition, planters often brought enslaved people into the country from Caribbean islands.

Southern Economy

The economy of the South was built on the labor of enslaved workers. The wealthiest Southerners owned large areas of land and had thousands of enslaved workers. Most Southern farmers planted crops on small pieces of land. They did not have enslaved workers. Even so, both plantation owners and small farmers depended on cotton.

Farmers grew food for the plantations, repaired roads, and built wagons. When the cotton was harvested, some farmers earned money transporting crops to Southern ports by wagon.

QUICK CHECK

Fact and Opinion **What is a fact about cotton?**

B POLITICAL BALANCE

In 1819 Missouri applied to be admitted to the Union as a **slave state**, a state in which slavery is allowed. At the time, the nation had 11 slave states and 11 **free states**, or states in which slavery was not allowed. Allowing Missouri to enter the Union as a slave state would upset the balance in Congress. Slave states would have more votes in the Senate than free states. Northern states wanted to keep the political balance in Congress.

Both sides argued over Missouri for a year. Finally, Senator Henry Clay of Kentucky solved the problem with the **Missouri Compromise**. Under this plan, Missouri was admitted as a slave state. Maine, which had been part of Massachusetts, came in as a free state. The compromise stated that in the future, slavery would not be allowed in any new states north of Missouri's southern border.

Economic Differences

Slavery was not the only issue that divided the North and South. The regions had important economic differences. Cotton was king in the South. Even people who did not grow cotton worked in some way to help bring it to market.

Unlike the South, the Northern economy was based on industry. These industries did not use enslaved workers. This fact led states in the North to outlaw slavery. In 1777 Vermont became the first state to outlaw slavery. Then, in 1804, New Jersey became the last Northern state to outlaw slavery.

Map Skill

LOCATION **Which states made up a larger area of the United States—slave states or free states?**

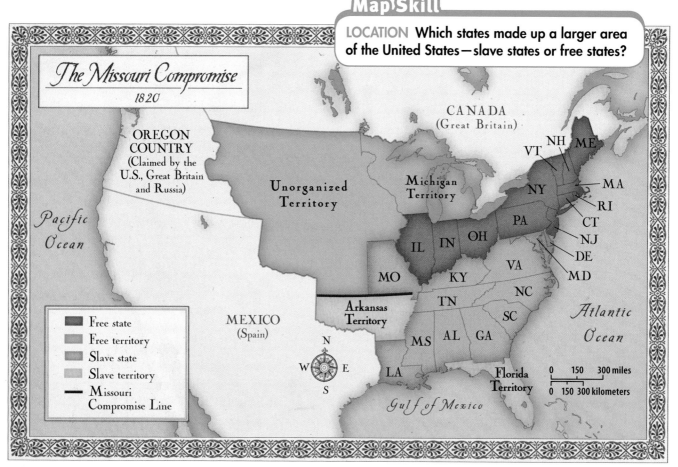

The Missouri Compromise
1820

OREGON COUNTRY
(Claimed by the U.S., Great Britain and Russia)

CANADA
(Great Britain)

Pacific Ocean

Unorganized Territory

Michigan Territory

VT NH ME
NY MA
RI
PA CT
NJ
DE
MD

IL IN OH

MO KY VA

Arkansas Territory

MEXICO
(Spain)

TN NC

SC

MS AL GA

LA

Florida Territory

Atlantic Ocean

Gulf of Mexico

N W E S

0   150   300 miles
0   150 300 kilometers

Free state
Free territory
Slave state
Slave territory
— Missouri Compromise Line

▲ Many Northern factories used women and children as workers. Cotton dresses, such as the dress on the left, were made in Northern factories.

In the North, men, women, and even children worked in factories making cloth, iron tools, rope, and other products. These factories were small compared to those of Great Britain. Also, British factories used new technology to make many of the same products more cheaply. That meant they could sell their products to Americans at prices lower than those charged by U.S. manufacturers.

Lower prices made it difficult for Americans who owned small factories to compete with British factories. American businesses that could not sell their more costly products failed. As a result, business owners asked Congress to pass **tariffs**, or special taxes on goods coming into the United States. Tariffs raised the price of foreign-made products and helped American industries. In 1828 Congress passed tariffs on British goods, which pleased Northern business owners.

QUICK CHECK

Fact and Opinion Why would a Northern factory owner want tariffs on British goods?

TARIFFS DIVIDE STATES

The new tariffs angered people in the South. Small farmers complained that tariffs raised the price of imports, or goods brought into the country. In fact, imported goods often cost more anyway. The tariffs also angered plantation owners. High tariffs meant that British manufacturers sold fewer goods in the United States. Fewer sales meant Great Britain had less money to buy cotton. This hurt Southern exports, or goods shipped out of the country.

▲ Senator John C. Calhoun of South Carolina spoke out against tariffs.

Speaking Out Against Congress

Southerners believed the tariffs threatened their way of life. Senator John C. Calhoun of South Carolina spoke out against the tariffs. He claimed Congress was trying to destroy the Southern economy. He said Congress was using tariffs to force the South to end the use of enslaved workers.

Calhoun said the Constitution gave states the right to ignore the laws passed by Congress if those laws hurt the state. Many Americans, including President Andrew Jackson, strongly disagreed with Calhoun. They thought that allowing states to decide which federal laws to obey could destroy the Union.

Jackson sent U.S. forces to South Carolina to enforce the tariffs. This use of federal troops caused even greater anger in the South. It would eventually be one cause of the bloodiest war in United States history.

QUICK CHECK

Fact and Opinion Why did John C. Calhoun speak out against tariffs?

Check Understanding

1. **VOCABULARY** Write a sentence using the word that is not related to the other three.

   slave state   Missouri Compromise

   free state   tariff

2. **READING SKILL Fact and Opinion.** Use the chart from page 244 to write your opinions about the facts you have listed.

Fact	Opinion

3. **Write About It** Why did Southerners fight to bring slavery into Missouri?

Chart and Graph Skills

Climographs

VOCABULARY

climate

climograph

You have read that the climate in the South was perfect for growing cotton. One way to learn more about **climate**, or the weather of a place over a number of years, is to study a **climograph**. A climograph shows the temperature, precipitation, and other climate information of a place over time. The climograph below shows the climate of Memphis, Tennessee.

Learn It

- Study the labels on the climograph. Notice that it is really two graphs in one: a bar graph and a line graph.

- Study the scales of measurement on the climograph. Precipitation is shown in the blue bar graph that measures inches, shown on the left. Temperature is shown by a line graph that measures the average temperature in degrees Fahrenheit, shown on the right.

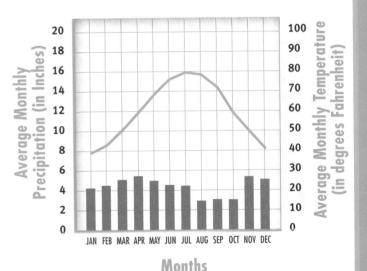

Memphis, Tennessee

Try It

- What is Memphis's average temperature in July?

- Which months have the greatest amount of precipitation? Which have the least?

Apply It

- Research the climate of a place you would like to visit.

- What are some ways you could use a climograph?

Heading Toward War

Lesson 2

VOCABULARY

abolitionists p. 251

debate p. 255

treason p. 256

secede p. 257

civil war p. 257

READING SKILL

Fact and Opinion
Copy the chart below. As you read, fill in the right side with opinions about slavery and abolition.

Fact	Opinion

MISSOURI COURSE LEVEL EXPECTATIONS

1.A.2, 3a.F.2, 3a.I.1, 5.A.1, 5.J.1, 6.I.1, 7.B.1, 7.C.1

Many people who escaped slavery headed North on the Underground Railroad.

Visual Preview

How did the issue of slavery affect the United States?

A Abolitionists from the North and South helped enslaved people in different ways.

B New laws increased conflict over slavery in the North and South.

C Political events, such as the Dred Scott decision, further divided Americans.

D After Lincoln was elected President, the South left the Union.

Ⓐ THE FIGHT OVER SLAVERY

Between 1820 and 1860, no issue divided the United States more than slavery. Some people said slavery was morally wrong. Others claimed it was necessary to preserve their way of life.

By the 1830s, many Americans wanted to abolish, or end, slavery. These people were called **abolitionists**.

Among the abolitionists were two sisters who grew up in South Carolina—Angelina and Sarah Grimké. Angelina said the abolition of slavery was:

Frederick Douglass

❝a cause worth dying for.❞

Immediate Release

One abolitionist leader was William Lloyd Garrison of Massachusetts. In 1831 he founded *The Liberator*, an abolitionist newspaper. In 1833 Garrison founded the American Anti-Slavery Society.

Another well-known person who spoke out against slavery was Frederick Douglass. He was born into slavery. After escaping, Douglass gave speeches about his early life. He also published an antislavery newspaper, *The North Star*.

In 1852 Harriet Beecher Stowe wrote *Uncle Tom's Cabin*. Her novel described a cruel slaveholder's treatment of enslaved people. This book turned many people against slavery.

The Underground Railroad

In the 1830s, enslaved people, free African Americans, and white abolitionists started the Underground Railroad, a secret network of trails, river crossings, and hiding places.

Many railroad terms had double meanings on this network. Enslaved people who decided to escape were called *passengers*. *Conductors* helped enslaved people escape. The houses where enslaved people could eat and rest were called *stations*.

Jermain Loguen was one of the many sucessful conductors on the Underground Railroad. He had escaped from slavery and wanted to help other people gain their freedom. His home in Syracuse, New York, became a well-known station. Harriet Tubman, an escaped enslaved woman, was a famous conductor who led many enslaved people North to freedom.

QUICK CHECK

Fact and Opinion Was Angelina Grimké's statement a fact or an opinion?

Congress tried to settle the slavery issue with compromises. As new territories applied to enter the Union, however, slavery continued to divide lawmakers and the American people.

Compromise of 1850

The U.S. victory in the War with Mexico of 1846–1848 brought large areas of land under U.S. control. In 1849 California applied to join the Union as a free state. This would change the balance of 15 free and 15 slave states. As in 1820, neither side wanted the other to gain control in the Senate. Southern lawmakers refused to admit California. In the end, Congress agreed to the Compromise of 1850. This allowed California to enter the Union. In return, Congress passed the Fugitive Slave Law. This law forced Americans to return runaway enslaved people to the person who had held them, or go to jail. Many Northerners were angered by the law.

John Brown

The Southern attack on Lawrence, Kansas, was the first battle of what newspapers called "Bleeding Kansas." ▼

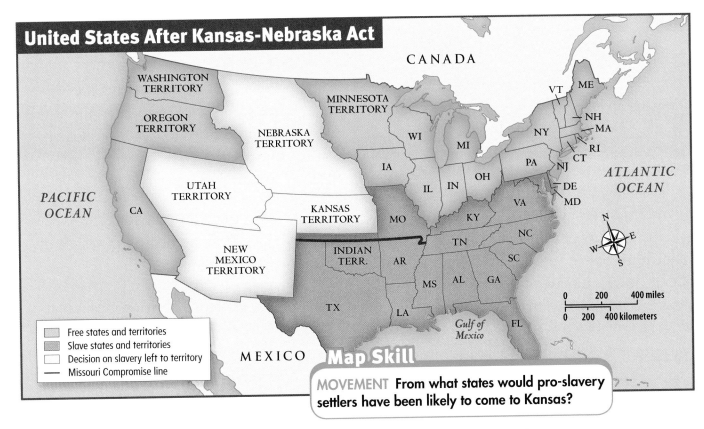

United States After Kansas-Nebraska Act

WASHINGTON TERRITORY

OREGON TERRITORY

NEBRASKA TERRITORY

MINNESOTA TERRITORY

CANADA

UTAH TERRITORY

CA

PACIFIC OCEAN

NEW MEXICO TERRITORY

KANSAS TERRITORY

MO

INDIAN TERR.

AR

TX

LA

WI

IA

IL

MI

IN

OH

KY

TN

MS

AL

GA

MEXICO

Gulf of Mexico

FL

NY

PA

VA

NC

SC

VT

ME

NH

MA

RI

CT

NJ

DE

MD

ATLANTIC OCEAN

Free states and territories
Slave states and territories
Decision on slavery left to territory
Missouri Compromise line

0   200   400 miles
0   200   400 kilometers

Map Skill

MOVEMENT **From what states would pro-slavery settlers have been likely to come to Kansas?**

Kansas-Nebraska Act

In 1854 Congress created two new territories, Kansas and Nebraska. Under the Missouri Compromise, neither territory could allow slavery. This changed when Senator Stephen Douglas of Illinois introduced the Kansas-Nebraska Act. In this act, Douglas used the term *popular sovereignty*. This meant that people—not the federal government— would vote to accept or ban slavery. This act overturned the Missouri Compromise.

New Political Party

The passage of the Kansas-Nebraska Act led Northern abolitionists to form a new political party, the Republicans. A lawyer from Illinois named Abraham Lincoln joined the Republican Party. Lincoln believed slavery was wrong, but he did not call for it to be abolished immediately. Lincoln wanted to stop slavery from spreading to new states.

"Bleeding Kansas"

After the passage of the Kansas-Nebraska Act, many Southerners moved to Kansas. They came to vote under popular sovereignty. Northern abolitionists responded by moving to Kansas. Suddenly armed settlers supporting both sides of the issue flooded the area.

Violence finally broke out in 1856, when settlers who favored slavery burned the free town of Lawrence, Kansas, to the ground. A few days later, abolitionist John Brown and his sons killed five Southerners. Newspapers began to describe the territory as "Bleeding Kansas." The violence in Kansas did not become all-out war, but it was a preview of events to come.

QUICK CHECK

Fact and Opinion **What opinion would abolitionists have had about the Fugitive Slave Law?**

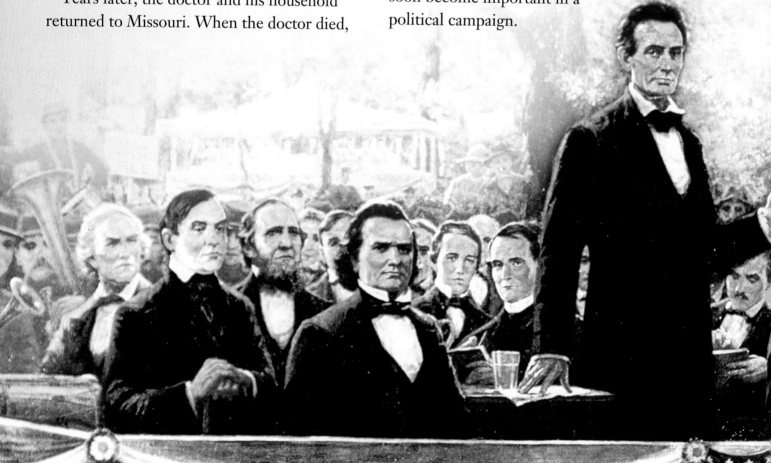

C A NATION DIVIDED

By 1857, the United States was close to breaking apart. Many Americans wondered whether the country could survive half-free and half-slave.

A Case About Freedom

In 1857 a case about the rights of enslaved people came before the United States Supreme Court. It was the case of *Dred Scott* v. *Sanford*. Dred Scott was an enslaved person bought by a doctor in Missouri, a slave state. The doctor moved his household to Illinois, a free state, and then to the Wisconsin Territory, where slavery was banned by the Northwest Ordinance of 1787.

Years later, the doctor and his household returned to Missouri. When the doctor died,

▲ Dred Scott

Scott said he was a free man because he had lived on free soil. Eleven years later, the Supreme Court refused to free Scott. Chief Justice Roger Taney wrote that enslaved people could be:

❝ . . . bought and sold and treated as an ordinary article of merchandise. ❞

The court's decision meant that enslaved workers could be taken anywhere, even free states, and remain enslaved.

In 1857, most Northerners didn't want to abolish slavery in the South. They didn't want slavery in new territories. This issue would soon become important in a political campaign.

Lincoln Against Douglas

In 1858 two candidates from Illinois attracted national attention. Abraham Lincoln, a Republican, ran against Stephen Douglas, a Democrat, for the Senate. Compared to the popular Douglas, Lincoln was unknown.

The two candidates held seven **debates**, or public discussions, on political issues. The three-hour debates drew crowds as large as 15,000. The candidates argued over many issues, but the issue of slavery drew the most attention.

Although Douglas disliked slavery, he refused to speak out against it. He believed popular sovereignty was the way to resolve disagreement over slavery. Douglas tried to paint Lincoln as a reckless abolitionist.

Lincoln believed that slavery was wrong for a nation founded on freedom. In a speech during the campaign, Lincoln said,

“This government cannot endure permanently half-slave and half-free.”

Lincoln received more votes than Douglas in the election. At that time, state legislatures chose Senators for the state. The Democrats held more seats in the Illinois legislature, and they picked Douglas, a Democrat. In the end, the campaign helped Lincoln. Republicans from the North and the Midwest agreed that he would be a good presidential candidate.

QUICK CHECK

Fact and Opinion Write one fact and one opinion about the Lincoln-Douglas campaign.

▼ The Lincoln-Douglas debates drew large crowds. Newspapers across the country reported on the debates.

D AT THE EDGE OF WAR

By 1859 many Americans feared that war would soon tear apart the nation. There seemed to be no way to avoid violence.

John Brown's Raid

For John Brown, there was no compromise on slavery. The fierce abolitionist had been a conductor on the Underground Railroad in New York. He was also involved in the violent events in "Bleeding Kansas." In 1859 Brown tried to start a revolt among enslaved people. He planned to attack an Army arsenal in Harpers Ferry, Virginia. Brown then planned to give the weapons to enslaved people who he believed would rise up against plantation owners. On October 16, Brown and a small force captured the arsenal. Enslaved people nearby did not join him, or revolt against the slaveholders. Two days later, U.S. soldiers, commanded by Colonel Robert E. Lee, recaptured the arsenal. Brown was convicted of **treason**, or betraying one's country, and hanged. His raid struck fear across the South.

The Election of 1860

In the presidential election of 1860, Abraham Lincoln ran as the Republican candidate. Stephen Douglas ran as a Democrat.

▼ The Civil War began with an attack by Confederate artillery on Fort Sumter in Charleston, South Carolina, on April 12, 1861.

Two other candidates also joined the race. Only Lincoln took a stand against slavery in the new territories. Southern lawmakers warned that if Lincoln won, they would **secede**, or withdraw, from the Union.

In November 1860, Lincoln was elected. Then, in December, South Carolina was the first state to secede. By February, six more states had seceded. They established the Confederate States of America, also called the Confederacy, and elected Jefferson Davis as their President.

▲ Abraham Lincoln

First Shots Fired

In the spring of 1861, Confederate troops seized several U. S. Army arsenals in the South. Fort Sumter, an island arsenal in the harbor of Charleston, South Carolina, refused to surrender. The commander asked the federal government for more supplies and weapons. Before supplies could arrive, Confederate guns fired on the fort on April 12, 1861. The Civil War had begun. A **civil war** is a war among people who live in the same country.

QUICK CHECK

Fact and Opinion What event between 1859 and 1861 was most responsible for causing the Civil War?

Check Understanding

1. **VOCABULARY** Write a summary of this lesson using the vocabulary terms.

   abolitionist   **secede**

   debate   **civil war**

2. **READING SKILL Fact and Opinion** Use the chart from page 250 to write your personal opinion about John Brown.

Fact	Opinion

3. **Write About It** Why were the settlers in Kansas ready to use violence?

The Nation Divided by War

Lesson 3

VOCABULARY

draft p. 259

Anaconda Plan p. 262

total war p. 264

READING SKILL

Fact and Opinion

Copy the chart below. As you read, record the opinions of each side.

Fact	Opinion

MISSOURI COURSE LEVEL EXPECTATIONS

5.A.1, 5.J.1, 6.I.1, 7.A.1, 7.B.1, 7.C.1

Union troops were defeated at the Battle of Bull Run.

Visual Preview

How did the challenges of wartime divide the nation?

A The South won the first major battle of the war at Bull Run.

B Both the North and South had specific strengths and weaknesses.

C Early battles proved the war would be long and bloody.

D The Civil War was a total war, one in which each side also strikes against civilians.

A THE WAR BEGINS

In the beginning, leaders in both the North and South thought the Civil War would last about two months. Some soldiers even feared the war would be over before they had a chance to fight.

By 1862 people on both sides realized the war was turning into a long, drawn-out conflict. The Civil War would become the bloodiest war in American history.

Battle of Bull Run

The first major battle of the Civil War was fought on July 21, 1861. It took place at a stream called Bull Run, near the town of Manassas, Virginia. Manassas is located between Washington, D.C., and Richmond, Virginia. Richmond was the capital of the Confederacy. That day, sightseers followed the Union troops. Many expected to watch a rapid Union victory. Then Richmond would fall quickly. What they saw instead was bloodshed and death.

For hours, Union soldiers attacked the line of Confederate soldiers, but could not break through. General Thomas Jackson was standing firm with his troops. One Confederate officer shouted:

"There stands Jackson like a stone wall!"

From that day forward, "Stonewall" Jackson became a Confederate hero.

With the battlefield littered with bloody bodies, fresh Southern troops arrived by railroad. Soon, Northern troops retreated in panic. Frightened soldiers and panicked sightseers fled to Washington. The South had won the first major battle of the war.

At first, excitement about the war made many Northern and Southern men eager to join the fight. As the war dragged on, the death toll rose. Both sides had to use a **draft**. A draft is the selection of men who must serve in the military. Draft riots broke out in many Northern cities.

QUICK CHECK

Fact and Opinion What opinion did leaders on both sides share at the beginning of the war?

PLACES

The Battle of Bull Run was fought at **Manassas, Virginia.** Today Manassas is a suburb of Washington, D.C. You can visit the museum at Manassas National Battlefield Park, where the battle was fought.

Manassas, Virginia

B STRENGTHS AND WEAKNESSES

Many Southerners believed they would win the war because they had a stronger military tradition than the North. Its generals had more experience. Confederate soldiers grew up riding horses and hunting. Large numbers of Southerners volunteered to fight. They were eager to protect their homes and way of life.

THE CONFEDERACY

STRENGTHS	WEAKNESSES
• It planned a defensive war, which is easier for the military to win.	• It had less than half the population of the North, and one-third were enslaved people.
• A third of the nation's officers joined the Confederate army, including Robert E. Lee, the most respected general in the Army.	• The South had less money to support the war effort than did the North.
• It had a strong military tradition, with 7 of the nation's 8 military schools located in the South.	• The South had only one factory producing cannons and no major factory for making gunpowder.
• Southerners were more skilled in shooting, hunting, and riding.	• The South had half as many miles of railroad track as the North, making it difficult to get food, weapons, and other supplies to troops.
• Soldiers began preparing for war before the attack on Fort Sumter.	

Northerners were also brave fighters. But many lived in cities, so the military tradition was not as strong as it was in the South. Even so, Northerners believed they would win simply because they had more people, industry, and money than the South.

QUICK CHECK

Fact and Opinion **What did Southerners think about their military tradition?**

THE UNION

STRENGTHS

- In 1861 the North had more than twice the population of the South.

- More than three-quarters of U.S. Navy officers came from the North, and 90 percent of the Navy stayed with the North.

- About 80 percent of U.S. factories were in the North.

- The majority of railroads were in the North.

- Almost all firearms were manufactured in the North.

- Northern farms grew more food than Southern farms.

WEAKNESSES

- Union troops fought mostly in Southern areas, where people were defending their homes.

- Long supply lines made it difficult for Union troops to move quickly.

- Many Northern soldiers came from areas where there was little military tradition.

- Most Union soldiers had little military training.

- Union armies would have to take control of most of the South to bring it back into the Union.

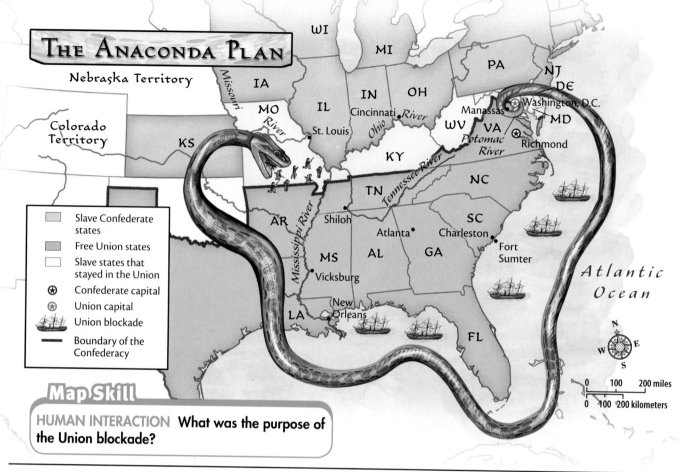

THE ANACONDA PLAN

Nebraska Territory

Colorado Territory

Legend:
- Slave Confederate states
- Free Union states
- Slave states that stayed in the Union
- ⊛ Confederate capital
- ⊛ Union capital
- Union blockade
- Boundary of the Confederacy

Map labels: WI, MI, PA, NJ, DE, IA, IN, OH, Washington, D.C., MO, IL, Cincinnati, Manassas, MD, St. Louis, Ohio River, WV, VA, KS, KY, Richmond, Potomac River, Missouri River, TN, NC, Tennessee River, AR, Shiloh, SC, Charleston, Atlanta, Fort Sumter, MS, AL, GA, Vicksburg, Mississippi River, New Orleans, LA, FL, Atlantic Ocean

0 100 200 miles
0 100 200 kilometers

Map Skill

HUMAN INTERACTION **What was the purpose of the Union blockade?**

ⓒ THE WAR CONTINUES

General Winfield Scott, the commander of the Union Army, made a plan to win the war. This plan would make it more difficult for the South to get the supplies it needed to fight the war. He called it the **Anaconda Plan**. Look at the map of the Anaconda Plan on this page.

The Anaconda Plan

An anaconda is a giant snake that strangles its prey. That is exactly what General Scott wanted to do to the South. Scott's Anaconda Plan had three parts. First, Northern ships would cut off, or blockade, Southern seaports. Without trade, the South would be unable to buy weapons and supplies. Second, the North would take control of the Mississippi River. This would divide the South and prevent Confederates from using the river to move supplies. In the final part of the plan, Union troops would invade the South, squeezing the region from both the east and the west.

The South's Strategy

While the North worked on its Anaconda Plan, the South prepared to defend its homeland. Jefferson Davis, president of the Confederacy, knew that a Union blockade of Southern ports could destroy the Confederate economy. Davis also knew that Great Britain and France needed Southern cotton. He believed British ships would break the Union blockade. Davis soon realized he was wrong. Europe had a surplus of cotton in the 1860s. Also, the British and French did not want to get involved in a foreign war. Look at the datagraphic on page 263. Which side, the North or the South, had the greater number of resources to fight the war?

The Battle of Shiloh

The number of casualties, or dead and wounded, at Bull Run shocked people on both sides. But those numbers were slight compared to those at the Battle of Shiloh, in Tennessee. There, on April 6, 1862, a Confederate army under General Albert Sidney Johnston surprised a Union army commanded by General Ulysses S. Grant.

It was the first time under fire for most of the soldiers. Still, the South pushed back one Union position after another. At one spot along a sunken road, bullets buzzed through the air. The place became known as "The Hornet's Nest."

The next day, dead bodies covered the bloody battlefield. The Union troops were near defeat. Suddenly, a second Union army arrived. The tired Confederates could not hold off a fresh Union attack. The North won at Shiloh, but both sides paid a heavy price. Twice as many Americans died in this one battle as died in the entire American Revolution. Shiloh showed both sides that the war would be long and bloody. Never again would people go sightseeing at the scene of a battle. What they saw would be too terrible.

QUICK CHECK

Fact and Opinion How did opinions about the war change after the Battle of Shiloh?

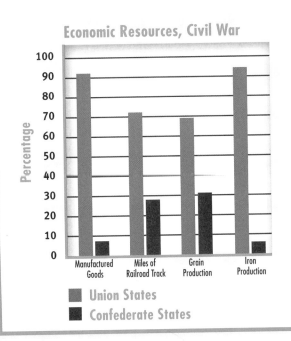

DataGraphic

Resources of the North and the South

Both the North and the South expected to win the Civil War. Study the chart and graph below. Then answer the questions.

Human Resources, Civil War

	Troops	Population
Union States	2,000,000	23,000,000
Confederate States	800,000	9,000,000

Economic Resources, Civil War

Bar graph showing Percentage (y-axis, 0–100) for Manufactured Goods, Miles of Railroad Track, Grain Production, and Iron Production (x-axis).

- Union States
- Confederate States

Think About Resources

1. Why did the North have more troops?

2. Why was iron an important resource?

◀ Twice as many Americans were killed at Shiloh as were killed in the American Revolution.

D A NEW KIND OF WAR

The Civil War was different from earlier American wars because it reached beyond battlefields. Farms and cities were burned. People were terrorized. Some historians call the Civil War the first **total war**. In a total war, each side strikes against the economic system and civilians of the other. Civilians are people who are not in the armed forces. In total war, entire populations are pulled into the conflict.

New Technology

Technology transformed the way the Civil War was fought. Railroads and telegraphs changed the way generals made battlefield decisions. Technology also made the Civil War more deadly than earlier wars. Rifles could fire bullets longer distances with greater accuracy. Mines were used to surprise and kill the enemy. Iron-covered battle ships, called ironclads, made wooden ships seem outdated overnight—cannon balls bounced off the hard metal sides.

The Confederates built the first ironclad ship, the CSS *Virginia*, formerly the USS *Merrimack*. To counter this new threat, the Union built the ironclad, USS *Monitor*. On March 9, 1862, the two ironclads fought off the Virginia coast. Neither ship could sink the other. Still, it was a victory for the North because they kept their blockade in place. Then one month later, the Union captured the port of New Orleans. Continuing the

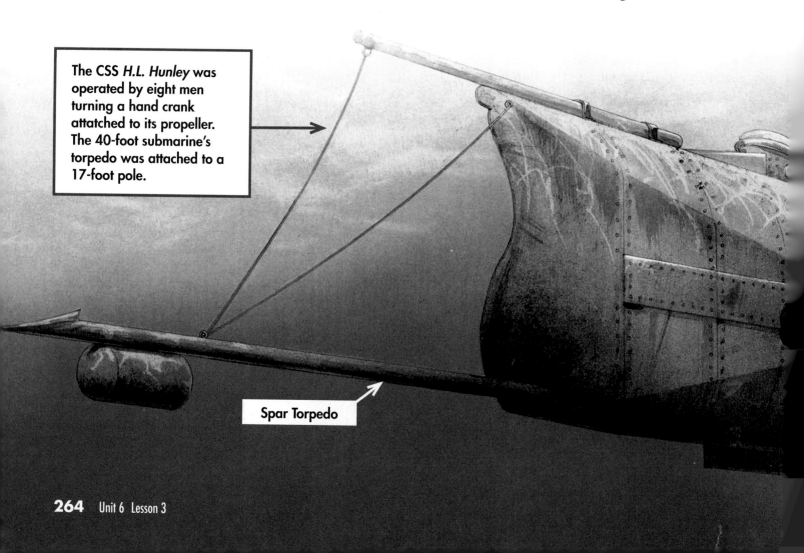

The CSS *H.L. Hunley* was operated by eight men turning a hand crank attatched to its propeller. The 40-foot submarine's torpedo was attached to a 17-foot pole.

Spar Torpedo

Anaconda Plan, Union ships began to sail up the Mississippi River. Soon, the Union navy controlled the river.

After the battle of the ironclads, "*Monitor* fever" swept the nation. Ironclad railroad cars were manufactured. With their thick armor plates and cannons, they were similar to modern tanks. Both sides also experimented with mines, torpedoes, and submarines. The South tried many ways to break the Union blockade of its ports. One Confederate, Horace L. Hunley, invented a submarine to sink warships. On February 16, 1864, the CSS *H.L. Hunley* sank the USS *Housatonic* near the Port of Charleston. Soon after the attack, however, the *Hunley* also sank. It may have been damaged during the blast. Even though the mission was a success, the port remained under Union control. The Union's ability to cut off the South's supplies would have a significant effect on the outcome of the Civil War.

QUICK CHECK

Fact and Opinion How did new technology change the Civil War?

Check Understanding

1. **VOCABULARY** Choose one word and write a paragraph explaining how it was used as a strategy in the Civil War.

    Anaconda Plan **total war**

2. **READING SKILL Fact and Opinion** Use your chart from page 258 to write your opinion about the most important strength of each side.

Fact	Opinion

3. **Write About It** Write about the reasons soldiers from the South and North fought in the Civil War.

Handcrank

Propeller

Lesson 4

VOCABULARY

Emancipation
Proclamation p. 267

Gettysburg Address
p. 271

READING SKILL

Fact and Opinion

Copy the chart below. As
you read, fill in the chart
with two facts and two of
your own opinions about
the Gettysburg Address.

Fact	Opinion

**MISSOURI COURSE
LEVEL EXPECTATIONS**

1.A.2, 3a.F.2, 6.I.1, 7.A.1, 7.C.1

The Union Moves Toward Victory

A reenactment of the Battle of Antietam

Visual Preview

How did civil war impact life in the United States?

A The Emancipation Proclamation ended slavery in Confederate states.

B Free African Americans enlisted, and the Union won at Vicksburg.

C The Union victory at Gettysburg changed the course of the war for the North.

D Women supported war both at home and on the war front.

Ⓐ BATTLE OF ANTIETAM

For months, Lincoln wanted to make an announcement that would change the purpose of the Civil War. He needed to do it after a Union victory. That victory finally came on September 17, 1862, the bloodiest day in American history.

After winning several battles in Virginia, Robert E. Lee's Confederate army marched north into Maryland in September 1862. Lee planned to continue east and surround Washington, D.C. The Confederates encountered the Union army at Antietam Creek near Sharpsburg, Maryland, on September 17. When the fighting ended that day, nearly 6,000 Confederate and Union soldiers were dead and another 17,000 were seriously wounded. The Union had won the battle. Many people questioned the purpose of so much bloodshed.

Lincoln's Important Announcement

Five days after the Battle of Antietam, Lincoln issued the **Emancipation Proclamation**. This document stated that on January 1, 1863, all enslaved people in the Confederacy were emancipated, or freed. It did not apply to slave states that had stayed in the Union—Delaware, Kentucky, Maryland, and Missouri.

The Emancipation Proclamation was an executive order based on powers given to the President by the Constitution. Lincoln hoped it would give Union troops a new sense of purpose, weaken the South and, eventually, help the North win the war.

Public Opinion Changes

The Emancipation Proclamation changed ideas about the reasons for fighting the Civil War. Now the fighting was about more than Southern independence or saving the Union. It was also about slavery and freedom.

QUICK CHECK

Fact and Opinion What opinion do you think enslaved people had about the Emancipation Proclamation?

EVENT

Early in the Civil War, Lincoln's goal was to keep the Union together. Later he decided to use the **Emancipation Proclamation** to change public views and the course of the war.

The Emancipation Proclamation

B THE WAR RAGES ON

Lincoln's Emancipation Proclamation encouraged thousands of free African Americans to join the Union army and navy. The Governor of Massachusetts asked an experienced officer and abolitionist, Robert Gould Shaw, to organize one of the first African American fighting forces.

The Fighting 54th

In February 1863 Shaw began training the 54th Massachusetts Colored Regiment at Camp Meigs, Massachusetts. This all-volunteer regiment included the two sons of Frederick Douglass. It became known as "The Fighting 54th."

On July 18, 1863, the 54th Regiment attacked Fort Wagner, South Carolina. Many men from the 54th died in the bloody fighting that ended in a Union defeat. In spite of the loss, the men of the Fighting 54th proved their bravery. Harriet Tubman, who helped care for the wounded, later described the battle:

> **"** And then we saw the lightning, and that was the guns; and then we heard the thunder, and that was the big guns; and then we heard the rain falling, and that was the drops of blood falling; and when we came to get the crops, it was dead men that we [gathered]. **"**

Although they were not treated as equals of white soldiers off the battlefield, they fought with courage in battle. By the end of the war, nearly 200,000 African Americans had joined the Union forces.

The Fighting 54th attacked Fort Wagner in South Carolina.

▲ Ulysses S. Grant watches his troops march into Vicksburg, Mississippi.

The Fall of Vicksburg

As you have read, one goal of the Anaconda Plan was for the Union to gain control of the Mississippi River. General Ulysses S. Grant achieved this goal in July 1863, when Union troops took control of Vicksburg, Mississippi.

For months, the city had been under siege by Grant's forces. In a siege, a military force surrounds a city and cuts it off. Grant's artillery pounded Vicksburg for weeks. Lack of food forced some people to eat rats! Finally the city fell on July 4, 1863. Grant was sickened by the sight of thousands of dead and wounded soldiers after the battle. Later, Grant wrote:

. . . after the battle . . . one naturally [wants] to do as much to [stop] the suffering of an enemy as a friend.

—ULYSSES S. GRANT

The victory gave the Union control of the Mississippi River. More importantly for the Union, the Confederacy was now split in two. The Anaconda Plan was almost complete.

QUICK CHECK

Fact and Opinion How did Grant feel about people he had defeated after a battle?

C THE TURNING POINT

By the spring of 1863, Lee's army had defeated the Union in several battles, including an important clash at Chancellorsville, Virginia. Unfortunately for the Confederates, General Stonewall Jackson was killed in the battle at Chancellorsville. This loss soon hurt the South. In June, Lee decided to take the war north again. His army marched through towns in southern Pennsylvania looking for badly needed supplies, especially shoes.

On July 1, 1863, Lee's army met Union troops under General George Meade in the small farm town of Gettysburg, Pennsylvania. Neither army had planned to fight there, but the nation would soon learn of the bloody Battle of Gettysburg. For two days, the armies fought each other. Ground was taken and lost, but neither side was able to win.

Pickett's Charge

On July 3, 1863, with the Confederate ammunition running low, Lee ordered General George Pickett to charge the Union lines. Confederate soldiers formed lines about a mile wide and half a mile deep. They began what came to be called "Pickett's Charge." More than 12,000 men ran almost one mile across an open field into cannon and rifle fire from Union troops. More than 6,000 men were killed and wounded in that attack. Lee was forced to retreat. The line of wagons carrying wounded soldiers back to Virginia was 17 miles long.

In all, about 51,000 soldiers were killed or wounded at the Battle of Gettysburg. It was the bloodiest battle ever fought in North America. Union victories at Gettysburg and Vicksburg turned the war in favor of the North.

▼ Thousands of Confederates died during Pickett's Charge. More than 51,000 men in all were killed or wounded at Gettysburg.

Confederate troops

Union troops

The Gettysburg Address

In November 1863, Lincoln gave a short speech at Gettysburg to dedicate a cemetery for dead Union soldiers. When he finished, the audience was silent. Lincoln thought his speech was a failure. But the people were silent out of respect for the powerful words.

The **Gettysburg Address** is known as one of the greatest speeches in American history. Read it in the Primary Sources feature.

QUICK CHECK

Fact and Opinion What was Lincoln's opinion of his speech at Gettysburg?

Primary Sources

The Gettysburg Address

"Four **score** and seven years ago our **fathers** brought forth on this continent, a new nation, **conceived** in liberty, and **dedicated** to the **proposition** that all men are created equal.

Now we are engaged in a great civil war, testing whether that nation, or any nation so conceived and so dedicated, can long endure. We are met on a great battlefield of that war. We have come to dedicate a portion of that field, as a final resting place for those who here gave their lives that that nation might live. It is altogether fitting and proper that we should do this.

But, in a larger sense, we cannot dedicate—we can not **consecrate**—we can not **hallow**—this ground. The brave men, living and dead, who struggled here, have consecrated it far above our poor power to add or detract. The world will little note nor long remember what we say here, but can never forget what they did here.

It is for us the living, rather, to be dedicated here to the unfinished work which they who fought here have thus far so nobly advanced. It is rather for us to be here dedicated to the great task remaining before us—that from these honored dead we take increased devotion to that cause for which they gave the last full measure of devotion; that we here highly resolve that these dead shall not have died in vain; that this nation, under God, shall have a new birth of freedom; and that government of the people, by the people, for the people, shall not perish from the earth."

by Abraham Lincoln • Gettysburg, Pennsylvania 1863

score: times twenty
fathers: forefathers or ancestors
conceived: formed
dedicated: set apart for a special purpose
proposition: intention or plan
consecrate: set apart as holy
hallow: consider holy

Write About It What reasons did Lincoln give for continuing the war?

An infantry camp

Rose Greenhow

A Civil War nurse

D THE WAR EFFORT

During the Civil War, civilians of all ages contributed to the war effort on both sides. Factory workers made weapons. Railroad workers transported troops and supplies. Even children played a role. Young people worked in family shops and helped on farms. Boys as young as 11 joined the army to serve as buglers or drummers. Men in their 60s and 70s signed up to fight. Others lied about their age to serve as soldiers.

Women and the War

Women in the North and South supported the war effort in many ways. On the home front, women worked in factories or ran family businesses while men were fighting in the war. They worked in shops, plowed fields, and harvested crops.

Women also helped the military. They cared for wounded soldiers, sewed uniforms, and made tents and ammunition. Some women took dangerous jobs as spies or nurses near the front lines. Rose Greenhow served as a Confederate spy. Before being caught, she directed a group of spies from her home in Washington, D.C. After getting information about Union plans, she sent coded messages

Harriet Tubman

A boy soldier

to the Confederate army. Greenhow also traveled to Europe to gain financial support for the South.

Harriet Tubman, the well-known conductor on the Underground Railroad, served the Union as a spy, scout, and nurse. Clara Barton served on the battlefield, bringing food, medicine, and supplies to the wounded. In 1881 she founded the American Red Cross.

QUICK CHECK

Fact and Opinion Why did civilians help in the war effort?

Check Understanding

1. **VOCABULARY** Write a paragraph about Abraham Lincoln using both vocabulary terms.

   Emancipation Proclamation

   Gettysburg Address

2. **READING SKILL Fact and Opinion** Use your chart from page 266 to write your opinion of the Gettysburg Address.

Fact	Opinion

3. **Write About It** Write about why you think men joined the Fighting 54th during the war.

VOCABULARY

malice p. 278

assassination p. 278

READING SKILL

Fact and Opinion
Copy the chart below. As you read, fill it in with facts and your own opinions about Sherman's March.

Fact	Opinion

MISSOURI COURSE LEVEL EXPECTATIONS

3a.I.1, 5.A.1, 5.J.1, 6.I.1, 7.A.1, 7.B.1, 7.C.1

THE WAR ENDS

The Battle of Cold Harbor

Visual Preview

How did the end of the Civil War change the United States?

A General Grant sieged Richmond in order to capture the Confederate capital.

B Sherman marched through the South to bring an end to the Civil War.

C In April 1865, Richmond fell, Lee surrendered, and Lincoln was assassinated.

A   THE FINAL BATTLES

Ulysses S. Grant was a strong general who had won important victories in the West. In 1864 Lincoln put Grant in command of the entire Union army. He hoped Grant would bring the war to an end.

Grant had two major goals. He wanted to destroy Lee's army in Virginia, and he wanted to capture Richmond, Virginia, the Confederate capital. For 40 days, from April to June 1864, he battled Lee's army.

The number of dead and wounded in these battles was enormous. At the Battle of Cold Harbor, Grant lost 7,000 men in about an hour. The Union army was so much larger than the Confederate army that it was able to continue its attacks. Finally, Grant reached Petersburg, a key railroad center south of Richmond. From there, he hoped to capture Richmond. Lee could not leave Petersburg. If he did, Grant would have a clear path to Richmond. With Lee trapped, Grant put Petersburg under siege for ten grim months.

People wondered if the war would ever end. Some Northerners wanted to let the Confederacy secede. Many blamed President Lincoln for continuing the fight to keep the Union together. As a result, Lincoln felt he had little hope of winning reelection in 1864.

QUICK CHECK

Fact and Opinion What opinion did some Northerners have about Lincoln's handling of the war?

▼ Richmond, Virginia, lay in ruins after the war.

B SHERMAN'S MARCH

General William Tecumseh Sherman led Union forces in the West. Following the Anaconda Plan, he marched his troops across Tennessee and Georgia to squeeze the South. He told his men to destroy anything of value to the enemy. Sherman's soldiers terrorized the South. They burned crops and buildings.

They destroyed railroads and factories. They even killed livestock and left the animals for vultures. Sherman believed that the North needed to launch a total war, which would break the South's fighting spirit.

In September 1864, Sherman captured and burned Atlanta, Georgia, one of the South's

Battles of the Civil War

Legend:
- Confederate states
- Union states
- ✸ Confederate victory
- ✸ Union victory
- ✩ Undecided battle
- → Sherman's march
- General Sherman

Map Skill

DIRECTION **Where did General Sherman go after Savannah?**

largest cities and a railroad center. Sherman's 60,000-man army cut a 60-mile-wide and 300-mile-long path across Georgia to the city of Savannah on the Atlantic Coast. The Union force took Savannah in December. From there, the army marched into South Carolina—the state some people believed had started the war. Many cities in Sherman's path were left in ashes. One soldier said:

> **Here is where treason began and . . . here is where it shall end!**

With the fall of Atlanta, it seemed the end of the war was finally in sight. Northerners began to regain confidence in Lincoln and his ability to lead the Union to victory. In November 1864, voters reelected him. See the the results of the election in the datagraphic on this page.

QUICK CHECK

Fact and Opinion What opinion did many Northern soldiers have about South Carolina?

▼ Union troops destroyed many parts of the South during Sherman's March.

DataGraphic

The Election of 1864

In 1864 the Democratic nominee for President, George McClellan, ran against Abraham Lincoln. Use the map and the graphs to answer the questions about the election of 1864.

Electoral Votes in Election of 1864

Lincoln (Republican)
McClellan (Democratic)
Nonvoting state or territory
3 Number of electoral votes

*One of Nevada's three electors did not vote.

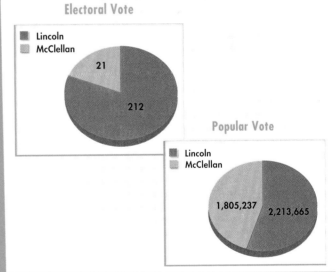

Electoral Vote

Lincoln
McClellan

21
212

Popular Vote

Lincoln
McClellan

1,805,237
2,213,665

Think About the 1864 Election

1. What states did McClellan win?

2. Why was the popular vote much closer than the electoral vote?

Robert E. Lee surrendered to Ulysses S. Grant at Appomattox Court House in Virginia.

Ⓒ THE SOUTH SURRENDERS

In March 1865 Grant was closing in on Lee at Petersburg. After the Union siege, Confederate soldiers defending the city were near starvation. On April 2, Lee took his army west, hoping to find food and gather more Confederate troops. As a result, Petersburg fell. The next day, Richmond, the Confederate capital, also fell. Lee knew that more killing would be meaningless. The war was over.

On April 9, 1865, Lee surrendered to Grant at Appomattox Court House in Virginia. Grant did not take any prisoners. Instead, he offered Lee generous terms. For example, Lee and his soldiers were allowed to return to their homes. They could also keep their horses to help with the spring plowing.

After Lee's surrender, Jefferson Davis fled westward, where he hoped to keep the Confederacy alive. On May 10, 1865, he was captured by Union soldiers. Davis was later imprisoned for two years in Virginia.

Lincoln Is Shot

Lincoln did not want to punish the South. In his second inaugural address, he encouraged Americans to put away their **malice**, or desire to harm, with these words: "With malice toward none, with charity for all."

Less than a week after Lee's surrender, Lincoln was watching a play at Ford's Theater in Washington, D.C. Suddenly a gunshot rang out. John Wilkes Booth had shot the President. The next morning, April 15, 1865, Lincoln died. Abraham Lincoln's **assassination** shocked the nation. Assassination is the murder of an important leader. The poet Walt Whitman expressed the country's sadness:

> O CAPTAIN! my Captain! our fearful trip is done; The ship has weather'd every [storm], the prize we sought is won;
>
> —WALT WHITMAN

Check Understanding

1. **VOCABULARY** Write a paragraph about Abraham Lincoln using both vocabulary words.

   malice   **assassination**

2. **READING SKILL Fact and Opinion** Use your chart from page 274 to help you write about Sherman's March.

Fact	Opinion

3. **Write About It** Why did most Northern voters support Lincoln and want to continue the war?

Troops Return Home

At the end of the war, the South had few farms left in working condition. Troops returned not only to the property that had been destroyed, but to a way of life that had ended. In the South, one of every four white men had been killed. Two-thirds of its wealth had been lost. It would take many years for the South to recover. One Confederate soldier, returning home to Richmond, wrote:

> **"**I shall not attempt to describe my feelings. The city [is] in ruins. . . . With a raging headache and a swelling heart I reach my home, and here the curtain falls.**"**

The Union had survived, but the cost of the Civil War had been huge. The North's victory ended slavery for millions of African Americans. At the same time, it left the South in ruins. United once again, the nation faced the task of rebuilding the South.

QUICK CHECK

Fact and Opinion Why did Lincoln say he would show "malice toward none"?

▼ Abraham Lincoln's funeral procession passed through several states on its way to Springfield, Illinois.

79

Lesson 6

VOCABULARY

Reconstruction p. 281

black codes p. 281

sharecropping p. 282

segregation p. 285

Jim Crow laws p. 285

READING SKILL

Fact and Opinion

Copy the chart below. As you read, fill it in with facts about Reconstruction and the opinions people had about Reconstruction.

Fact	Opinion

MISSOURI COURSE LEVEL EXPECTATIONS

1.A.2, 3a.l.1, 5.A.1, 6.l.1, 7.C.1

RECONSTRUCTION AND AFTER

The Freedmen's Bureau started schools such as this one in Charleston, South Carolina.

Visual Preview

How did the South change after the war?

A The Freedmen's Bureau provided valuable services to help blacks and whites.

B Amendments to the Constitution gave people more rights, but life was still difficult.

C Southern states began a policy of segregation after Reconstruction ended.

A REBUILDING THE SOUTH

After the Civil War, President Lincoln wanted to end the harsh feelings between the North and South. Before letting the defeated Confederate states back into the Union, he asked them to take an oath to support the Constitution and the Union.

Before his death, Lincoln created a plan for **Reconstruction**, or rebuilding the South. In March 1865, he had signed a bill that created the Freedmen's Bureau. This government program was part of Reconstruction. It provided food, clothing, shelter, medical care, jobs, and legal help to both African Americans and whites. It also set up 4,000 schools for newly freed people.

African Americans also set up schools. By 1870 African Americans had spent over $1 million on education. Several colleges and universities for African Americans were founded in the South. Among these were Fisk University in Tennessee and Spelman College in Georgia.

Congress and President Andrew Johnson supported the Freedmen's Bureau. But they clashed over who would control other parts of Reconstruction.

Johnson Is Impeached

Few Presidents have been more unpopular than Andrew Johnson. Southerners disliked him because he had supported the Union. Northerners disliked him because he allowed former Confederate leaders to serve in Congress.

▲ This political cartoon criticizing President Andrew Johnson shows him being crushed the by U.S. Constitution.

He also took no action when Southern states passed **black codes**, laws that restricted the rights of African Americans.

The House of Representatives voted to impeach Johnson. To impeach is to charge an official with wrongdoing. If two-thirds of the 36 Senators had voted against Johnson, he would have been removed from office. The vote was 35 to 19. He remained in office, but the division between the North and South also remained.

QUICK CHECK

Fact and Opinion What opinion did many in the South have about Andrew Johnson?

After two years of struggling with President Johnson over who would control Reconstruction, Congress passed the first Reconstruction Act in 1867. This act divided the South into five districts. The districts would remain under the control of the U.S. Army until new governments could be formed. Each state had to write a new constitution.

Amendments to the Constitution

Before Lincoln's death in 1865, Congress approved the Thirteenth Amendment. This amendment abolished slavery. During Reconstruction, a Southern state had to ratify the Thirteenth Amendment in order to return to the Union. Other amendments that passed after Lincoln's death guaranteed rights to African Americans. In 1868 the Fourteenth Amendment made African Americans citizens of the United States and guaranteed them the same legal rights as whites. In 1870 the Fifteenth Amendment made it illegal for states to deny a man's right to vote. Women were not included in the amendment.

A New Way of Life

After the Civil War, most plantation owners had little money to pay workers. Instead, they rented out their fields. Landowners usually accepted part of the crop grown on their land as rent—sometimes as much as one-half of the crop. This system of renting land in return for a share of the crop raised on it is called **sharecropping**. It sounds fair, but most people who worked in the fields remained poor.

They did not make much money because the price for cotton was low. Many farmers had to borrow money to survive. By doing this, they slipped deeply into debt.

Citizenship
Rights and Responsibilities

As an American citizen, you have the responsibility to protect not only your own rights but the rights of others. Suppose you were asked to attend a meeting to suggest rules for the playground. You have a right to speak and give your suggestions. You also have a responsibility to be careful about what you say and to respect the ideas of others.

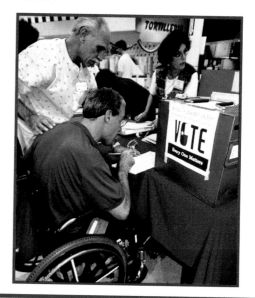

Write About It Explain the responsibilities citizens have when voting and what might happen if people were not allowed to vote.

Northerners in the South

At the same time, many Northerners moved to the South to start businesses. They soon became active in the fight for African Americans' rights. Southerners often called these Northerners "carpetbaggers" because many carried suitcases made of carpeting. Many Southerners believed that carpetbaggers were taking advantage of the South's suffering. Many carpetbaggers were former Union soldiers or members of the Freedmen's Bureau who wanted to settle in the South.

QUICK CHECK

Fact and Opinion What opinion did Southerners have about carpetbaggers?

▼ This newspaper cartoon shows a carpetbagger from the North. What was the cartoonist's opinion of carpetbaggers?

▼ A family of sharecroppers in Virginia in 1899

▲ Hiram R. Revels (left) and Blanche K. Bruce (right)

C RECONSTRUCTION ENDS

During Reconstruction, more than 600 African Americans were elected to state office and 16 were elected to Congress. Among them were Hiram R. Revels and Blanche K. Bruce from Mississippi, who were both elected to the United States Senate. Some Southern whites were not ready to accept and treat African Americans as equals.

Violence in the South

Many white Southerners didn't want African Americans to hold public office. They did not want to pay higher taxes for schools and roads that helped African Americans. Some Southerners turned to violence to terrorize African Americans and their white supporters.

In 1866 six former Confederate officers formed the Ku Klux Klan. Disguised in white robes and hoods, they terrorized African Americans, driving them from their homes and destroying their property. They used "night raids" and murder to keep African Americans from voting. African Americans working for whites were often told they would be fired

▼ The Ku Klux Klan terrorized African Americans.

if they voted. Sometimes whites kept the locations of voting places secret from African American voters. In some places, African Americans were forced to pay an illegal "poll tax" in order to vote. Many people could not afford to pay the tax.

Jim Crow Laws

In the presidential election of 1876, Democrat Samuel J. Tilden of New York won the popular vote. The electoral vote, however, was in question in some states, including three in the South. The Republican candidate, Rutherford B. Hayes, promised to remove all Union troops from the South if the electoral votes were cast for him. The Democrats from the South, who were white, voted for the Republican in order to end Reconstruction.

President Hayes quickly ordered the removal of federal troops, bringing an end to Reconstruction. After federal troops left, Southern states began a policy called **segregation**. Segregation is the separation of people based on race. The **Jim Crow laws** made segregation legal in the South. Under the Jim Crow laws, blacks and whites could not use the same schools, restaurants, railroad cars, hotels, or parks. In 1896 the Supreme Court in *Plessy* v. *Ferguson* ruled that "separate but equal"

services were Constitutional. In reality, such services were rarely equal.

In the late 1800s, African Americans experienced discrimination in the North as well as the South. African Americans in the North were often not allowed in many public places. Although Reconstruction granted equal citizenship, segregation resulted in unequal treatment. African Americans did not gain many of the rights guaranteed by the Thirteenth, Fourteenth, and Fifteenth Amendments until the Civil Rights movement of the 1950s and 1960s.

QUICK CHECK

Fact and Opinion **How did the decision in *Plessy* v. *Ferguson* hurt African Americans?**

Check Understanding

1. **VOCABULARY** Write a paragraph about African Americans after the Civil War using these vocabulary terms.

   Reconstruction   sharecropping

   black codes   segregation

2. **READING SKILL Fact and Opinion** Use your chart from page 280 to write an opinion about Reconstruction.

Fact	Opinion

 3. **Write About It** Write about the ways African Americans improved their lives in the South.

Unit 6

Review and Assess

Vocabulary

Number a paper from 1 to 4. Beside each number, write the word from the list that matches the description.

blockade   black codes

malice   segregation

1. The separation of people based on race

2. The closing of an area to keep supplies from moving

3. Laws passed by the Southern states that limited the rights of the African Americans

4. The desire to harm someone

Comprehension and Critical Thinking

5. How did Harriet Tubman help enslaved Africans?

6. **Reading Skill** Identify one fact and one opinion about carpetbaggers.

7. **Critical Thinking** Why did Sherman believe that only total war would lead to a Union victory?

8. **Critical Thinking** In what ways was Reconstruction unsuccessful in improving the lives of African Americans?

Skill

Use Climographs

Write a complete sentence to answer each question.

9. Which are Richmond's two driest months?

10. How would you describe Richmond's temperature during the wettest month of the year?

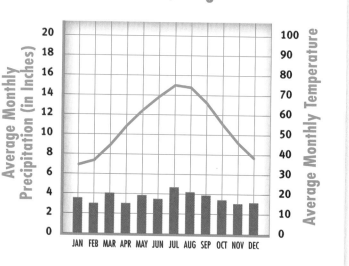

Richmond, Virginia

# MAP Test Preparation

During the Civil War, the Union had several advantages over the Confederacy. The North had a larger population and more workers, as well as greater factory and textile production. It had more farmland, miles of railroad, and ships. It could feed, arm, and move a large army easily. The Confederacy also had some advantages. Southerners were fighting for their way of life. The army fought on familiar land and had officers with years of military experience. One of them, Robert E. Lee, became commander of the Confederate army.

1   **What two things does this passage compare?**

○   the Civil War and the Korean War

○   advantages of the Union and Confederacy

○   Northern factories and Southern factories

○   railroads and ships

2   **What does this sentence from the passage show? "It had more farmland, miles of railroad, and ships."**

○   Most soldiers rode on horseback.

○   Farms helped the South produce food.

○   The North had advantages in the Civil War.

○   The South had advantages in the Civil War.

3   **What advantages did the South have in the Civil War?**

Write your answer on a separate piece of paper.

The Big Idea Activities

What are some things people are willing to fight for?

Write About the Big Idea

Expository Essay
Use the Unit 6 Foldable to help you write an expository essay that answers the Big Idea question, *What are some things people are willing to fight for*? Use the Notes you wrote under each tab in the Foldable for details to support each main idea. Be sure to begin with an introduction that includes facts. Include one paragraph that explains the reason for each fact. End with a concluding paragraph that includes your opinion.

Things people fight for

North | South

Make a Poster

Make a poster of a person or event you read about in Unit 6. Here's how to make your poster.

1. Find or draw a picture of the person's face, the person in action, or the event you chose.

2. Research the person or event you chose to find five interesting facts.

3. Use resources available from your library or historical sites on the Internet.

Illustrate your poster with drawings of some of the interesting facts.

Frederick Douglass

1. Douglass escaped slavery

2. Gave a speech at the . . .

3. Became publisher of several abolitionist newspapers

4. Best-selling autobiography

5. Gave a speech at Lincoln's memorial

Unit 7

EXPLORE The Big Idea

Essential Question
How do geography, economics, and government affect people's lives?

FOLDABLES
Study Organizer

Summarize
Make and label a Trifold Book Foldable before you read this unit. Label the three sections **Geography, Economics,** and **Government**. Use the Foldable to organize information as you read.

Geography
Economics
Government

LOG ON
For more information about Unit 7 go to www.macmillanmh.com

Life in the United States

Denver, Colorado

289

PEOPLE, PLACES, AND EVENTS

John Wesley Powell

John Muir

Grand Canyon

1869
Powell explores the Grand Canyon

Yosemite

1890
Muir helps make Yosemite a national park

1865   1885   1905   1925

Powell led an expedition down the Green and Colorado rivers that included the first passage through the **Grand Canyon**.

Today you can see the Grand Canyon, one of the natural wonders of the world.

Muir's actions helped to save the **Yosemite** Valley and other wilderness areas. Muir also founded a conservation club, the Sierra Club.

Today you can go to Yosemite National Park and see the park's beauty close up.

Muriel Siebert

Condoleezza Rice

New York City

1967
Muriel Siebert joins the
New York Stock Exchange

Washington, D.C.

2005
Condoleezza Rice becomes
Secretary of State

1945 1965 1985 2005

Muriel Siebert was elected as a member of the New York Stock Exchange in 1967, making her the first woman to hold a seat in the body.

Today you can visit the New York Stock Exchange on Wall Street in **New York City**.

Dr. Rice is the first female African American Secretary of State.

Today you can visit **Washington, D.C.,** and see United States government buildings, monuments, and landmarks.

Lesson 1

VOCABULARY

region p. 294

climate p. 294

precipitation p. 294

humid p. 294

arid p. 294

READING SKILL

Summarize
Copy the chart below. Use it to summarize the regions of the United States.

```
[  ]   [  ]   [  ]
        ↓     ↓     ↓
      [    Summary    ]
```

MISSOURI COURSE LEVEL EXPECTATIONS

5.B.2, 5.B.3, 5.C.1, 5.F.1, 7.B.1

REGIONS OF THE UNITED STATES

The Colorado River carved out the Grand Canyon over a period of 6 million years.

Visual Preview

How does geography create regions?

A The landscape of the United States varies greatly.

B The United States is divided into five regions.

A THE UNITED STATES

The landscape and history of North America greatly influenced the development of the United States. Today interaction with the environment and the rest of the world continues to play a role in the growth of our country.

Studying the past helps us understand what is happening today. Geography, economics, and government have influenced how the United States developed and how it runs today.

Geography, economics, and government interact as they shape the society in which we live. Economic concerns, such as jobs, influence environmental policies the government makes. Lawmakers may create rules to encourage economic growth and protect the environment. A region's natural resources often determine the industries employing people in the area.

Layout of the United States

The United States is the world's fourth-largest country in size. Land elevation changes from the west coast to the east coast. Forty-eight of the country's fifty states stretch across the middle of North America. Two states lie elsewhere. Alaska lies in the northwestern part of the continent. Hawaii is in the Pacific Ocean.

The western coast of the United States faces the Pacific Ocean. The eastern coast faces the Atlantic Ocean. In the north the very cold Arctic Ocean borders Alaska. In the south the Gulf of Mexico's warm currents border the land.

QUICK CHECK

Summarize Describe the position of the United States in North America.

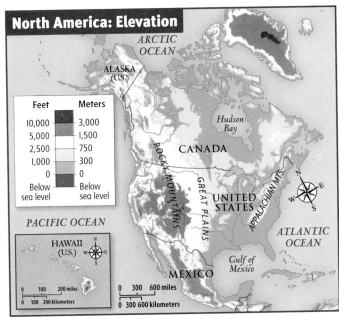

North America: Elevation

Feet	Meters
10,000	3,000
5,000	1,500
2,500	750
1,000	300
0	0
Below sea level	Below sea level

Map Skill

PLACE **About how high are the Appalachian Mountains?**

B THE FIVE REGIONS

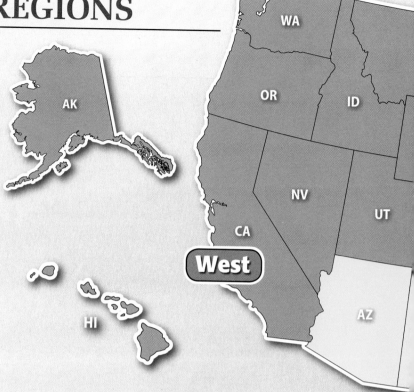

The United States can be divided into five geographic regions: the Northeast, Southeast, Northwest, Southwest, and West. A **region** is a large area with features, such as climate and landforms, which set it apart from other areas.

Weather Patterns

Climate is weather over a number of years. The weather of a place includes its wind pattern, temperature, and the amount of **precipitation**, or rain or snow, that falls. If you divide the United States roughly in half from north to south, the eastern part is **humid**, or wet. The humid half gets more than 20 inches of precipitation each year. In contrast, the western half is **arid**, or dry. Arid areas get less than 20 inches of precipitation each year.

QUICK CHECK

Summarize How does precipitation divide the United States?

Midwest

The Midwest is a region of plains and prairies. The Mississippi River begins in the Midwest, in northern Minnesota. The Midwest has extreme weather conditions. From spring through autumn, thunderstorms and tornadoes are a constant danger.

West

The West region includes eleven states. Two states, Alaska and Hawaii, do not have borders on the rest of the United States. Natural forces shape the region. In 2000, fires caused by lightning destroyed about 7 million acres of forest. The Rocky Mountains run north and south through the West region.

Southwest

The Southwest includes four states: Arizona, New Mexico, Texas, and Oklahoma. One of the best-known landforms in the United States, the Grand Canyon, is in the Southwest. Natural forces changed this region as well. The force of water over hundreds of millions of years changed a plateau into the ecosystem we call the Grand Canyon.

Midwest

MT • ND • MN • SD • WI • MI • IA • NE • IL • IN • OH • CO • KS • MO • WY

Northeast

ME • VT • NH • NY • MA • CT • RI • PA • NJ • MD • DE • WV • VA

Southwest

NM • OK • AR • TX • LA • MS

Southeast

TN • AL • GA • SC • NC • FL • KY

Northeast

The Northeast region includes eleven states and the nation's capital, Washington, D.C. The Hudson, Susquehanna, and Delaware rivers are important waterways. This region has two smaller areas: New England and the Middle Atlantic States.

Southeast

The soil of the Southeast is ideal for farming. Rivers such as the Mississippi, Savannah, and James deposit rich soil on the lowlands around their mouths. The Ohio and Potomac rivers form part of the northern boundary of the Southeast. The region has a hurricane season from late summer to early autumn. In some cases, one natural force may set another natural force in motion. For example, in 2005, Hurricane Katrina caused a flood that covered New Orleans, Louisiana.

Check Understanding

1. **VOCABULARY** Write a sentence about the United States for each of the words below.

   region   **climate**

2. **READING SKILL Summarize** Use your chart from page 292 to summarize the regions of the United States.

3. **Write About It** How do natural forces such as hurricanes affect certain regions?

295

Lesson 2

VOCABULARY

megalopolis p. 297

prairie p. 298

navigable p. 300

Continental Divide p. 302

canyon p. 302

READING SKILL

Summarize
Copy the chart below. Use it to summarize information about the mountain ranges in the United States.

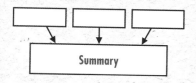

MISSOURI COURSE LEVEL EXPECTATIONS

5.B.1, 5.B.2, 5.B.3, 5.C.1, 5.J.1, 7.B.1

Geography of the United States

Bear Mountain Bridge on the Hudson River, New York

Visual Preview

How does the geography of the United States affect people's lives?

A Many large cities exist along the coasts of the United States.

B Rolling grasslands are a typical feature of the interior lowlands.

C Three major waterways connect cities and regions.

D A group of mountain ranges divides the North American continent.

Ⓐ LOWLANDS AND HIGHLANDS

The United States has many amazing physical wonders, such as the Grand Canyon, Rocky Mountains, and Great Lakes.

Many different landforms shape the United States. A broad lowland called the Atlantic Coastal Plain runs along the coast of the Atlantic Ocean. The cities of Boston, New York, Philadelphia, and Washington, D.C., form a **megalopolis** called "Boswash" along the coastal plain. A megalopolis is a group of cities that have grown so close together they seem to form one city. Boshwash has long been an important economic, cultural, and political center of the United States.

In northeastern areas of the Atlantic Coastal Plain, the soil is thin and rocky. Farming is limited. However, an area called the Piedmont has fertile soil. The Piedmont lies in the eastern foothills of the Appalachian Mountains.

The Gulf Coastal Plain

Another lowland, the Gulf Coastal Plain, lies along the Gulf of Mexico. It is wider than the Atlantic Coastal Plain. Large cities there include Houston and New Orleans. Soil in this region is richer than in the Atlantic Coastal Plain and is excellent for farming. Cotton is a major crop of the Gulf Coastal Plain.

The Appalachian Mountains

An area of highlands sits west of the Atlantic Ocean and north of the Gulf Coastal Plain. The Appalachian Mountains, which run from eastern Canada to Alabama, lie here and divide the East coast from the Midwest. The Appalachians are made up of several mountain ranges, including the Blue Ridge Mountains, the Great Smoky Mountains, and the Allegheny Mountains.

QUICK CHECK

Summarize Explain the geographic features of the Atlantic and Gulf Coastal Plains.

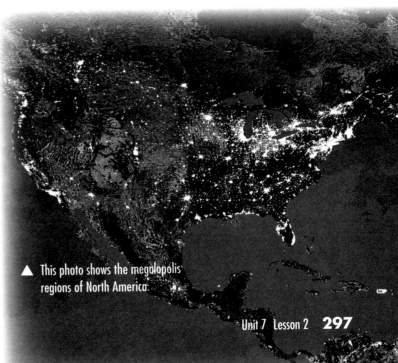

▲ This photo shows the megalopolis regions of North America.

B INTERIOR LOWLANDS

The Central Lowlands, or Central Plains, lie to the west of the Appalachian Mountains. Grassy hills, rolling flatlands, thick forests, and fertile farmland cover this area. The Great Lakes, the Mississippi River, and other waterways influence life here. Large cities, such as Chicago and Detroit, are located in the Central Plains.

The Great Plains

To the west of the Mississippi River stretch the Great Plains. West of the Mississippi River the land begins to rise. At the river's edge, the land is at sea level. Over many miles, though, the elevation changes quite a bit. Denver, Colorado in the western Great Plains, is about 5,000 feet above sea level.

Most of the Great Plains region is **prairie**, or flat, rolling lands covered with grass. Farmers use the fertile soil to grow grains, and ranchers raise cattle. The Great Plains are also rich in resources such as coal, oil, and natural gas.

Tornado Alley

The lowlands of the Plains between the Appalachian and Rocky Mountains is known as Tornado Alley. Frequent thunderstorms in this region provide conditions perfect for producing tornadoes. The United States averages over 1,000 tornadoes each year, most of which happen in Tornado Alley. May and June have the highest rates of tornadoes due to rapidly changing air temperatures. Texas has the highest average number of tornadoes each year.

EVENT

The deadliest tornado in U.S. history was the **Great Tri-State Tornado** of 1925. It crossed through Missouri, Illinois, and Indiana, killing 695 people.

Great Tri-State Tornado

TORNADO ALLEY

QUICK CHECK

Summarize **How do the Central Plains differ from the Great Plains?**

Map Skill

PLACE **Which state in Tornado Alley is furthest north?**

The rolling hills of the Midwest

Central Lowlands

▶ You may see rising and falling flatlands, green hills, and dense forests. This region has soil that is good for farming.

▶ There are important waterways such as the Mississippi River and the Great Lakes.

▶ The area is rich in minerals, such as nickel, copper, and iron ore.

▶ Major cities, such as Detroit, and Chicago, are located here.

Chart Skill

Why are cities located near waterways?

Great Plains

▶ Much of this vast region has flat, rolling lands covered with grass.

▶ The soil is very fertile.

▶ Farmers grow grains, and ranchers raise cattle.

▶ The region is rich in coal, oil, and natural gas.

Chart Skill

Why do people farm in the Great Plains?

A cattle ranch on the Great Plains

▲ A Great Plains wheat farm

There are many lakes and rivers in the United States Many of these rivers are **navigable**, or wide and deep enough to allow the passage of ships. This has allowed for easy travel and trade throughout the history of the United States.

The Mississippi River

The Mississippi River begins in Minnesota as a narrow, unnavigable river. It enlarges as it

Mississippi River Basin

Map Skill

REGION **Into what body of water does the Mississippi River drain?**

heads south to the Gulf of Mexico. It is the second longest river in the country at about 2,300 miles long. The Missouri River is the longest river, but it is a tributary of the Mississippi. A tributary is a river that flows into another river.

The central part of the United States is sometimes called the Mississippi River Basin. Here the Mississippi, along with its tributaries, drains over one million square miles of land. Since the land receives so much water, it some of the best farmland in the country.

At its widest point, the river is nearly four miles wide, making it easy for ships to navigate and move from port to port. Memphis, Tennessee and St. Louis, Missouri are two of the major port cities along the river.

The Great Lakes

Giant blankets of ice called glaciers carved out the Great Lakes about 10,000 years ago.

The mighty Mississippi River

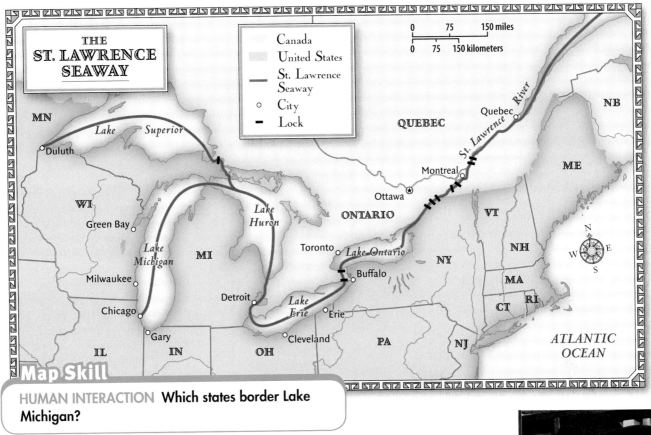

THE ST. LAWRENCE SEAWAY

Canada
United States
— St. Lawrence Seaway
○ City
— Lock

0   75   150 miles
0   75   150 kilometers

MN
Lake Superior
Duluth
WI
Green Bay
Lake Michigan
Milwaukee
MI
Chicago
Gary
IL   IN
Lake Huron
Detroit
OH
Lake Erie
Cleveland
Erie
Toronto
Lake Ontario
Buffalo
NY
PA   NJ
QUEBEC
Quebec
St. Lawrence River
Montreal
Ottawa
ONTARIO
VT
NH
MA
CT   RI
NB
ME
ATLANTIC OCEAN
N E W S

Map Skill

HUMAN INTERACTION **Which states border Lake Michigan?**

Lakes Huron, Ontario, Michigan, Erie, and Superior are located in the central part of North America and are the world's largest group of freshwater lakes. While Lake Superior is the largest, Lake Erie holds the least amount of water of all of the lakes. The lakes are important to Midwest trade and are popular tourist and recreation spots.

St. Lawrence River

The Great Lakes drain into the St. Lawrence River which flows from Lake Ontario to the Atlantic Ocean. The St. Lawrence Seaway, as it is often called, is important for trade.

In the past, the St. Lawrence river was unnavigable due to rapids, waterfalls, and uneven water levels. Ships could not travel from the Great Lakes to the Atlantic Ocean. Then the United States and Canada built a series of canals that change water levels using

PEOPLE

Marjory Stoneman Douglas fought to save the Florida Everglades. Her book, *The Everglades: River of Grass*, inspired people to protect the wetlands.

Marjory Stoneman Douglas

a system of locks. A lock is a part of a canal where water is pumped in or out in order to raise or lower ships.

Today, the St. Lawrence is navigable allowing ships to transport raw materials and manufactured goods from the Great Lakes region throughout the world.

QUICK CHECK

Summarize How are the Mississippi and the St. Lawrence rivers similar?

D MOUNTAINS AND PLATEAUS

West of the Great Plains is a group of mountain ranges. The Rocky Mountains begin in Alaska and run south to New Mexico. Although they are younger and higher than the Appalachian Mountains, the Rockies are not a barrier to travel. Mountain passes allow people to cross the mountain range.

An imaginary line called the **Continental Divide** runs through the Rockies. East of the Continental Divide, rivers drain into the Arctic Ocean, the Atlantic Ocean, and the Gulf of Mexico. To the west, rivers flow into the Pacific Ocean and the Gulf of California.

Near the Pacific coast are mountain chains that make up the western part of the group. The highest point in North America, Mount McKinley, rises to 20,320 feet. It is in one of these chains, the Alaska Range.

The Grand Canyon

Between the Pacific coast and the Rocky Mountains is a stretch of dry basins and high plateaus. In the southern part of this area, rivers have worn through rock to create magnificent **canyons**, or deep valleys with steep sides. One of the most beautiful is the Grand Canyon of the Colorado River. A man named John Wesley Powell led the first exploration of the Grand Canyon in 1869.

QUICK CHECK

Summarize How are canyons created?

▲ Rocky Mountain pass marking the Continental Divide

Diagram Skill
What does the Continental Divide do?

Check Understanding

1. **VOCABULARY** Write a paragraph about the geography of the United States using three of the words below.

   megalopolis   Continental Divide

   prairie   canyon

2. **READING SKILL Summarize** Use your chart from page 296 to summarize information about the mountain ranges in the United States.

3. **Write About It** Write about why people changed the St. Lawrence Seaway.

Map and Globe Skills

Use Time Zone Maps

VOCABULARY

time zone

In 1878 Sanford Fleming of Canada suggested dividing the world along the lines of longitude into 24 equal **time zones**—areas that have the same time throughout. After railroads were built, times zones were introduced because of confusion over train schedules. Study the map below.

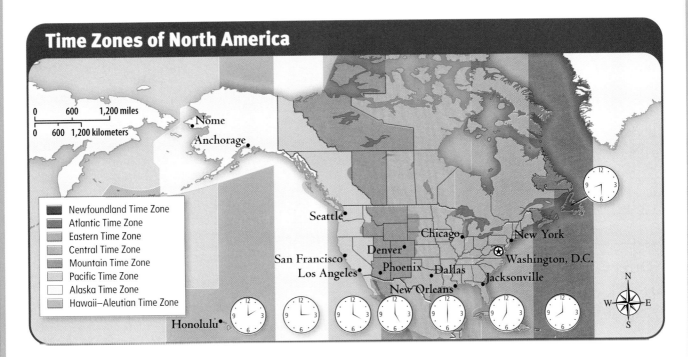

Time Zones of North America

Learn It

- Each stripe represents one time zone.

- Sometimes the time zones follow national or state borders.

- The time for each zone is shown at the bottom of the map when it is noon at the Prime Meridian.

- As you go west or to the left, one hour is subtracted for each time zone. As you go east to the right, one hour is added.

Try It

- If it is noon in Denver, what time is it in Washington, D.C.?

Apply It

- Suppose you traveled from Los Angeles to Honolulu by plane. When you arrive, how would you have to change your watch?

Natural Resources and Climate

VOCABULARY

scarcity p. 305

economy p. 305

current p. 308

temperate climate p. 308

drought p. 309

READING SKILL

Summarize
Copy the chart below.
Use it to summarize the
importance of resources in
the United States.

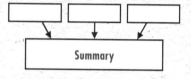

Summary

Redwood trees in California

Visual Preview

How do natural resources impact life in a region?

A Industries in the United States use natural resources to make products.

B Energy resources include oil, coal, natural gas, wind, the sun, and corn.

C Rich soil helps farmers grow crops in several regions.

D Landforms, location, bodies of water, and moisture affect climate.

Ⓐ NATURAL RESOURCES

Natural resources are materials found in nature that people use. The products and energy we use every day are made from natural resources. But not all natural resources will last forever.

Some natural resources are renewable resources, which can be replaced. Renewable resources can become scarce. Many people are working to improve the **scarcity** of trees. Scarcity happens when there is not enough of a resource to make all of the products people want.

The Timber Industry

Forests once covered much of the United States. Today, forests cover only about one-third of the country. People have cleared land to farm. They also cut forests to make timber products. Farming and timber are important parts of the **economy** of the United States. A country's economy is the way its people use natural

▲ Cleveland Cliffs Iron Ore Mine and Mill in Republic, Michigan

resources, knowledge, and money to produce goods and services.

Mineral Resources

The United States has vast mineral resources. A mineral resource is a natural substance found in the earth. Minerals have helped create industries in the United States.

Parts of the northern United States have large iron-ore deposits. Iron ore is used to make steel. The Rocky Mountains have gold, silver, and copper. Products made from copper include wire, pipes, and frying pans.

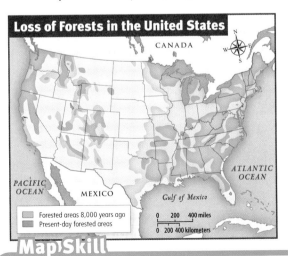

Loss of Forests in the United States

CANADA

PACIFIC OCEAN

MEXICO

Gulf of Mexico

ATLANTIC OCEAN

☐ Forested areas 8,000 years ago
☐ Present-day forested areas

0   200   400 miles
0 200 400 kilometers

Map Skill

PLACE **Which state has lost the most forests?**

QUICK CHECK

Summarize **What are some natural resources found in the United States?**

The United States has a variety of energy resources. Nonrenewable energy resources include oil, natural gas, and coal. Even with large supplies of oil in Texas and Alaska, the United States imports oil because it uses nearly three times the amount of oil it produces.

Renewable Energy

Renewable energy resources include wind, the sun, corn, and hydroelectric power. Hydroelectric power is energy generated by falling water.

Scientists have worked to produce renewable sources of energy. Ethanol is a fuel made from corn used to power cars and rockets. Solar energy is made from sunlight. Flat plates called solar panels collect sunlight and turn it into electricity. Wind and falling water also make energy. The force of the wind or falling water spins a turbine that produces electricity. Solar, wind, and hydroelectric power have the added benefit of creating very little pollution.

QUICK CHECK

Summarize **What are the benefits of using renewable energy?**

▲ Oil rigs in the Gulf of Mexico drill for oil 24 hours a day.

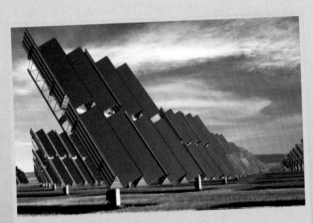

▲ Solar panels at a solar power plant in California track the sun across the sky.

▲ A wind farm near Palm Springs, California does not create pollution.

▲ A coal-burning power plant in Ohio creates energy from coal.

C SOIL RESOURCES

Flat land and fertile soil cover much of the Midwest. Farmers produce huge amounts of corn, soybeans, and grains such as oats and wheat. In some areas of the Great Plains, farmers use dry farming to grow a certain kind of wheat. Dry farming is a method in which land is left unplanted every few years so it will hold rainwater. Dairy products and livestock are also important to the Midwest economy.

The South's warm, wet climate favors crops that are not usually grown elsewhere in the United States. Farmers in Louisiana and Arkansas grow rice and sugarcane. In Florida and Texas, they grow citrus fruits such as oranges and lemons. Georgia, Alabama, and North Carolina produce peanuts.

Farming Dry Land

The Central Valley of California is located between two mountain ranges, the Sierra Nevada and the Coast Ranges. The land is fertile, and the weather is warm. Farmers have a problem, though. Very little rain falls there in the summer because it is the dry season. For many years farmers could only grow crops that needed little water. Today irrigation has made California a leading producer of grapes, olives, plums, peaches, tomatoes, artichokes, and more than 150 other fruits and vegetables.

QUICK CHECK

Summarize Describe farming in the United States.

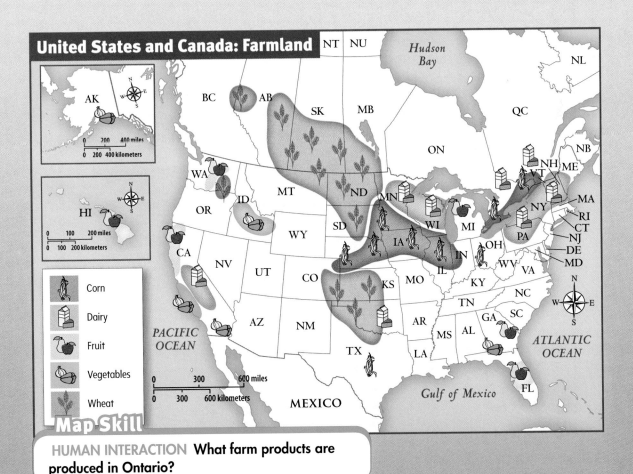

United States and Canada: Farmland

Corn
Dairy
Fruit
Vegetables
Wheat

Map Skill

HUMAN INTERACTION **What farm products are produced in Ontario?**

D   CLIMATE

Climate affects the quality of soil resources in an area. Climate is mainly determined by latitude. Other factors, such as mountains or nearby bodies of water, also influence an area's climate. The movement of air and water helps create Earth's climates. The sun's heat is moved around the globe by streaming waters and moving air. In the ocean, the moving streams of water are called **currents**.

Most of the United States is located in a **temperate climate**, which has changing seasons and mild weather that is neither too hot nor too cold. For example, the Northeast experiences snowy winters, rainy springs, and hot, wet summers. The Southeast has mild temperatures due to regular rainfall. Climate in the West varies with elevation.

Ocean Effect

The warmest parts of the country are areas near the Equator. The air and water here are heated and travel from the tropics toward Earth's poles. Areas near the tropics, such as Florida and Hawaii, are warm all year. The Gulf Stream is one of the strongest, warmest ocean currents in the world. It flows north from the Gulf of Mexico through the cool waters of the Atlantic Ocean.

Coastal areas tend to have moderate temperatures year round. This is because ocean temperatures don't change as much as the temperatures on land. Water temperatures stay constant. This means that the air over large bodies of water is warmer in winter and cooler in summer than the air over land.

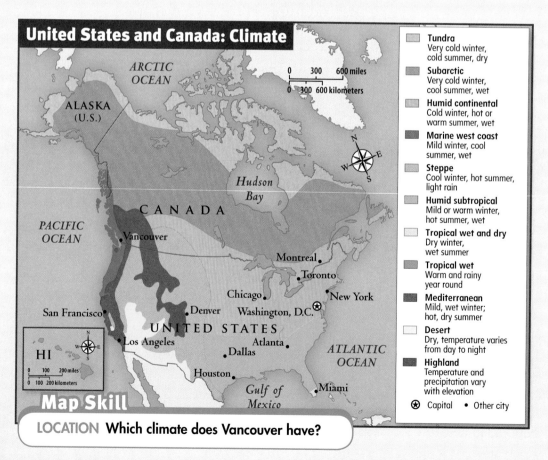

United States and Canada: Climate

Tundra
Very cold winter, cold summer, dry

Subarctic
Very cold winter, cool summer, wet

Humid continental
Cold winter, hot or warm summer, wet

Marine west coast
Mild winter, cool summer, wet

Steppe
Cool winter, hot summer, light rain

Humid subtropical
Mild or warm winter, hot summer, wet

Tropical wet and dry
Dry winter, wet summer

Tropical wet
Warm and rainy year round

Mediterranean
Mild, wet winter; hot, dry summer

Desert
Dry, temperature varies from day to night

Highland
Temperature and precipitation vary with elevation

⊛ Capital • Other city

Map Skill

LOCATION **Which climate does Vancouver have?**

In Alaska winters are long and cold (left). Many places in the Southwest, like this pueblo in New Mexico (below), are desert.

Lake Effect

Just as the ocean affects other parts of the country, the Great Lakes affect the climate of the Midwest. This is because of the lake effect. In this region, the climate is humid, with snowy winters and hot summers. During the summer, lake water and the air above it are cooler than the nearby land. Wind crossing the lake creates a cool, humid breeze. In the winter, the wind picks up moisture from the lake water and forms clouds, causing lake effect snow.

Deserts

Most areas of the southwestern United States are desert and have high temperatures all year. A desert gets less than 10 inches of rainfall each year. **Drought**, or a long period without rainfall, is a serious problem in this region. Many plants can adapt to the climate by storing water from rainfall so they can survive during the long dry season. However, farmers and ranchers in the region can lose crops and livestock when rainfall is low.

QUICK CHECK

Summarize How does the location of a place affect its climate?

Check Understanding

1. **VOCABULARY** Write a paragraph about the climate of the United States using the words below.

   current   drought

   temperate climate

2. **READING SKILL Summarize**  Use your chart from page 304 to summarize the resources of the United States.

 3. **Write About It** How has the timber industry affected forests in the United States?

ECONOMY OF THE UNITED STATES

VOCABULARY

market economy p. 311

stock p. 311

competition p. 311

interdependence p. 312

trade surplus p. 313

trade deficit p. 313

READING SKILL

Summarize

Copy the chart below. Use it to summarize how free trade helps the U.S. economy.

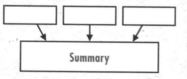

Summary

MISSOURI COURSE LEVEL EXPECTATIONS

4.F.1

The trading floor of the New York Stock Exchange

Visual Preview

How does interdependence shape the U.S. economy?

A People decide what to make, how much to make, and how much to charge.

B The United States trades goods with countries around the world.

A   MARKET ECONOMIES

*The United States has a **market economy**. Individuals make economic decisions about what to make, how much to produce, and what price to charge.*

Capitalism is another name for a market economy. In a capitalist system, people make decisions based upon their best interests. The economy of the United States can also be called a free enterprise system. In the American economy, people can start any business and buy any products they want. The United States has the highest gross domestic product (GDP) in the world. GDP is the total amount of goods produced in a nation in one year.

Stocks, Profits, and Competition

In a market economy, people are free to risk their savings in order to invest in a business. People invest in companies by buying **stock**. Stock is part ownership in a company. When a company makes money, it often pays some of this money to people who own stock. If the business fails, however, the stock becomes worthless.

Profit is the amount of money left over after all the costs of production have been paid. It is one measure stock owners use to determine how well a company is doing. Profit is the driving force that encourages companies and individuals to improve

their wealth. This motivation is largely responsible for the growth of capitalist systems.

In a free enterprise system, companies compete with one another. **Competition** happens when companies try to win customers from each other. Companies often compete by offering their goods and services at lower prices or better quality than other companies.

Voluntary exchange is part of capitalism. It occurs when buyers and sellers make a market trade with anyone they choose. Voluntary exchange is a way for us to improve our well-being.

QUICK CHECK
Summarize Describe the U.S. economy.

Shopping is part of the free enterprise system. ▶

B ECONOMIC TIES

The world's economies are connected in many ways. Trade not only allows countries to export their finished products, but also to import the raw materials and other goods they need. The United States depends on trade for economic growth.

Trade Cooperation

Global **interdependence**, or nations relying on each other to meet needs and wants, allows countries to specialize in certain products and materials. Because of global trade, Americans enjoy goods from all over the world, and products from the United States are used throughout the world. This trade creates jobs for American workers.

Trade agreements help countries do business. The North American Free Trade Agreement (NAFTA), has increased the value of the goods Canada, Mexico, and the United States ship to each other. Canada is now the largest trading partner of the United States, and Mexico is the second largest.

Another trade agreement, the Central America-Dominican Republic-United States Free Trade Agreement (CAFTA-DR). This deal, which went into effect during 2006, ended trade barriers among the participating nations. This free trade, or trade without tariffs, has helped the countries build stronger economies. Tariffs are taxes on goods brought into a country.

In addition to trade among the countries of the Americas, trade with other continents grows each year. For example, since the early 1990s, U.S. trade with Asia has nearly tripled.

▼ The port of Anchorage, Alaska

The United States not only relies on trade for economic growth, but it also depends on trade for energy resources. Americans use three times the amount of oil our country produces. Additional oil has to be imported from other countries such as Canada, Mexico, Venezuela, Saudi Arabia, and Nigeria.

In addition to building stronger economies, cooperation among countries fosters friendly relationships and encourages people to find solutions to problems. Warren Christopher, secretary of state at the time, said,

> **❝**[NAFTA] is a symbol of . . . a new structure of cooperation. . . . It is a turning point . . . among our countries.**❞**

Trade Differences

The value of a country's money is affected by the nation's balance of trade. Balance of trade is the difference between the value of a nation's exports and its imports. When a country earns more from exports than it spends for imports, a **trade surplus** occurs.

The United States spends more on imports than it earns from exports. The resulting **trade deficit**, or a situation when the value of a country's imports is higher than its exports, is hundreds of billions of dollars. The U.S. trade deficit continues to grow each year.

A country's balance of trade can be affected by its trade agreements. For instance, in 2005 the United States had a trade deficit with CAFTA-DR countries, while the following year it recorded a trade surplus.

QUICK CHECK

Summarize Why does the United States have a trade deficit?

Value of U.S. Imports and Exports

Dollar Value (in billions): 2,000 / 1,750 / 1,500 / 1,250 / 1,000 / 750 / 500 / 250 / 0

Years: 1980 1985 1990 1995 2000 2005

Source: U.S. Department of Commerce

Imports
Exports

Chart Skill

In which year did the trade deficit begin to increase dramatically?

Check Understanding

1. **VOCABULARY** Write a paragraph about the economy of the United States using the words below.

   stock   profit   trade deficit

   interdependence   market economy

2. **READING SKILL Summarize** Use your chart from page 310 to summarize how free trade helps the economy of the United States.

 3. **Write About It** Write about how the economy of the United States is tied to the economies of other countries.

VOCABULARY

supply p. 315

demand p. 315

biotechnology p. 316

READING SKILL

Summarize
Copy the chart below. Use it to summarize the economy of the Pacific region.

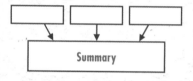

MISSOURI COURSE LEVEL EXPECTATIONS

4.A.1, 4.E.1, 5.C.2, 5.F.1

Economic Regions of the United States

An auto worker on an assembly line

Visual Preview

How do regional economies meet people's needs?

A The economy of the South is expanding into different industries.

B The Northeast and Midwest have cities with large and small businesses.

C Diverse industries thrive in the Interior West and Pacific.

Ⓐ THE SOUTH

The economic regions of the United States mirror the geographic regions: the Northeast, the Midwest, the South, the Interior West, and the Pacific.

All markets have a buying side and a selling side. Prices in a capitalist system are determined by supply and demand. **Supply** is the amount of a product or service available at a certain price at one time. **Demand** is the amount of a good or service consumers are willing to buy at any price. Supply and demand influence a region's economy.

The South's economy has a long history of being affected by market pressures. For example, when the supply of oil is low and the demand is high, the price tends to go up. When the demand for oil is low and the supply is high, the price tends to go down.

In recent decades the South has changed rapidly. Today the area has expanding cities, growing industries, and diverse populations. Workers make textiles, electrical equipment, computers, and airplane parts. Florida relies on tourism. Northern Virginia is now a telecommunications center, and North Carolina is one of the South's largest centers for biotechnology research.

THEN

In the 1900s, many Southerners worked in mill towns, or towns that grew up around textiles factories that manufactured cloth. Many people in the South also worked on small family farms and in the oil industry.

NOW

Today the economy of the South is booming in information technology, software development, biotechnology, and aerospace technology. Many Southerners work in high-tech environments such as North Carolina's Research Triangle Park, the largest research park in the world.

QUICK CHECK

Summarize How do supply and demand affect the price of a good?

THE NORTHEAST AND MIDWEST

B

Every economic region must answer the question: what goods and services will be produced and in what amount? Two regions, the Northeast and the Midwest, look at their resources for the answer. Both regions contain big cities where skilled workers are employed in businesses both large and small.

PLACES

In 1790 the **NYSE** began on Wall Street in New York City. Today it is the largest stock exchange in the world in terms of dollars traded.

NY Stock Exchange

The Northeast

With few mineral resources and poor soil for farming, the Northeast has long focused on business. Cities in the Northeast include New York City, the country's largest city, and Washington, D.C., the nation's capital. The federal government is responsible for about 50 percent of the jobs in Washington.

New York City has many financial and media, or communications, companies.

Most stocks traded in the United States are traded on the New York Stock Exchange (NYSE) and the American Stock Exchange. The city is also home to the NASDAQ, an electronic stock market.

Boston is an important center of **biotechnology** research. Biotechnology is the study of cells to find ways of improving health. Philadelphia's economy is heavily based upon manufacturing and financial services.

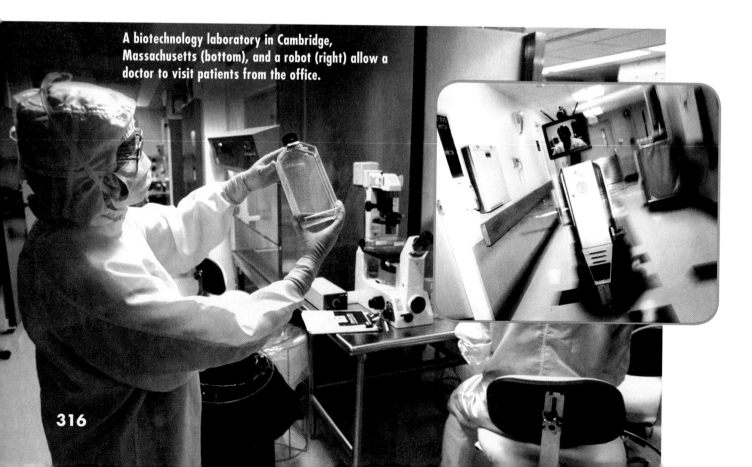

A biotechnology laboratory in Cambridge, Massachusetts (bottom), and a robot (right) allow a doctor to visit patients from the office.

In 2001 this aid cargo plane from Chicago helped earthquake survivors in India. ▶

The Midwest

Unlike the Northeast, the Midwest has plenty of fertile, or rich, soil. Midwestern farmers grow corn, wheat, soybeans, and other crops. Farms are bigger than they were fifty years ago, but there are fewer farmers. Only a small percentage of farms are owned by corporations, but these farms are extremely large.

Farming can be a difficult business. High costs, unpredictable weather, and hard and time-consuming work add to its difficulty. Advances in technology have made farming easier. But new machines are expensive. Small family farmers may not be able to afford the technology they need to make a profit.

The Midwest is also rich in mineral resources. These include iron ore, coal, lead, and zinc. Since the 1800s, these resources have fueled manufacturing. Manufacturing has been an important source of jobs in the cities of the Midwest. Detroit excelled in automobiles and Cleveland in steel. New technology, however, has led to the decline of older industries. As a result, the Midwest now focuses on other industries, such as telecommunications. Chicago, for example, has the third-largest economy in the United States. More and more companies are moving to the Chicago area to take advantage of the city's central location for shipping goods. Chicago has the second-largest workforce in the United States.

QUICK CHECK

Make Generalizations What are the major industries in the Northeast and the Midwest?

A Detroit automaker displaying an electric hybrid car in 2007 ▲

DataGraphic

The United States Economy

The graph shows how the U.S. economy is divided by category. The map shows the location of selected industries. Study the graph and map. Then answer the questions below.

United States Economy, 2006

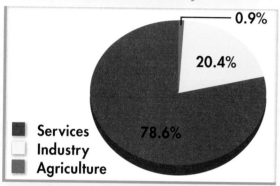

- ■ Services — 78.6%
- □ Industry — 20.4%
- ■ Agriculture — 0.9%

SOURCE: CIA Factbook, 2006   *Percentages are rounded

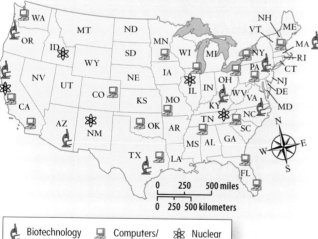

0   250   500 miles

0   250 500 kilometers

- 🔬 Biotechnology
- 🖥 Computers/ Electronics
- ✻ Nuclear research

Think About the U.S. Economy

1. What is the largest part of the U.S. economy?

2. Which states have nuclear research?

The Interior West and Pacific have long struggled with the question: how shall goods and services be produced? Because both areas are mainly arid, they often suffer from droughts. Most of the people in these regions depend on irrigation to keep their economies alive.

The Rugged Interior West

The magnificent mountains and plateaus of the Interior West draw many people. Grasses thrive in certain places, and where the land is irrigated, you find agriculture. For many decades, mining, ranching, and lumbering have been the Interior West's main economic activities. In recent years, other parts of the area's economy have grown rapidly. The cities of Denver and Salt Lake City both have growing information technology industries. Service industries are important to Albuquerque and Phoenix, two cities that attract many tourists each year.

Tourists in New Mexico buying Navajo crafts ▼

This worker is studying a magnified diagram of a computer microchip.

▲ This scientist is working with a new kind of tiny robot called a "nanobot."

The Diverse Pacific

The Pacific area includes the western coastal states plus Alaska and Hawaii. Farmers raise fruits and vegetables in the fertile valleys of California, Oregon, and Washington. Sugarcane, pineapples, and coffee are grown in the rich volcanic soil of Hawaii. Fish, timber, and mineral resources are also important in the Pacific area. California has gold, lead, and copper. Alaska has vast reserves of oil, and large timber and fishing industries.

Many diverse industries thrive in the Pacific area. Workers in California and Washington make airplanes and develop computer software. Los Angeles is the center of the movie industry for the world. Tourism is also a source of income. California has the largest economy and population in the United States. Nearly half of its people are Latino or Asian American.

QUICK CHECK

Make Generalizations Explain how irrigation supports the economies of the Interior West and Pacific.

Check Understanding

1. **VOCABULARY** Write a sentence for each vocabulary word below.

   demand   supply   biotechnology

2. **READING SKILL Make Generalizations** Use your chart from page 314 to summarize the economy of the Pacific region.

3. **Write About It** Describe the diversity of economic activity in the United States.

Lesson 6

VOCABULARY

income p. 321

tax p. 321

cost-benefit decision p. 322

opportunity cost p. 322

budget p. 323

expense p. 323

READING SKILL

Summarize

Copy the chart below. As you read, fill in the chart. Use it to summarize personal finance.

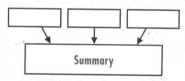

Summary

MISSOURI COURSE LEVEL EXPECTATIONS

4.A.1, 4.E.1, 4.F.1

PERSONAL FINANCE

Recording money helps a person save

How do finances affect the way a person lives?

A Education, work experience, and location affect income levels.

B Saving and spending money are consumer decisions.

Ⓐ EARNING INCOME

Education has a powerful effect on the money a person earns. Education can also influence the opportunities a person receives.

The level of education, amount of training, and work experience people have can affect their **income**, or money earned for doing a job. Typically people with more training and education earn higher incomes.

Regional Income Differences

Where a person lives can influence income as well. Wages in some regions of the United States are higher than in others. This is due to the cost of living in the area. Cost of living is the average cost of basic needs in an area.

Wage differences may also be due to a shortage of workers. For example, areas

▲ Families celebrating high school graduation

with population growth may need service professionals, such as nurses, and offer higher pay to attract these people.

An increase in population may also lead to an increased need for goods. Businesses will need to hire more employees in order to meet the growing demand for goods.

Paying Taxes

Disposable income is the total income a person receives after paying **taxes**. United States citizens are required pay a portion of the money they earn to the government. This money is used to pay for services provided by the government, such as education.

How Education Affects Income

Amount of Education	Average Income	
	Males	Females
Some high school	$19,802	$10,613
High school diploma	$27,526	$15,972
Some college	$35,023	$20,602
Bachelor's degree	$55,188	$34,292
Professional degree	$88,216	$44,748

Source: Statistical Abstract of the United States, 2006

Chart Skill

Which level of education earns the least income?

QUICK CHECK

Summarize What factors can affect the amount of income a person earns?

SPENDING AND SAVING MONEY

You and everyone around you are an important part of the economy because you are consumers. A consumer is a person who buys or uses goods and services to satisfy needs and wants. Consumers spend disposable income on goods and services. First they buy the necessities: food, clothing, and housing. They can save any leftover income or spend it on extras such as luxury items or entertainment.

Spending Money

Consumers who choose to spend their money today give up the chance to have goods and services in the future. People must also decide whether the value they receive is worth the money they spend. For example, a bicycle can cost hundreds of dollars. But having a bike would allow a person to travel faster than walking and also help the person stay healthy. This is a **cost-benefit decision**. If the benefits are greater than the cost, a consumer may buy the product or service.

When consumers make decisions about what to buy, they also make decisions about what they will not buy. For example, suppose you want to buy a CD and a T-shirt, but only have enough money to pay for one. The value of the second-best choice—the item you don't buy—is called your **opportunity cost**. If you buy the CD, the opportunity cost is the T-shirt.

▼ Buying groceries is a typical expense.

Saving Money

When people save money, they choose to give up goods and services now in order to have other things in the future. To help save money, people develop a **budget**, a plan for spending and saving. A budget includes a list of all the **expenses**, or payments for goods and services, a person must make. Expenses usually include a mortgage or rent, groceries, and utilities. There may be other expenses too, such as a car payment, credit card debt, or student loans.

Monthly Family Budget

	Expenses (money out)	Income (money in)
Paychecks		+3,300
Mortgage	−1000	
Car payments	−500	
Utilities	−130	
Cable	−50	
Telephone	−100	
Gas (car)	−120	
Groceries	−250	
Car insurance	−100	
Student loans	−300	
Entertainment/ dining out	−100	
Savings	−200	
Credit card debt	−150	
Balance		300

Chart Skill

What expenses could you eliminate in order to save more money?

Budgeting Your Money

Budgets show the amount of money left after all expenses have been paid. The incentive to stick to the budget, and not spend more than the budget allows, is the reason you began saving in the first place.

For example, let's imagine your family is planning a vacation that will cost $1,500. Your family's monthly income is $3,300. However, there are $3,000 in monthly expenses. That means there is $300 available to be spent each month. If you set a monthly budget to pay all expenses and save the $300, in just 5 months your family could be on vacation!

QUICK CHECK

Summarize **How does a budget help maintain control of a person's finances?**

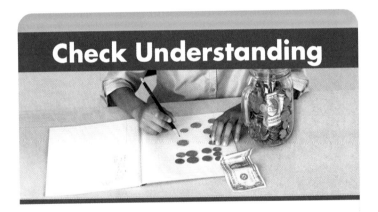
Check Understanding

1. **VOCABULARY** Write a paragraph about budgeting using the words below.

   income   tax   cost-benefit decision

   budget   expense

2. **READING SKILL Summarize** Use your chart from page 320 to summarize personal finance.

 3. **Write About It** How does education affect the amount of income an individual earns?

GOVERNMENT IN THE UNITED STATES

VOCABULARY

political party p. 325

democracy p. 326

republic p. 326

bill p. 327

veto p. 327

immigrant p. 330

READING SKILL

Summarize

Copy the chart below. Use it to summarize the levels of government in the United States.

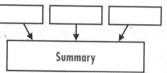

Summary

MISSOURI COURSE LEVEL EXPECTATIONS

1.A.1, 1.A.2, 1.A.3, 2.C.1

The U.S. Capitol houses the legislative branch of the government.

Visual Preview

How does government affect people's lives?

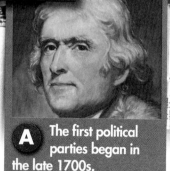

A The first political parties began in the late 1700s.

B Americans elect their leaders and lawmakers.

C Three levels of government provide for citizens.

D Citizens have responsibilities and rights.

A POLITICAL PARTIES

Did you know that George Washington was not a member of a political party? In fact, he warned that political parties could divide the nation.

The Constitution does not mention political parties. However, political parties began during the ratification of the Constitution. A **political party** is a group of people who share similar ideas about government.

Beginning of Political Parties

By the time of Washington's reelection in 1792, differences in political beliefs had begun to divide people into two groups of thought. Two members of Washington's cabinet, Alexander Hamilton and Thomas Jefferson, became the leaders of the first political parties.

Hamilton headed the Federalist Party, which supported the policies of Washington's administration. Federalists wanted a strong national government, a national banking system, and tax policies that supported manufacturing.

In contrast, the Democratic-Republican Party preferred strong state governments that were responsible to the people, an agricultural society, and free trade. Thomas Jefferson led this political party.

The Election of 1796

Candidates for President ran as members of a political party for the first time during the 1796 election. Candidates are people who seek to hold an office. John Adams was the Federalist candidate, and the Democratic-Republicans nominated Jefferson. Adams won and became the second President.

QUICK CHECK

Summarize Describe the differences between the Federalist and Democratic-Republican Parties.

Thomas Jefferson

Alexander Hamilton

ELECTIONS AND LAWMAKING

Under the Constitution, the people are the source of the government's power. The government of the United States can be described as both a democracy and a republic. In a **democracy,** power is held by the people. A **republic** is a country with elected leaders who represent the people. The people use their power when they vote in elections. Every American citizen age 18 and over is eligible to vote as long as he or she is registered with the state office of elections.

Types of Elections

Sometimes a political party has more than one candidate running for office, and the party holds a primary election. Members of the same political party compete against each other in primary elections. These elections can be open or closed. In a closed primary election, voters can choose only between candidates from the party to which they are registered. Open primaries are different because people can vote for either party regardless of the party they belong to.

The winner of the primary election becomes the party's candidate. This person then competes against candidates from other political parties in the general election. In a general election, each political party has only one person representing the whole party. All registered people vote in the general election to choose the overall winner.

Americans vote in national, state, and local elections. Every four years Presidential elections are held. At the state level, elections for members of Congress, governor, and other offices occur. Americans can vote for mayor, members of city council, and school board members in their local communities.

Running for Office

▲ People show their support at a political rally.

▲ During a debate politicians present their ideas.

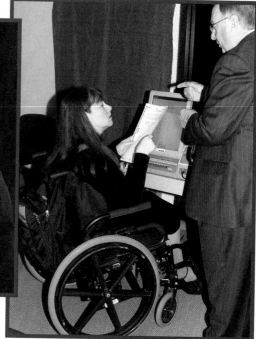

▲ Citizens vote for a candidate.

Creating Laws

The 535 members of the United States Congress are responsible for making laws that will promote the common good. Congress has two parts called houses—the House of Representatives and the Senate. Because of the system of checks and balances built into the Constitution, Congress has to work with the President in order to pass laws.

Any law begins with an idea. An idea for a law is called a **bill**. Once a bill has been introduced, the members of Congress spend time studying, researching, and debating the bill in various committees. Bills written by Representatives are first voted upon by the House. If the bill is passed, it is then sent to the Senate for approval. The opposite occurs when Senators write bills. After both houses have passed the bill with a majority vote, or approval by over half of the members, it is sent to the President.

If the bill is signed by the President, it becomes a law. The President can also choose to **veto**, or reject, the bill. If a bill is vetoed, it is sent back to Congress. The bill can still become a law, though. If two-thirds of the members of Congress again vote for the bill, the President's veto is overridden, or reversed, and the bill becomes a law.

Judicial Review

When a law is challenged, the nine justices of the Supreme Court can choose to review it. The Court can cancel the law if its members find it unconstitutional. This power is called judicial review.

QUICK CHECK

Summarize How does a bill become a law?

HOW A BILL BECOMES A LAW

A member of Congress introduces the bill.

The members of Congress discuss and debate the bill.

The House and Senate vote to approve the bill.

H.R. 0672
HOUSE OF REPRESENTATIVES
A BILL

The President signs or vetoes the bill.

Congress can override a veto with a two-thirds majority vote.

Supreme Court justices decide if the law is constitutional.

Chart Skill

How can Congress override a veto?

C LEVELS OF GOVERNMENT

In the United States, there are three levels of government: national, state, and local. The national, or federal, government serves the whole country. Local and state governments provide for the needs of people in towns, cities, counties, and an entire state.

Each level of government has its own executive, legislative, and judicial branches. As you have read, the President, Congress, and Supreme Court represent the three branches of the federal government. A state has a governor as its executive, a state legislature as its lawmaking body, and a state supreme court to interpret state laws. A local community usually has a mayor, city council, and local courts.

Federalism

The Constitution gives some powers to the federal government. Others are given to the states. This dividing of powers between the federal and state governments is called federalism. The chart on the next page shows some of the rights and responsibilities of each level of government. Some powers, such as collecting taxes and conducting elections, are shared by the federal and state governments. Shared powers are called concurrent powers.

QUICK CHECK

Summarize **How are national, state, and local governments similar?**

The capitol of Indiana is Indianapolis.

Main Responsibilities Under Federalism

National Government

▶ make treaties with other countries
▶ has the power to make laws about trade between states
▶ declare war
▶ run the post office
▶ mint money
▶ collect taxes

▲ A mint worker

State Governments

▲ Highway construction

▶ set up local governments
▶ collect taxes
▶ set up public schools
▶ make laws about transportation
▶ run local elections
▶ make laws about health issues

Local Governments

▶ make laws for the community
▶ provide police and fire departments
▶ maintain parks and recreation facilities
▶ collect garbage and recycling
▶ plan for city building projects
▶ collect taxes

Firefighters at work ▲

RESPONSIBLE CITIZENS

A citizen is someone who is born in a country or who becomes a member of that country by law. Citizens have certain rights and responsibilities.

Becoming a Citizen

Immigrants are people who live in a country in which they were not born. Immigrants to the United States gain citizenship through a process called naturalization.

In order to be eligible for citizenship, a person must be at least 18 years old. The applicant needs to have lived in the United States for at least five years and be able to read, write, and speak basic English. Immigrants must also promise to support the Constitution and must have a basic understanding of United States history and government.

Naturalization is a long process involving paperwork, fingerprinting, fees, interviews, and a citizenship test. Immigrants become citizens of the United States when they take an oath of allegiance to the United States at a ceremony.

Citizen Rights

Each citizen of the United States has certain rights that cannot be taken away by the government. The Declaration of Independence, Constitution, and Bill of Rights explain many of these rights.

The First Amendment of the Bill of Rights is one of the best known and most important rights of Americans. It says:

> **"**Congress shall make no law respecting an establishment of religion or prohibiting the free exercise thereof; or [limiting] the freedom of speech, or of the press; or the right of the people peaceably to assemble, and to [ask] the Government [to hear their complaints].**"**

Among other things, this amendment guarantees that Americans can speak freely about any topic and can practice the religion of their choice.

▼ Immigrants take the oath of allegiance.

▲ Freedom of the press allows newspapers to talk about any topic.

Citizen Responsibilities

Just as governments have a responsibility to their people, people have responsibilities as citizens.

Good citizens participate in government. They learn about political issues, and they vote in elections. Through voting, citizens become involved in government and help choose the leaders and lawmakers who shape the nation. Working on political campaigns, signing petitions, and writing letters to their representatives are ways citizens can contribute to government.

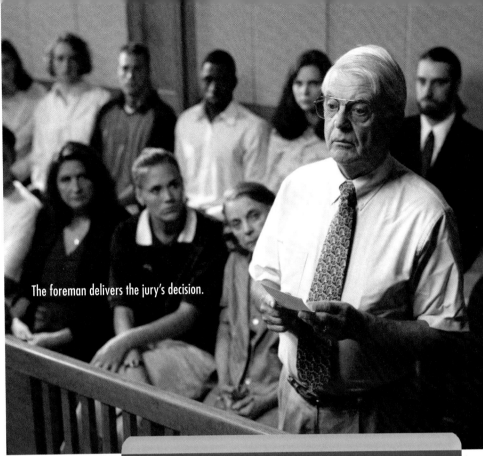

The foreman delivers the jury's decision.

Obeying the law is an important citizen responsibility that helps keep everyone safe and healthy. American citizens pay taxes to support the government. Taxes pay for services and projects that benefit all Americans. Males over age 18 also have the duty to register with the government for military service.

Citizens have the responsibility to respect the rights and ideas of others, even when they disagree with them. Treating all people equally is a way to show respect to others.

Jury Duty

One particular duty of citizens is to serve on juries. All Americans have the right to a public trial by an impartial jury. Serving jury duty helps the judicial system in the United States run effectively.

QUICK CHECK

Summarize How can people be good citizens?

Check Understanding

1. **VOCABULARY** Write a paragraph about the government of the United States using the words below.

   political party   **democracy**

   republic   **federalism**

2. **READING SKILL Summarize**
   Use your chart from page 324 to summarize the levels of government in the United States.

 3. **Write About It** Write about how local government helps people.

Unit 7 Review and Assess

Vocabulary

Number a paper from 1 to 4. Beside each number, write the word that matches the description.

climate   scarcity

republic   budget

1. A country with elected leaders that represent the people

2. A situation where there is not enough of a resource to make all the things people want

3. A list that includes all expenses a person has to pay

4. The weather in an area over a number of years

Comprehension and Critical Thinking

5. How were the Great Lakes formed?

6. How can water in a region affect climate?

7. **Reading Skill** Summarize the federal system of government in the United States.

8. **Critical Thinking** Why does free trade lead to economic growth?

Skill

Use Time Zone Maps

Write a complete sentence to answer each question.

9. Is the time earlier or later in the time zones west of where you live?

10. If you live in Honolulu and need to call a friend in Alaska at 10 A.M., at what time should you make the call from your home?

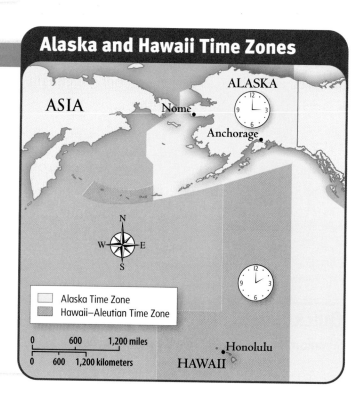

Alaska and Hawaii Time Zones

ASIA

ALASKA

Nome

Anchorage

N
W — E
S

Alaska Time Zone
Hawaii–Aleutian Time Zone

0   600   1,200 miles
0   600   1,200 kilometers

Honolulu

HAWAII

MAP Test Preparation

Directions   Read the passage. Then answer Numbers 1 through 3.

The Everglades are a large area of wetlands in southern Florida. A wetland is an area of land that does not completely drain of water, such as a swamp. Wetlands depend on both water and land to support diverse, sometimes endangered, plant and animal life. The Everglades are home to many animals and plants. Alligators, crawfish, falcons, and the rare Florida panther all live in the Everglades.

During the late 1800s and early 1900s, people built buildings and roads through the Everglades. To protect and save the natural homes of rare plants and animals, Everglades National Park was created in 1947. Marjory Stoneman Douglas worked tirelessly to preserve the Everglades.

1   **Which word means the SAME as *rare*?**

○ regular

○ uncommon

○ colorful

○ strong

2   **What other animal might live in the Everglades?**

○ giraffe

○ polar bear

○ ostrich

○ manatee

3   **Why did the Everglades need to be protected?**

Write your answer on a separate piece of paper.

The Big Idea Activities

How do geography, economics, and government affect people's lives?

Write About the Big Idea

Expository Essay
Use the Unit 7 Foldable to help you write an expository essay that answers the Big Idea question, *How do geography, economics, and government affect people's lives?* Be sure to begin your essay with an introduction. Add a paragraph for each section on your Foldable. End with a concluding paragraph that explains how geography, economics, and government influence each other.

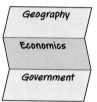

FOLDABLES™
Study Organizer

Geography
Economics
Government

Write a Newspaper Article

Work in small groups to create a news story about an issue in your area. Choose a topic dealing with either local geography, economics, or government. There are several parts to an article. Follow these steps to create your own story.

1. Decide who should write the article.

2. Other members of your group should find and cut out or copy photographs and illustrations for the article.

3. As a group, decide how you want your page to look. Then choose a headline for your article.

NEW ICE CREAM STORE

Ice Cream Delights recently opened a new store in Blackton. The store features many flavors of ice cream and over 30 different toppings. The store currently employs 25 people and has had great sales since its opening weekend. It is located near Tower Mall.

Reference Section

The Reference Section is a collection of tools that can be used to help you understand the information you read in this textbook.

Compare and Contrast

When you compare, you notice how things are alike. When you contrast, you notice how they are different. Comparing and contrasting will help you understand the people and events you read about in social studies.

Learn It

● To compare two things, note how they are similar. The words *alike*, *same*, and *both* are clues to similarities.

● To contrast two things, note how they are different. The words *different, however,* and *by contrast* show differences.

● Now read the passage below. Think about how you would compare and contrast Native American groups.

Native Peoples of North America

Contrast
The first paragraph is a contrast between environments.

For Native Americans in the West, environment helped to determine culture. The Arctic is extremely cold. By contrast, the hot, dry deserts of southern California are very hot. Each culture adapted to the climate and natural resources of their surroundings.

The Inuit in Alaska found ways to live in the bitterly cold Arctic. On hunting trips, men built igloos, temporary shelters, of snow blocks. In warm weather, hunters made tents from wooden poles and animal skins. The Inuit hunted walruses, seals, fish, and whales.

Contrast
This sentence tells how groups were different.

Life in the desert of southern California was very different from life in the Arctic. Desert groups such as the Cahuilla used desert plants for food. They also grew crops using irrigation. The Cahuilla dug wells in the desert sand. They watered fields of maize, squash, and beans. Like the Inuit, desert groups hunted animals.

Compare
This shows how groups were alike.

Try It

Copy the Venn diagram. Then fill in the left-hand side with Inuit activities. Fill in the right-hand side with desert group activities. Fill in the center with activities that both groups did.

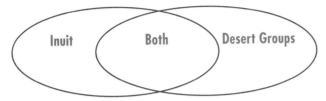

Inuit   Both   Desert Groups

How did you figure out the similarities and differences?

Apply It

● Review the steps for comparing and contrasting in Learn It.

● Read the passage below. Use a Venn diagram to show the similarities and differences between the Creek and the Iroquois.

One Southern woodlands group, the Creek, arranged their towns around a large council house or "Chokofa." Family homes called wattle-and-daub huts were made from poles and covered with grass, mud, or thatch. Unlike the Creek, the Iroquois of the northern woodlands lived in longhouses. Longhouses were large enough for several families and were made of bent poles covered with sheets of bark. The longest longhouse is thought to have been about 340 feet. That's longer than a football field!

Both the Creek and Iroquois celebrated the Green Corn Festival, honoring the summer's first maize crop. They also played a sport with sticks that French explorers later called Lacrosse. Lacrosse games were sometimes played to settle disagreements.

Cause and Effect

A cause is an action or event that makes something else happen. An effect is the result of the cause. When one event causes another event to happen, the two events have a cause-and-effect relationship. Connecting causes with effects will help you understand more about what you read in social studies.

Learn It

- After you finish reading a section, ask yourself, "What happened?" The answer to that question will help you identify an effect.

- Then ask yourself "Why did that happen?" The answer to this question helps you identify a cause.

- Look for the clue words *because, so,* and *as a result.* These words point to cause-and-effect relationships.

- Now read the passage below. Use the steps above to pick out cause-and-effect relationships.

Exploration and Colonization

Cause
This is a cause. It tells why.

Effect
This is an effect. It tells what happened.

Cause and Effect
This has a cause and an effect.

The first people of the Middle Ages to travel to distant regions were the Norse, or "north people," who lived in what are today Denmark, Sweden, and Norway. To gain wealth, they sailed throughout Europe by ocean and rivers trading goods. Some people knew them as Vikings, a Norse word for "raiders."

Around A.D. 1000, Viking explorers were the first to reach North America. But their settlements there did not last. As a result, the Vikings' discoveries were forgotten for many years.

Try It

Copy and complete the cause and effect chart below. Then fill in the chart with another cause and effect from the paragraph.

Cause	→	Effect
	→	
	→	
	→	

How did you figure out the causes and effects?

Apply It

- Review the steps for understanding cause and effect in Learn It.

- Read the passage below. Then use a chart to list the causes and effects from the passage.

In 1096 thousands of Europeans began the long journey southeast to Jerusalem. The city had great religious importance to Jews, Christians, and Muslims. European Christians hoped to capture the city from the Muslim Turks who ruled the city at the time. These journeys were called Crusades. The Crusaders captured Jerusalem, but were driven out after about 100 years.

Many European travelers returned with products of these cultures, such as cloth or spices, that were unknown in Europe. Traders found that Europeans were willing to pay a lot for items such as cotton, pepper, and cinnamon.

Make Generalizations

When you read, sometimes it helps to make a generalization. A generalization is a broad statement that shows how different facts, people, or events have something in common. Being able to make generalizations will help you uncover similarities that you might otherwise not notice. Generalizations can also help you make sense of new information you will learn later.

Learn It

- Identify text clues with similarities or relationships.
- Apply what you already know about the topic.
- Make a generalization that is true about all of your text clues and what you know.
- Read the passage below. Think about a generalization you could make.

Text Clue
Puritans wanted self-government.

Text Clue
Elections were held at town meetings.

Text Clue
Only white men who were Puritans voted.

Colonial America

The Puritans' charter allowed them to govern themselves. They held elections at town hall meetings, but only white men who were Puritans could vote. John Winthrop was elected the first governor of the Puritans. Winthrop wrote about building "a city upon a hill" that would show how God wanted people to live.

Try It

Copy and complete the generalization chart below. Then make a generalization about the Puritan government.

Text Clues	What You Know	Generalization

How did you figure out how to make a generalization?

Apply It

- Review the steps to make generalizations in Learn It.

- Read the next paragraph. Then make a generalization about Roger Williams using a generalizations chart.

One person who disagreed with Puritan leaders was Roger Williams. He believed that government should tolerate people with different religious views. To tolerate means to allow people to have beliefs or behaviors that are different from others. Puritans accused Williams of spreading "new and dangerous opinions" and tried to silence him. Williams decided to move south where he lived with the Narragansett Indians. In 1636 Williams bought land from the Narragansett and founded the settlement of Providence in what became Rhode Island. It was the first colony to allow freedom of religion.

Main Idea and Details

As you read, it is important to look for the main idea and supporting details. The main idea is what a paragraph is all about. The details tell about, or support, the main idea. Often the main idea is stated in the first sentence of a paragraph. At other times, you have to figure out the main idea. Either way, keeping track of the main idea and details will help you understand what you read.

Learn It

- Think about what a paragraph is all about. Look to see if the first sentence states the main idea.

- Look for details. Think about the idea that the details tell about.

- Now read the paragraph below. Look for the main idea and details.

Main Idea:
This sentence states the main idea.

Supporting Detail
This detail explains that some colonists worked for the British government.

Supporting Detail
This detail also supports the main idea.

The American Revolution

While most colonists wanted to end what they saw as British bullying, not all colonists wanted to end their ties to Great Britain. They hoped that the British government would compromise to end the fighting. Some of these colonists worked for the British government. Others feared that they might lose their property during the fighting. Still others simply did not want to separate from Great Britain; they hoped for compromise.

Try It

Copy and complete the chart below. Then fill in the chart by listing the main idea and details from the paragraph on page R8.

Main Idea	Details

How did you choose the main idea and details?

Apply It

● Read the paragraph below. Then create supporting details using the information.

● Review the steps for finding the main idea and details. Then read the paragraph below. Create a main idea and supporting details chart using the information.

Most colonists understood that a compromise would not be reached. They knew that once British soldiers were killed, the British government would not back down. The events around Boston made colonists see themselves in a new way. They were no longer British citizens living in colonies. They were citizens of a new country that was fighting to free itself from British rule. They were Americans.

Draw Conclusions

Reading for understanding is more than noticing the details in a passage. Readers need to think about what the details tell them. Often the details in a passage will help you draw a conclusion. Drawing a conclusion is reaching an opinion based on the details you read.

Learn It

- Gather details and other evidence in a reading passage.

- Identify the subject of the passage.

- Look for connections between the pieces of information. Ask yourself what the evidence says about the subject.

- Draw a conclusion based on what you have read.

- Read the passage below and think about what conclusions you can draw from it.

Text clue
  The British march into the nation's capital.

Text clue:
  Dolley Madison had finished preparations for a dinner party.

Text clue
  British troops reached the White House.

Text clue
  The British ate a meal before burning the White House.

The War of 1812

On the evening of August 24, 1814, British troops marched into Washington, D.C. After setting fire to the Capitol building, they marched down Pennsylvania Avenue toward the White House. First lady Dolley Madison had just finished preparations for a dinner for forty people when she heard the British cannons. She grabbed several paintings and fled the White House as the British arrived. After eating a meal, the British set fire to the White House.

Try It

Copy and complete the graphic organizer below. Fill in lines on the left with the text clues. Fill in the box on the right with a conclusion based on the evidence you gathered.

Text Clues	Conclusion

What conclusion did you draw about where the British ate dinner?

Apply It

- Review the steps for drawing conclusions in Learn It.

- Read the paragraph below. Then use a graphic organizer to draw a conclusion about where Francis Scott Key was when he watched the battle of Fort McHenry.

     The British attack on Fort McHenry began September 13. For 25 hours, the fort was bombarded by more than 1,500 cannonballs and rockets. Francis Scott Key, an American prisoner on a British ship, watched the night sky light up with "the rockets' red glare." The next morning, Key saw that the American flag still flew over Fort McHenry. Key expressed his feelings in "The Star-Spangled Banner," a poem that later became our national anthem.

Fact and Opinion

When people write about events, they often include both facts and opinions. Facts are statements that can be proven true. Opinions state feelings and beliefs. Opinions cannot be proven true or false. Being able to distinguish facts from opinions will help you understand what you read in social studies.

Learn It

- Facts can be checked and proven true.
- Opinions are personal views. They cannot be proven true or false.
- Clue words such as *think, felt, believe,* and *it seems* often state opinions.
- Now read the passage below. Look for facts and opinions.

The Underground Railroad

Fact
After traveling 90 miles, she reached the free soil of Pennsylvania.

Opinion
I felt like I was in heaven.

In 1849 Harriet Tubman heard that she and other enslaved workers on her Maryland plantation were to be sold farther south. Tubman believed that life there would be more difficult. She fled from the plantation in the middle of the night. After traveling 90 miles, she reached the free soil of Pennsylvania. She later said, "I felt like I was in heaven."

Try It

Copy and complete the chart below. Fill in the chart with two facts and two opinions from the paragraph about the Underground Railroad on page R12.

Fact	Opinion

How did you figure out which phrases were facts and which were opinions?

Apply It

● Review the steps for understanding fact and opinion from Learn It.

● Read the paragraph below. Then make a chart that lists two facts and opinions from the paragraph.

Ulysses S. Grant was Lincoln's best general and he seemed fearless. Lincoln decided to put Grant in charge of the entire Union army. He hoped Grant would bring the ugly war to an end.

Grant had two major goals. First, he planned to destroy Lee's army in Virginia. After that, he planned to capture Richmond, the capital of the Confederacy.

For 40 days, from April to June 1864, Grant battled Lee again and again across Virginia. Finally, Grant surrounded Lee in Petersburg, and put the city under siege. In the end, Grant captured Richmond. But he wasted the lives of thousands of Union troops. The Confederacy would have fallen without Grant's attacks.

Summarize

Summarizing is a good way to remember what you read. After you read a paragraph or section in your textbook, make a summary of it. A summary is a brief statement about the topic of a passage. Since a summary leaves out minor details, it should be short.

Learn It

- Find key details that tell more about a subject.
- Leave out details that are not important.
- Restate the important points briefly in a summary.
- Read the passage below and think about how you would summarize it.

Topic Spending Money	**SPENDING MONEY**

Key detail
An economy must have consumers.

Key detail
Income allows people to meet their needs and wants.

Unimportant detail
Two kinds of extras are luxury items and entertainment.

You and everyone around you are an important part of the economy because you are consumers. A consumer is a person who buys or uses goods and services to satisfy needs and wants. Consumers spend their disposable income on many kinds of goods and services. First they buy the necessities: food, clothing, and housing. They can save any leftover income or spend it on extras such as luxury items or entertainment.

Try It

Copy and complete the summary chart below. Fill in the top box with pieces of information from the passage on page R14. Add one important detail of your own. Then write a summary based on the information you gathered.

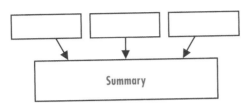

Summary

What is the difference between a summary and a main idea?

Apply It

- Review the steps for summarizing in Learn It.
- Read the paragraphs below. Then summarize the passage using a summary chart.

Capitalism is another name for a market economy. In a capitalist system, people make decisions based upon their best interests. The economy of the United States can also be called a free enterprise system. In the American economy, people can start any business and buy any products they want.

Geography Handbook

Geography and You

Many people think geography means learning about the location of cities, states, and countries, but geography is much more than that. Geography is the study of our Earth and all its people. Geography includes learning about bodies of water such as oceans, lakes, and rivers. Geography helps us learn about landforms such as plains and mountains. Geography also helps us learn about using land and water wisely.

People are an important part of the study of geography. Geography includes the study of how people adapt to live in new places. How people move, how they transport goods, and how ideas travel from place to place are also parts of geography.

In fact, geography has so many parts that geographers have divided the information into smaller groups to help people understand its ideas. These groups are called the six elements of geography.

Six Elements of Geography

The World in Spatial Terms: Where is a place located, and what land or water features does that place have?

Places and Regions: What is special about a place, and what makes it different from other places?

Physical Systems: What has shaped the land and climate of a place, and how does this affect the plants, animals, and people there?

Human Systems: How do people, ideas, and goods move from place to place?

Environment and Society: How have people changed the land and water of a place, and how have land and water affected the people who live in a place?

Uses of Geography: How has geography influenced events in the past, and how will it influence events now and in the future?

Five Themes of Geography

You have read about the six elements of geography. The five themes of geography are another way of dividing the ideas of geography. The themes, or topics, are **location, place, region, movement,** and **human interaction**. Using these five themes is another way to understand events you read about in this book.

1. Location

The White House

In geography, *location* means an exact spot on the planet. A location is usually a street name and number. You write a location when you address a letter.

2. Place

The Grand Canyon

A *place* is described by its physical features, such as rivers, mountains, or valleys. Human features, such as cities, language, and traditions can also describe a place.

3. Region

Wheat field in the Midwest

A *region* is larger than a place or location. The people in a region are affected by landforms. Their region has typical jobs and customs. For example, the fertile soil of the Mississippi lowlands helps farmers in the region grow crops.

4. Movement

Passenger Train

Throughout history, people have moved to find better land or a better life. Geographers study why these *movements* occurred. They also study how people's movements have changed a region.

5. Human Interaction

Hoover Dam

Geographers study the ways that people adapt to their environment. Geographers also study how people change their environment. The *interaction* between people and their environment explains how land is used.

Dictionary of Geographic Terms

1 **BASIN** A bowl-shaped landform surrounded by higher land

2 **BAY** Part of an ocean or lake that extends deeply into the land

3 **CANAL** A channel built to carry water for irrigation or transportation

4 **CANYON** A deep, narrow valley with steep sides

5 **COAST** The land along an ocean

6 **DAM** A wall built across a river, creating a lake that stores water

7 **DELTA** Land made of soil left behind as a river drains into a larger body of water

8 **DESERT** A dry environment with few plants and animals

9 **FAULT** The border between two of the plates that make up Earth's crust

10 **GLACIER** A huge sheet of ice that moves slowly across the land

11 **GULF** Part of an ocean that extends into the land; larger than a bay

12 **HARBOR** A sheltered place along a coast where boats dock safely

13 **HILL** A rounded, raised landform; not as high as a mountain

14 **ISLAND** A body of land completely surrounded by water

15 **LAKE** A body of water completely surrounded by land

16 **MESA** A hill with a flat top; smaller than a plateau

17 MOUNTAIN A high landform with steep sides; higher than a hill

23 PLATEAU A high, flat area that rises steeply above the surrounding land

28 VALLEY An area of low land between hills or mountains

18 MOUNTAIN PASS A narrow gap through a mountain range

24 PORT A place where ships load and unload their goods

29 VOLCANO An opening in Earth's surface through which hot rock and ash are forced out

19 MOUTH The place where a river empties into a larger body of water

25 RESERVOIR A natural or artificial lake used to store water

30 WATERFALL A flow of water falling vertically

20 OCEAN A large body of salt water; oceans cover much of Earth's surface

26 RIVER A large stream that empties into another body of water

21 PENINSULA A body of land nearly surrounded by water

27 SOURCE The starting point of a river

22 PLAIN A large area of nearly flat land

Reviewing Geography Skills

Read a Map

Maps are drawings of places on Earth. Most maps have standard features to help you read the map. Some important information you get from a map is direction. The main directions are north, south, east, and west. These are called cardinal directions.

The areas between the cardinal directions are called intermediate directions. These are northeast, southeast, southwest, and northwest. You use these directions to describe one place in relation to another.

In what direction is Iowa from North Carolina?

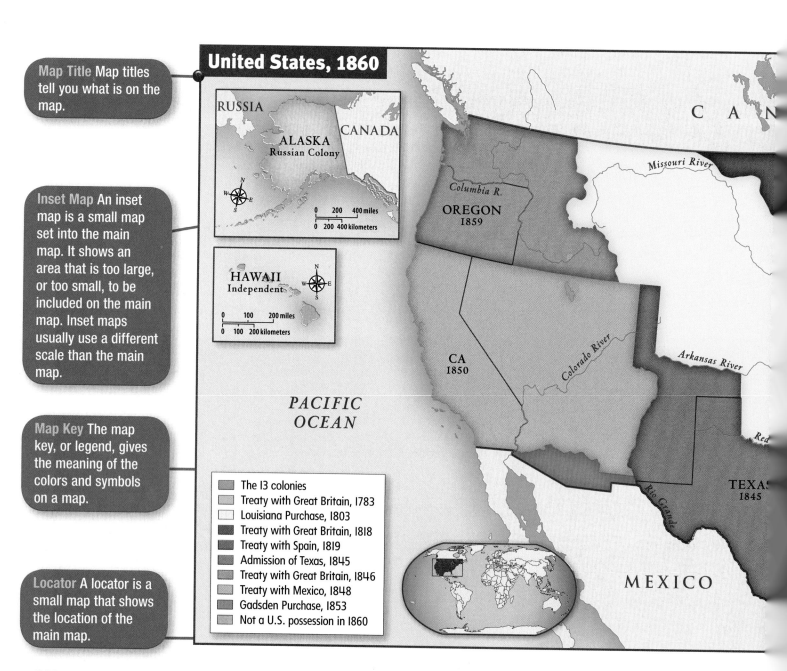

Map Title Map titles tell you what is on the map.

Inset Map An inset map is a small map set into the main map. It shows an area that is too large, or too small, to be included on the main map. Inset maps usually use a different scale than the main map.

Map Key The map key, or legend, gives the meaning of the colors and symbols on a map.

Locator A locator is a small map that shows the location of the main map.

United States, 1860

RUSSIA

CANADA

ALASKA
Russian Colony

0 200 400 miles
0 200 400 kilometers

HAWAII
Independent

0 100 200 miles
0 100 200 kilometers

C A N

Missouri River

Columbia R.

OREGON
1859

CA
1850

Colorado River

Arkansas River

PACIFIC OCEAN

Red

Rio Grande

TEXAS
1845

MEXICO

- The 13 colonies
- Treaty with Great Britain, 1783
- Louisiana Purchase, 1803
- Treaty with Great Britain, 1818
- Treaty with Spain, 1819
- Admission of Texas, 1845
- Treaty with Great Britain, 1846
- Treaty with Mexico, 1848
- Gadsden Purchase, 1853
- Not a U.S. possession in 1860

Read Historical Maps

Some maps capture a period in time. These are called historical maps. They show information about past events or places. For example, this map shows the United States in 1860 just before the beginning of the Civil War. Read the title and the key to understand the information on the map.

What year did California become a state?

Which states entered the Union after California?

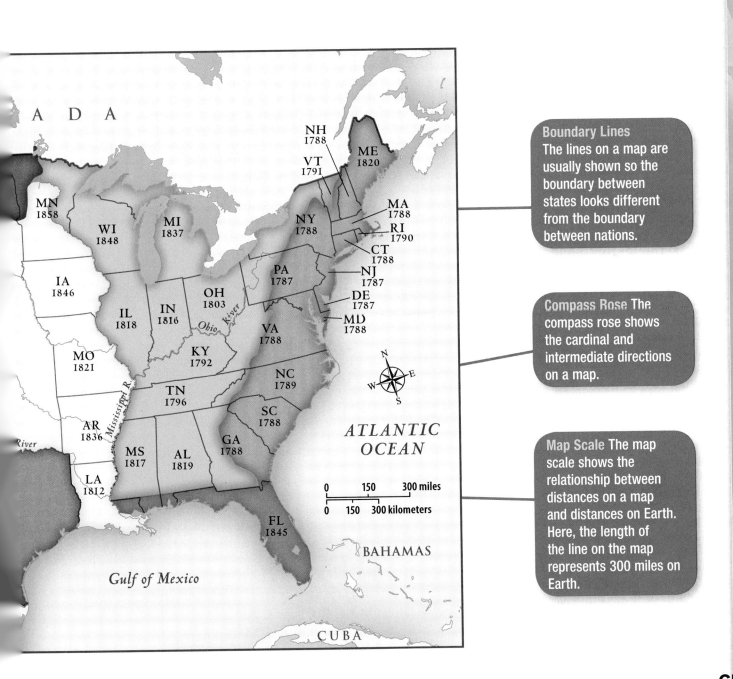

Boundary Lines The lines on a map are usually shown so the boundary between states looks different from the boundary between nations.

Compass Rose The compass rose shows the cardinal and intermediate directions on a map.

Map Scale The map scale shows the relationship between distances on a map and distances on Earth. Here, the length of the line on the map represents 300 miles on Earth.

Use Elevation Maps

An elevation map is a physical map that uses colors to show the elevation, or height of land above or below sea level. The height is usually measured in feet or meters. Sea level is measured as 0 feet or meters around the world. Read the key to understand what each color means. The map on this page uses purple to show land below sea level.

Identify the area of your town or city on the map. How high above sea level is your area?

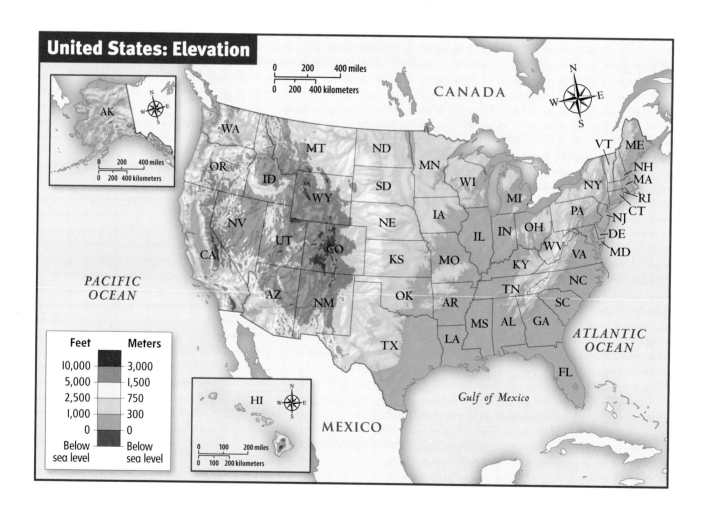

United States: Elevation

Use Road Maps

Suppose you want to go somewhere you have never been before. How do you know what road to take? You could use a road map. Road maps show where the roads in a certain area go. By reading a road map you can figure out how to get from one place to another.

Look at the road map of Indiana. The map key tells you which kinds of roads are shown on the map. Interstate highways run through two or more states and have two or more lanes in each direction. U.S. highways are usually two lane highways that also connect states. State highways stop at a state's borders. The name of each highway is a number. Notice the different symbols for each of the three kinds of highways.

Which roads would you use to get from South Bend to Terre Haute?

Hemispheres

The equator is an imaginary line on Earth. It divides the sphere of Earth in half. A word for half a sphere is *hemisphere*. The prefix "hemi" means half. Geographers divide Earth into four hemispheres.

All land and ocean north of the equator is in the Northern Hemisphere. All the land and ocean south of the equator is in the Southern Hemisphere.

Another imaginary line on Earth runs from the North Pole to the South Pole. It is called the prime meridian. It divides Earth into the Eastern Hemisphere and the Western Hemisphere.

Is North America in the Northern Hemisphere or Southern Hemisphere?

Is North America in the Eastern Hemisphere or the Western Hemisphere?

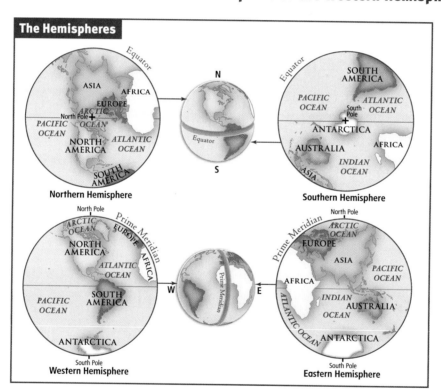

The Hemispheres

Northern Hemisphere

Southern Hemisphere

Western Hemisphere

Eastern Hemisphere

Earth-Sun Relationships

Earth revolves around the sun once a year. As it revolves, Earth also rotates on an axis. An axis is an imaginary line through the center of an object. Earth's axis is tilted 23.5° from due north. That tilt, plus the revolution of Earth around the sun, causes the seasons. The seasons are opposite in the Southern and Northern Hemispheres. For example, when it is winter in the Northern Hemisphere, it is summer in the Southern Hemisphere.

Latitude and Longitude

Geographers have created an imaginary system of lines on the Earth. These lines form a grid to help locate places on any part of the globe. Lines of latitude go from east to west. Lines of longitude go from north to south.

Lines of latitude are called parallels because they are an equal distance apart. The lines of latitude are numbered from 0 at the equator to 90 degrees (°) North at the North Pole and 90° South at the South Pole. Latitude lines usually have N or S to indicate the Northern or Southern Hemisphere.

Lines of longitude, or meridians, circle the Earth from pole to pole. These lines measure the distance from the Prime Meridian, at 0° longitude. Lines of longitude are not parallel. They usually have an E or a W next to the number to indicate the Eastern or Western Hemisphere.

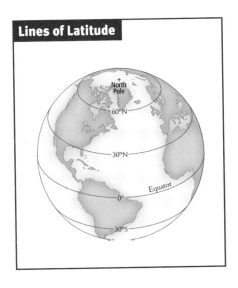

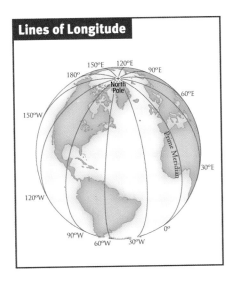

Absolute and Relative Location

You can locate any place on Earth using lines of latitude and longitude. Each line is identified by degrees (°). Each location has a unique number where one line of latitude intersects, or crosses, a line of longitude. This is called its absolute location. Each spot on Earth has an absolute location.

Relative location is the location of a place in relation to other landmarks. For example, St. Louis, Missouri, is located in eastern Missouri, along the Mississippi River.

What is your absolute location? Use a map of the United States to find the latitude and longitude of the city or town where you live.

Maps at Different Scales

All maps are smaller than the real area that they show. To figure out the real distance between two places, most maps include a scale. The scale shows the relationship between distances on a map and real distances.

The scales on the maps in this book are drawn with two horizontal lines. The top line shows distances in miles. The bottom line shows distances in kilometers. You can use a ruler or mark a strip of paper under the scale to measure the distance between places on the map.

The maps on this page are drawn at different scales. Map A and Map B both show the Hawaiian Islands, but Map B shows a larger area with less detail. It is a small-scale map. Map A is a large-scale map. It shows a smaller area with more detail. The scales are different, but the distance between the places shown on both maps is the same.

On both maps, what is the distance in miles between Niihau and Molokai?

What details on Map A are not on Map B?

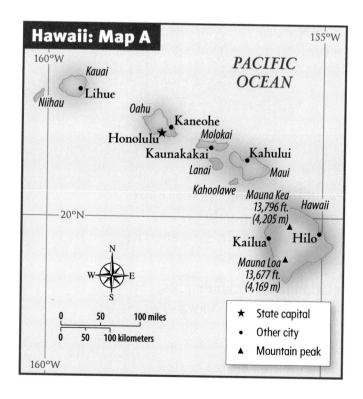

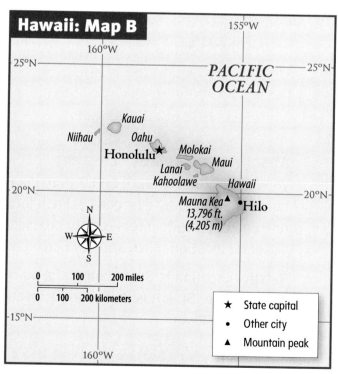

Use Population Maps

When you need to know the number of people who live in a place, or where people live, you can look at a population map. Most population maps show population density—how many people live in a certain area. Another kind of population map shows population distribution—where in an area people live.

Look at the population distribution map of the United States below. Population distribution maps often use different colors to stand for numbers of people per square mile or kilometer. The map key shows the number each color stands for. For example, between 5 and 24 people per square mile live in areas that are shaded yellow.

Which color is used to show the areas with the most people?

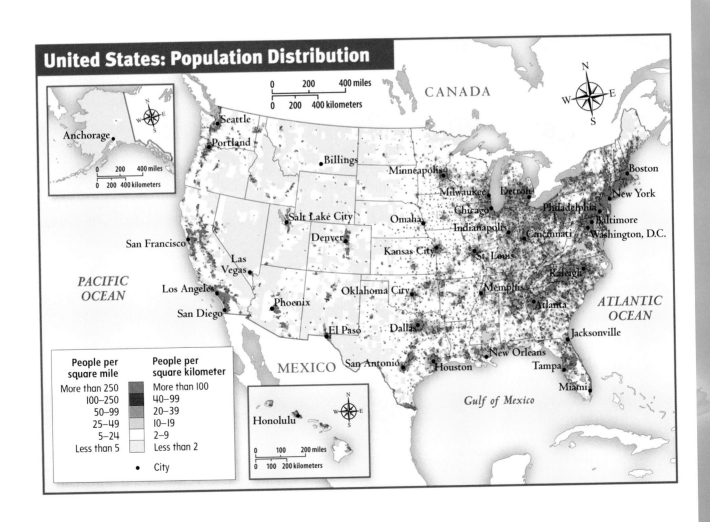

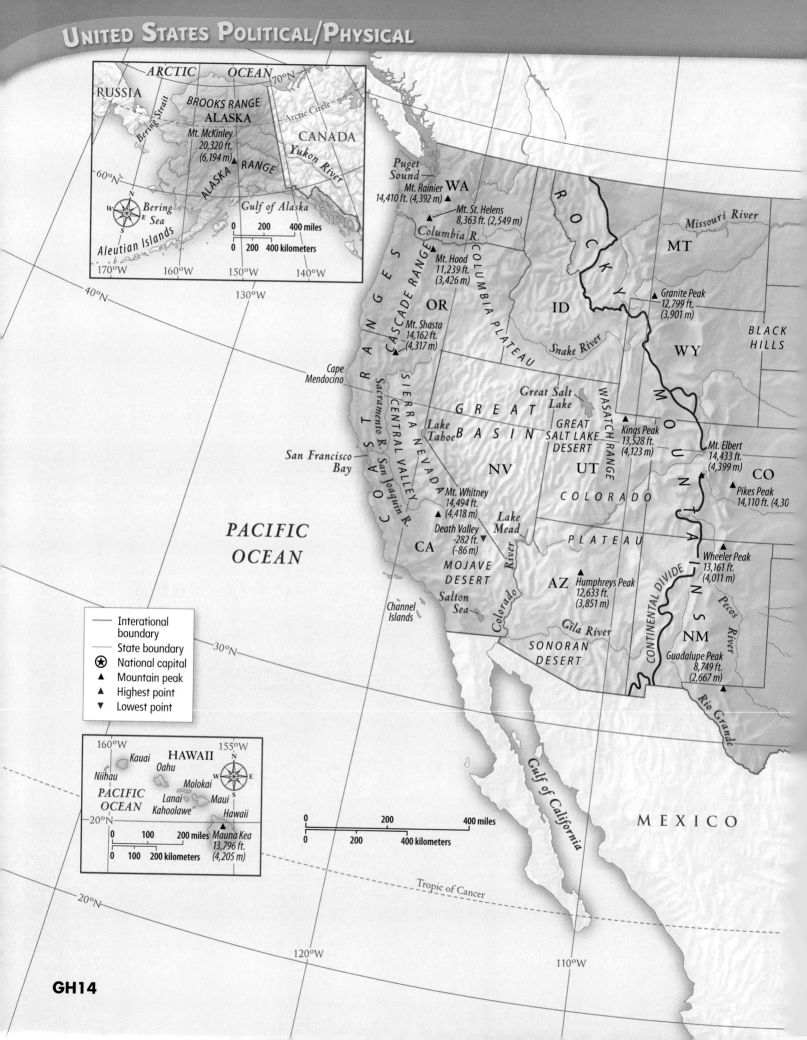

ARCTIC OCEAN

RUSSIA

70°N

BROOKS RANGE

ALASKA

Mt. McKinley
20,320 ft.
(6,194 m)

CANADA

Yukon River

Bering Strait

ALASKA RANGE

Arctic Circle

60°N

Bering Sea

Gulf of Alaska

Aleutian Islands

N
W   E
S

0   200   400 miles
0   200   400 kilometers

170°W   160°W   150°W   140°W

40°N

130°W

PACIFIC
OCEAN

Cape
Mendocino

San Francisco
Bay

COAST RANGES

CASCADE RANGE

Puget
Sound

Mt. Rainier
14,410 ft. (4,392 m)   ▲

WA

Mt. St. Helens
8,363 ft. (2,549 m)   ▲

Columbia R.

Mt. Hood
11,239 ft.
(3,426 m)   ▲

OR

Mt. Shasta
14,162 ft.
(4,317 m)   ▲

Sacramento R.

CENTRAL VALLEY

SIERRA NEVADA

San Joaquin R.

Lake
Tahoe

Mt. Whitney
14,494 ft.
(4,418 m)   ▲

Death Valley
-282 ft. ▼
(-86 m)

CA

MOJAVE
DESERT

Channel
Islands

Salton
Sea

ROCKY

COLUMBIA PLATEAU

Snake River

ID

GREAT
BASIN

Great Salt
Lake

WASATCH RANGE

GREAT
SALT LAKE
DESERT

NV

UT

COLORADO

Lake
Mead

Colorado River

AZ

Humphreys Peak
12,633 ft.
(3,851 m)   ▲

Gila River

SONORAN
DESERT

MT

Missouri River

Granite Peak
12,799 ft.
(3,901 m)   ▲

WY

BLACK
HILLS

Kings Peak
13,528 ft.
(4,123 m)   ▲

MOUNTAINS

Mt. Elbert
14,433 ft.
(4,399 m)   ▲

CO

Pikes Peak
14,110 ft. (4,30

PLATEAU

Wheeler Peak
13,161 ft.
(4,011 m)   ▲

CONTINENTAL DIVIDE

NM

Guadalupe Peak
8,749 ft.
(2,667 m)   ▲

Pecos River

Rio Grande

30°N

Gulf of California

MEXICO

Tropic of Cancer

20°N

120°W   110°W

Legend

——	Interational boundary
—	State boundary
⊛	National capital
▲	Mountain peak
▲	Highest point
▼	Lowest point

160°W

Kauai

Niihau

Oahu

HAWAII

Molokai

Lanai   Maui
Kahoolawe

155°W

N
W   E
S

PACIFIC
OCEAN

Hawaii

20°N

Mauna Kea
13,796 ft.
(4,205 m)   ▲

0   100   200 miles
0   100   200 kilometers

0   200   400 miles
0   200   400 kilometers

CANADA

Lake of the Woods

MESABI RANGE

Lake Superior

GREAT LAKES

St. Lawrence River

ME

ND

MN

Mt. Washington
6,288 ft.
(1,917 m)

VT

Lake Huron

ADIRONDACK MOUNTAINS

NH

WI

MI

Lake Michigan

Lake Ontario

NY

Hudson River

MA

CT RI

Cape Cod

SD

Mississippi River

ALLEGHENY PLATEAU

Lake Erie

PA

Susquehanna River

Long Island

NJ

40°N

CENTRAL PLAINS

ALLEGHENY MOUNTAINS

NE

IA

OH

WV

MD DE

Delaware Bay

Platte River

Missouri River

River

IL

IN

Potomac River

Washington, D.C.

KS

Wabash River

Ohio River

VA

Chesapeake Bay

Arkansas River

INTERIOR PLAINS

MO

PIEDMONT

Cape Hatteras

(1 m)

KY

TN

Tennessee River

Mt. Mitchell
6,684 ft.
(2,037 m)

NC

OZARK PLATEAU

OK

Red River

OUACHITA MOUNTAINS

AR

Mississippi River

SC

ATLANTIC COASTAL PLAIN

ATLANTIC OCEAN

Savannah River

AL

Alabama River

GA

TX

Brazos River

MS

Chattahoochee River

Colorado River

LA

GULF COASTAL PLAIN

Mobile Bay

EDWARDS PLATEAU

Galveston Bay

Mississippi River Delta

FL

Lake Okeechobee

BAHAMAS

Gulf of Mexico

N

W E

S

Florida Keys

Straits of Florida

CUBA

20°N

100°W

90°W

80°W

50°N

30°N

GH15

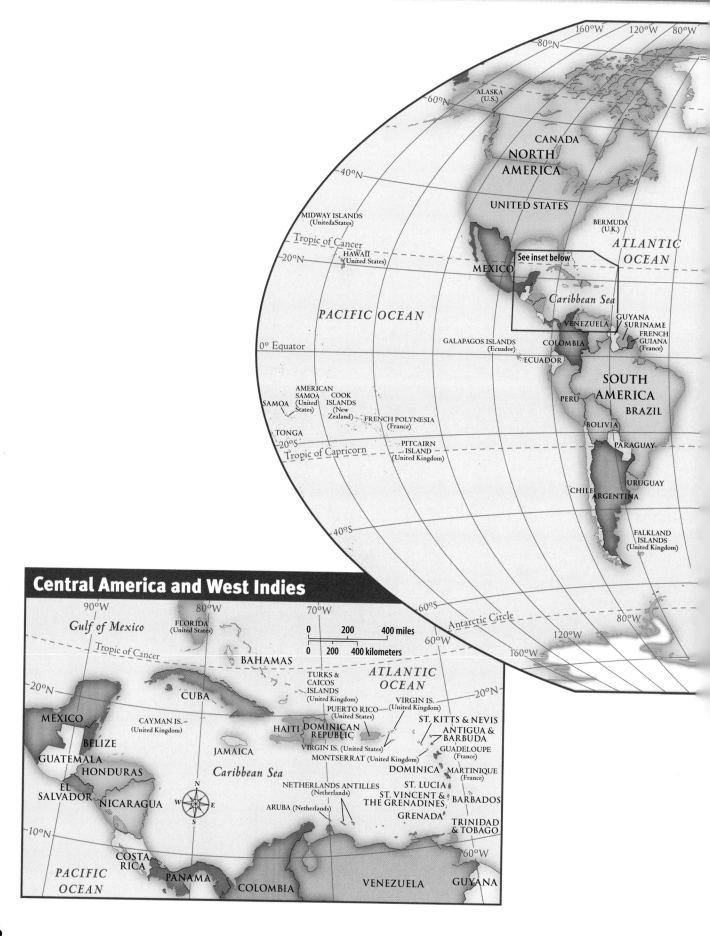

Central America and West Indies

SOUTH AMERICA POLITICAL/PHYSICAL

NORTH AMERICA

ISTHMUS OF PANAMA

Caribbean Sea

15°N

15°N

Maracaibo

Caracas

Orinoco R.

VENEZUELA

GUIANA HIGHLANDS

Bogotá

Cali

COLOMBIA

Georgetown

GUYANA

Paramaribo

SURINAME

Cayenne

FRENCH GUIANA
(France)

ATLANTIC OCEAN

Negro River

Quito

Equator

Equator

0°

ECUADOR

Guayaquil

Galápagos Islands (Ecuador)

Amazon River

River

Tapajos River

Xingú River

Tocantins River

São Francisco River

AMAZON BASIN

Madeira River

PERU

Lima

BRAZIL

BRAZILIAN

Lake Titicaca

Arequipa

La Paz

BOLIVIA

Santa Cruz

Brasília

River

HIGHLANDS

15°S

15°S

Sucre

Paraguay R.

Paraná

ATACAMA DESERT

Mt. Ojos del Salado
22,572 ft.
(6,880 m)

PARAGUAY

Asunción

River

Rio de Janeiro

São Paulo

Tropic of Capricorn

Tropic of Capricorn

CHILE

ANDES MOUNTAINS

Paraná

Mt. Aconcagua
22,834 ft. (6,960 m)

Valparaíso

Santiago

Rosario

Salto

ARGENTINA

URUGUAY

Montevideo

Buenos Aires

Rio de la Plata

30°S

30°S

PACIFIC OCEAN

Concepción

PAMPAS

PATAGONIA

ATLANTIC OCEAN

Falkland Islands
(Islas Malvinas)
(U.K.)

45°S

45°S

Strait of Magellan

TIERRA DEL FUEGO

Cape Horn

South Georgia (U.K.)

	International boundary
⊛	National capital
•	Other city
▲	Mountain peak

0 250 500 miles
0 250 500 kilometers

GH19

105°W   90°W   75°W   60°W   45°W   30°W

Glossary

This Glossary will help you to pronounce and understand the meanings of the vocabulary terms in this book. The page number at the end of the definition tells you where the word first appears.

A

A.D. (ā dē) "Anno Domini." Latin for "in the year of the Lord." Used before a numeral to indicate a year occurring since the birth of Jesus Christ (p. 27)

abolitionist (ab ə lish'ə nist) a person who wanted to end slavery in the United States (p. 251)

absolute location (ab sə lüt' lō kā'shən) the exact location of a place expressed by longitude and latitude or street address (p. 59)

Adams-Onís Treaty (ad' əmz ō'nēs' trē'tē) Spain's agreement to sell Florida to the United States (p. 219)

adobe (a dō'bē) a type of clay traditionally used as a building material by Native Americans and, later, Spanish colonists in the Southwest (p. 24)

ally (a'lī) a person, group, or nation united with another in order to do something (p. 83)

amendment (ə mend'mənt) an addition to the U.S. Constitution. (p. 209)

ammunition (am ū nish'ən) objects, such as bullets, that can be fired from a weapon (p. 163)

Anaconda Plan (an ə kon'da plan) the Union's three-part plan for defeating the Confederacy and ending the Civil War (p. 262)

apprentice (ə pren' tis) a person learning a craft or trade from a master (p. 120)

archaeologist (är kē ol'ə jist) a scientist who looks for and studies artifacts. See **artifact** (p. 21)

arid (ar'id) dry areas that receive very little precipitation each year (p. 294)

arsenal (ar'sə nəl) a storage place for weapons (p. 198)

Articles of Confederation (är'ti kalz uv kən fed ə rā'shən) the first plan of government of the United States. It gave more power to the states than to the central government. (p. 197)

artifact (är'ti fakt) an object made by humans long ago (p. 3)

assassination (ə sas ə nā 'shən) the murder of an important person (p. 278)

assembly (ə sem'blē) a lawmaking body (p. 137)

B

B.C. (bē sē) Before Christ. Used after a numeral to indicate a year occurring before the birth of Jesus Christ (p. 27)

B.C.E. (bē sē ē) Before the Common Era. See **B.C.** (p. 27)

backcountry (bak kun′trē) Colonial area between the Appalachian Mountains and the Atlantic Coastal Plain (p. 122)

barter (bär′ tər) the trading of goods for goods (p. 54)

battle map (bat′əl map) a map that shows the events of a conflict between two groups of armed forces (p. 177)

bill (bil) an idea for a law which has not been approved (p. 327)

bill of rights (bil əv rīts) a formal statement of rights and liberties guaranteed to the people by a state. See **amendment** (p. 209)

biotechnology (bī ō tech nol′ə gē) technology that uses living cells to create new medicines (p. 316)

black codes (blak kōdz) laws passed by the Southern states after the Civil War that severely limited the rights of the newly freed African Americans (p. 281)

blockade (blok ād′) a barrier preventing the movement of troops and supplies (p. 187)

boycott (boi′kot) to refuse to do business or have contact with a person, group, company, country, or product (p. 157)

budget (buj′it) a plan for saving and spending money (p. 323)

C.E. (sē ē) "Common Era" (p. 27)

canyon (kan′yən) a deep valley with very high, steep sides (p. 302)

cash crop (kash krop) a crop that is grown to be sold for profit (p. 88)

century (sen′chə rē) a period of 100 years (p. 27)

charter (chär′tər) an official document giving a person permission to do something, such as settle in an area (p. 87)

circa (sûr′kə) in approximately (p. 27)

circle graph (sûr′kəl graf) a kind of chart that shows how something can be divided into parts (p. 77)

civil war (siv′əl wôr) an armed conflict between groups within one country. In the United States, the war between the Union and the Confederacy from 1861 to 1865 (p. 257)

civilization (siv ə lə zā′shən) A culture that has developed complex systems of government, education, and religion. Civilizations usually have large populations with many people living in cities (p. 22)

clan (klan) a group of families who share the same ancestor (p. 44)

climate (klī′mit) the weather of an area over a number of years (p. 249, 294)

climograph (klī′mō graf) a graph that shows information about the temperature and precipitation of a place over time (p. 249)

colony (kol′ə nē) a settlement far away from the country that rules it (p. 63)

Columbian Exchange (kə lum′bē ən eks chānj′) the movement of people, plants, animals, and germs in either direction across the Atlantic Ocean following the voyages of Columbus (p. 64)

common (kom′ən) the village green or center of Puritan villages characterized by the presence of a Puritan church or meeting house (p. 102)

competition (kom′pi tish′ən) the act of trying to win or gain something from another or others (p. 311)

conquistador (kon kēs′tə dôr) a name for the Spanish conquerors who first came to the Americas in the 1500s (p. 67)

Continental army (kon′tə nen′təl är′mē) the army created by the Second Continental Congress in May 1775 with George Washington as commander-in-chief (p. 149)

Continental Divide (kon′tə nen′təl di vīd′) an imaginary line made of high points in the Rockies from where our nation's rivers flow east or west (p. 302)

cost-benefit decision (kost 'ben ə fit dis izh'ən) a choice made to buy a product by taking into consideration the future benefits that will result from the product (p. 322)

cotton gin (kot'ən jin) a machine that separates cotton from its seeds, invented by Eli Whitney in 1793 (p. 223)

coup stick (kü stik) a weapon used by a Lakota Sioux fighter to show bravery by touching, but not killing, an enemy (p. 39)

coureurs de bois (kü rər' də bwä') in New France, a person who trapped furs without permission from the French government (p. 84)

covenant (ku' və nənt) a contract, an agreement (p. 102)

credibility (kre də'bilə tē) the correctness or reliability of a source of information (p. 9)

Creek Confederacy (krēk kən fed'ər ə sē) the union formed by several groups of Creek Native Americans to protect themselves (p. 44)

culture (kul'chər) the entire way of life of a people, including their customs, beliefs, and language (p. 3)

current (kûr'ənt) a portion of water or air that flows continuously in approximately the same path (p. 308)

D

data (dat'ə) facts from which inferences or conclusions can be made (p. 15)

debate (dē bāt') a formal argument about different political ideas (p. 255)

debtor (det'ər) a person who owes money (p. 115)

Declaration of Independence (dek lə rā'shən əv in də pen'dəns) the official document issued on July 4, 1776, announcing that the American colonies were breaking away from Great Britain (p. 150)

delegate (del'ə git) a member of an elected assembly. See **assembly** (p. 159)

demand (di mand') the desire for a product or service. See **supply** (p. 315)

democracy (di mok'rə sē) a government in which the power is held by the people (p. 326)

desert (di'zərt) to go away and leave a person or thing that should not be left (p. 179)

decision making (dē sizh'ən māk'ing) choosing between two or more things (p. 13)

discrimination (di skrim ə nā'shən) an unfair difference in the treatment of people (p. 231)

draft (draft) the selecting of persons for military service or some other special duty (p. 259)

drought (drout) a long period of little or no rainfall (p. 309)

E

economy (i kon'ə mē) the way a country's people use natural resources, money, and knowledge to produce goods and services (p. 305)

Emancipation Proclamation (ē man si pā'shən prok lə mā'shən) the official announcement issued by President Abraham Lincoln in 1862 that led to the end of slavery in the United States (p. 267)

empire (em'pīr) an area in which different groups of people are controlled by one ruler or government (p. 67)

enslave (en slāv') to force a person to work for no money without the freedom to leave (p. 75)

Era of Good Feelings (ir'ə uv gůd fē'lingz) the name given to the period of peace and prosperity that followed the War of 1812 (p. 219)

ethnic group (eth'nik grüp) people who share the same customs and language, and often a common history (p. 7)

expedition (ek spi dish'ən) a journey made for a special purpose (p. 61)

expense (ek spens') a payment for goods and services (p. 323)

export (ek'spôrt) to send goods to other countries for sale or use (p. 84)

F

fact (fakt) information that is known to be true (p. 8)

federal system (fed′ər əl sis′təm) a system of government in which power in the nation is shared between the central government and the state governments (p. 205)

free state (frē stāt) state where slavery was banned (p. 246)

French and Indian War (french ənd in′dē ən wôr) a conflict between Great Britain and France in North America from 1756 to 1763 (p. 153)

frontier (frun tēr′) the name given by colonists to the far end of a country where people are just beginning to settle (p. 73)

fundamental (fun də men′təl) something basic or necessary (p. 103)

G

Gettysburg Address (get′iz burg ə dres′) a speech made by President Lincoln at the site of the Battle of Gettysburg in 1863 (p. 271)

glacier (glā′ shər) a large mass of ice (p. 21)

global grid (glō′bəl grid) a set of squares formed by crisscrossing lines that can help you determine the absolute location of a place on a globe (p. 59)

Gold Rush (gōld rush) the sudden rush of people to an area where gold has been discovered (p. 236)

government (guv′ərn mənt) the rules used to organize how people live together (p. 4)

Great Awakening (grāt ə wā′ kən ing) a religious movement of the 1700s (p. 121)

growth rate (grōth rāt) an increase or decrease of something expressed in percentage (p. 121)

H

historian (hi stōr′ē ən) a person who studies the past (p. 14)

historical map (his tôr′i kəl map) a map that shows information about the past or where past events took place (p. 123)

hogan (hō′gən) a Navajo dwelling (p. 35)

House of Burgesses (hous uv bər′jis əz) the lawmaking body of colonial Virginia, established in Jamestown in 1619 (p. 89)

humid (hū′mid) moist areas or regions that receive more than 20 inches of precipitation each year (p. 294)

I

immigrant (im′ə grənt) a person who lives in a country in which he or she was not born (p. 330)

import (im′pōrt) to bring goods from another country for sale or use (p. 84)

impressment (im pres ′ mənt) the act of seizing for public use or service (p. 215)

indentured servant (in den′chərd sûr′vənt) a person who worked for someone in colonial America for a set time in exchange for the ocean voyage (p. 89)

income (in′kum′) money earned for doing work (p. 321)

indigo (in′di gō) a plant that is used to produce a blue dye. See **cash crop** (p. 114)

Industrial Revolution (in dəs′trē əl rev ə lü′shən) the change from making goods by hand at home to making them by machine in factories (p. 223)

industry (in′ dəs trē) a branch of business, trade, or manufacturing (p. 134)

inflation (in flā′ shən) a rise in the usual price of goods and services (p. 176)

informational text (in'fər mā'shənəl tekst) a book that explains a topic (p. 6)

interchangeable part (in tər chan'jə bəl part) parts of a product built to a standard size so that they can be easily replaced (p. 223)

interdependence (in'tər di pen'dəns) dependence on each other to meet needs and wants (p. 312)

Iroquois Confederacy (îr'ə kwä kən fed'ər ə sē) the union of the five major Iroquois groups beginning about 1570 (p. 45)

irrigation (ir i gā'shən) a method of supplying dry land with water though a series of ditches or pipes (p. 24)

key word (kē wûrd) an important word or phrase that is used to describe pieces of information (p. 9)

large-scale map (lärj skāl map) a map that shows a smaller area in greater detail (p. 177)

latitude (lat'i tüd) an imaginary line, or parallel, measuring distance north or south of the equator. See **parallel** (p. 59)

legislation (le jəs lā'shən) laws passed by a lawmaking body (p. 137)

legislature (lej'is lā' chər) a body of people that has the power to make or pass laws (p. 200)

line graph (līn graf) a kind of graph that shows changes over time (p. 77)

lodge (loj) a type of home made of logs, grasses, sticks, and soil, which Native Americans of the Plains used when living in their villages. See **teepee** (p. 37)

longhouse (lông'hous) a home shared by several related Iroquois families (p. 43)

longitude (lon'ji tüd) an imaginary line, or meridian, measuring distance east or west of the prime meridian. See **meridian** and **prime meridian** (p. 59)

loyalist (loi'ə list) a colonist who supported Great Britain in the American Revolution (p. 172)

malice (ma' ləs) to want to harm someone (p. 278)

manifest destiny (man'ə fest des'tə nē) belief in the early 1800s that the United States was to stretch west to the Pacific Ocean and south to the Rio Grande (p. 229)

map scale (map skāl) a line drawn on a map that uses a unit of measurement, such as an inch, to represent a real distance on Earth (p. 221)

market economy (mär'kit ē kon'ə mē) individuals make economic decisions about what to make, how much to produce, and what to charge (p. 311)

megalopolis (meg ə lop'ə lis) a large urban area formed by several cities (p. 297)

mercenary (mûr'sə nər ē) a soldier paid to fight for another country (p. 172)

merchant (mûr'chənt) a person who buys, sells, and trades goods for a profit (p. 54)

merchant company (mûr'chənt kum'pə nē) a group of merchants who share the cost and profits of a business (p. 80)

meridian (mə rid'ē ən) any line of longitude east or west of Earth's prime meridian. See **longitude** and **prime meridian** (p. 59)

mestizo (me stē'zō) a person of mixed Spanish and Native American heritage (p. 76)

Middle Passage (mid'əl pas'ij) the middle leg of the colonial trade route in which captive Africans were shipped to the West Indies. See **slave trade** and **triangular trade** (p. 133)

migrant farm worker (mī′grənt färm wûr′kər) a laborer who moves from one farm to another as the seasons change (p. 356)

migrate (mī′grāt) to move from one place to another (p. 34)

militia (mə lish′ə) a group of volunteers who fought in times of emergency during the colonial period and the American Revolution (p. 161)

missionary (mish′ə ner ē) a person who teaches his or her religion to those who have different beliefs (p. 75)

Missouri Compromise (mə zûr′ē kom′prə mīz) an agreement in 1820 that allowed Missouri and Maine to enter the Union and divided the Louisiana Territory into areas allowing slavery and areas outlawing slavery (p. 246)

Monroe Doctrine (mən rō dok′trin) a declaration of United States foreign policy made by President James Monroe in 1823 that opposed European colonization or interference in the Western Hemisphere (p. 220)

navigable (na′vi gə bəl) describes a waterway that is deep enough and wide enough for ships to steer through (p. 300)

navigation (nav ə gā′shən) the science of determining a ship's location and direction (p. 57)

neutral (nü′trəl) not taking sides (p. 341)

Northwest Passage (nôrth′west pas′ij) a water route believed to flow through North America to Asia that European explorers searched for from the 1500s to the 1700s (p. 79)

opportunity cost (äp ôr tün′ə tē kost) the value of the second best choice when choosing between two things (p. 322)

oral history (ôr′əl his′tə rē) information that is told, rather than written down (p. 14)

opinion (ə pin′yən) a statement that tells what a person thinks, believes, or feels (p. 8)

P

parallel (par′ə lel) a line of latitude. See **latitude** (p. 59)

parallel time line (par′ə lel tīm′līn) two different sets of events on the same time line (p. 27)

Patriot (pā′trē ət) an American colonist who supported the fight for independence (p. 171)

patroon (pə trün′) the name given to wealthy Dutch landowners who were given land to farm along the Hudson River by the Dutch West India Company in the 1600s (p. 107)

pilgrim (pil′ grəm) a person who travels to a place for religious reasons (p. 90)

pioneer (pī ə nîr′) a person who is among the first of nonnative people to settle a region (p. 213)

plantation (plan tā′shən) a large farm that often grows one cash crop (p. 114)

point of view (poin′t uv vü) the way in which people see the world (p. 7)

political party (pə lit′i kəl pär′tē) a group of people who share similar ideas about government (p. 324)

potlatch (pot′lach) a feast given by Native Americans of the northwest coast, in which the guests receive gifts (p. 31)

prairie (prâr′ē) flat, rolling land covered with grass (p. 298)

precipitation (pri sip i tā′shən) moisture that falls to the ground in the form of rain, sleet, hail, or snow (p. 294)

primary source (prī′mer ē sôrs) a firsthand account of an event or an artifact created during the period of history that is being studied. See **artifact** and **secondary** source (p. 10)

prime meridian (prīm mə rid′ē ən) the line of longitude labeled 0° longitude. Any place east of the prime meridian is labeled E. Any place west of it is labeled W. See **longitude** (p. 59)

problem solving (prob′ləm solv′ing) finding a solution to a difficult issue (p. 12)

Proclamation of 1763 (prok lə mā'shən) an official announcement by King George III of Great Britain that outlawed colonial settlement west of the Appalachian Mountains (p. 154)

profit (prof' it) the money made on goods that exceeds the cost of production (p. 54)

profiteering (prof'it ēr ing) making excess profits from goods that are in short supply (p. 176)

proprietor (prə prī'ə tər) a person who owns property or a business (p. 108)

R

ratify (rat'ə fi) to officially approve (p. 208)

reaper (rē'pər) a machine that cuts grain for harvesting (p. 224)

reform (ri fôrm') a change to improve the lives of many people (p. 325)

region (rē'jən) a large area with common features that set it apart from other areas (p. 294)

relative location (rel ə tiv lō kā'shən) a place in relation to another (p. 59)

repeal (ri pēl') to cancel (p. 157)

republic (ri pub'lik) a government with elected leaders who represent the people (p. 326)

research (rē'sûrch) information discovered about the past (p. 14)

S

sachem (sā'chəm) an Iroquois chief or tribal leader (p. 92)

scarcity (skâr'si tē) a shortage of available goods and services (p. 305)

secede (si sēd') to withdraw from the Union (p. 257)

secondary source (sek'ən der ē sôrs) an account of the past based on information from primary sources and written by someone who was not an eyewitness to those events. See **primary source** (p. 11)

segregation (seg ri gā'shən) separation of people based on race (p. 285)

sharecropping (shâr'krop ing) a system in which farmers rented land in return for crops (p. 282)

slash-and-burn (slash and bûrn) to cut and burn trees to clear land for farming (p. 41)

slave codes (slāv cōdz) rules made by colonial planters that controlled the lives of enslaved Africans (p. 125)

slave state (slāv stāt) state where slavery was allowed (p. 246)

slave trade (slāv trād) the business of buying and selling people (p. 119)

slavery (slā'və rē) the practice of treating people as property and forcing them to work (p. 104)

small-scale map (smôl skāl map) a map that shows a large area but not much detail (p. 221)

social studies (sō'shəl stud'ēz) the study of people (p. 2)

spiritual (spi' ri tū əl) the religious songs of enslaved Africans (p. 127)

Stamp Act (stamp akt) a law passed by the British requiring colonists to pay a tax on paper products (p. 157)

steam engine (stēm en'jin) an engine that is powered by compressed steam (p. 224)

stock (stok) a share in the ownership of a company (p. 311)

suffrage (suf'rij) the right to vote (p. 333)

supply (sə plī') a quantity of something needed or ready for use. See **demand** (p. 315)

Supreme Court (sü prēm' kôrt) the head of the judicial branch of the federal government. It is the highest court in the country (p. 205)

T

tariff (tar' ef) a tax placed on imports or exports to control the sale price (p. 247)

tax (taks) money that people and businesses must pay to the government for its support (p. 321)

temperate climate (tem′pər it klī′mit) mild weather that is neither too hot nor too cold with changing seasons (p. 308)

tenement (ten′ə mənt) rundown building (p. 308)

tepee (tē′pē) a cone-shaped tent made from animal hides and wooden poles used by Native Americans of the Plains (p. 37)

territory (ter′i tôr ē) an area of land controlled by a nation (p. 149)

time line (tīm′ līn) a diagram showing the order in which events took place (p. 27)

time zone (tīm zōn) one of the 24 areas into which Earth is divided for measuring time (p. 303)

tolerate (tol′ə rāt) to allow people to have different beliefs from your own (p. 103)

total war (to′ təl wôr) attacking an enemy's soldiers, civilians, and property (p. 264)

totem pole (tō təm pōl) a tree trunk that is carved with sacred images by Native Americans (p. 30)

trade deficit (trād def′ə sit) when the value of a country's imports is higher than the value of its exports (p. 313)

trade surplus (trād sûr′plus) when the value of a country's exports is higher than the value of its imports (p. 313)

Trail of Tears (trāl uv tîrz) the name given to the 800-mile forced march of 15,000 Cherokee in 1838 from their homes in Georgia to the Indian Territory (p. 229)

travois (trə voi′) a kind of sled that is dragged to move supplies (p. 38)

treason (trē′zən) the act of betraying one's country (p. 256)

Treaty of Alliance (trē′tē əv ə lī′əns) the treaty signed between France and the United States during the American Revolution (p. 181)

Treaty of Guadalupe Hidalgo (trē′tē uv gwäd ə lü′pā ēdäl′gō) the treaty under which Mexico sold territory to the United States (p. 235)

Treaty of Paris 1763 (trē′tē uv par′əs) the agreement signed by Great Britain and France that brought an end to the French and Indian War (p. 154)

Treaty of Paris 1783 (trē′tē uv par′əs) the peace agreement in which Great Britain recognized the United States as an independent country (p. 187)

tributary (trib′ yə ter ē) a river or stream that flows into a larger river (p. 149)

U

Union (yün′yən) states that are joined together as one political group (p. 277)

V

veto (vē′tō) to refuse to approve (p. 327)

Voting Rights Act (vō′ting rīts akt) a 1965 law that guarantees U.S. citizens the right to vote (p. 355)

voyageur (vwä yä zhûr′) a trader who transported furs by canoe in New France (p. 84)

W

wagon train (wag′ ən trān) a group of covered wagons that follow one another closely to a destination (p. 229)

wampum (wom′pəm) polished beads made from shells strung or woven together used in gift-giving and trading by Native Americans (p. 43)

War Hawks (wôr hôks) members of Congress from the South and the West in the early 1800s who wanted the United States to go to war against Great Britain. See **War of 1812** (p. 217)

Index

Note: This index lists many topics that appear in the book, along with the pages on which they are found. Page numbers after a *c* refer you to a chart or diagram, after a *g*, to a graph, after an *m*, to a map, after a *p*, to a photograph or picture, and after a *q*, to a quotation.

technology in, 264–65, p264–65
as total war, 264, 276
women in, 272–73, p272
Civilizations, 22
Clan mother, 44
Clans, 44
Clark, George Rogers, 183, 214
Clark, William, p212
exploration of Louisiana Territory, m214, 214–15, p215
Clay, Henry, Missouri Compromise and, 246
Cleveland, 317
Cleveland Cliffs Iron Ore Mine and Mill, p305
Climate, 249
definition of, 294
differences in, m308, 308–9
Climographs, 249, g249
Clinton, DeWitt, 224
Coal industry, p306, 317
Cold Harbor, battle of, p274
Colonial governments
assemblies in, 137, p137, 138
governors in, 138–39
self-government, 137, p137
Colonial militia, 161
Colonial trade, 131
Colonists
daily life of, 120–21, p120, p121
early communities of, 120–21
reasons for becoming, 119
Colorado, 298
Colorado, settlement of, 235
Colorado River, p292, 302
Columbian Exchange, 60, c64, 64–65, 96
Columbus, Christopher, p50, p60, 61, q63
discovery of America, 63
voyages of, m62, 62–63
Common, village, 102
Common good, working for, 121
Compasses, Chinese, 57
Competition, 311
Compromise of 1850, 252
Concord, 161, 162
Confederacy (Confederate States of America), 257
Jefferson Davis as president of, 257, 262

strengths and weaknesses of, c260
See also Civil War (1861-1865)
Confederacy, Creek, 44
Congress, U.S., 205
and lawmaking, 327
and presidential vetos, 327
Reconstruction under, 282
See also House of Representatives, U.S.; Senate, U.S.
Connecticut, 126
Colonial government in, 138
Conquistadors, 67, 73, 74
Constitution ("Old Ironsides"), 218
Constitution, U.S., p204
Article 1 (Congress), 205
Article 2 (Executive Branch), 205
Article 3 (Supreme Court), 205
Bill of Rights in, 208, p208, 209
changing, 209
checks and balances in, 206–7, p206–7
debate over, 208
importance of, 4
Preamble to, 205
ratification of, 208–9
See also Amendments
Constitutional Convention, 200–201, p202
Electoral College and, 202–3
Great Compromise at, 202
New Jersey Plan in, 201
signing at, 203
Three-Fifths Compromise at, 202
Virginia Plan in, 200–201
Continental Army in American Revolution, 167, 175, 187
Continental Congress
First, 159
Second, 167
Continental Divide, 302, m302, p302
Continentals, 176
Cooper, Peter, 225
Copán, 23
Copper, 305
Corn as renewable energy, 306
Cornwallis, Charles, 185, p185, 186

Coronado, Francisco Vásquez de, 74
Corps of Discovery, 214
Cortés, Hernan, 67, 75
Cosby, William, 140
Cost-benefit decisions, 322
Cotton as cash crop, 244, p244, 245, 297
Cotton gin, 223, 245, p245
Coup stick, 39
Coureurs de bois, 84
Covenants, 102
Credibility, 9
Creek, 42, p42
government of, 44
James Oglethrope and, 116–17, p116
The Crisis (Paine), 179
Crockett, Davy, p195
Crows, 37
Crusades, 54
CSS H.L. Hunley, p264–65, 265
CSS Virginia, 264
Cultures, 3
Cumberland Gap, 213
Currents, 308
Currier & Ives, p112
Cuzco, 68

Da Gama, Vasco, p52, 58
Dallas, m303
Data, 15
DataGraphics
Election of 1864, 277
Native American Languages, 44
Resources of North and South, c263, g263
Davis, Jefferson, 278
as president of Confederate States of America, 257, 262
Dawes, William, 161
De La Salle, Robert, 149, p149
De Las Casas, Bartolomé, 75, p75, q75
De Soto, Hernando, 73
Debates, 255
Lincoln-Douglas, p254–55, 255
Debtors, 115
settlement of, in Georgia, 115
Decision making, 13
Declaration of Independence (1776), 168–69, 189
signing of, 169

Deganawida, 45, p45
Delaware
settlement of, 111
as Union State, 267
Delaware River, 108, 295
Demand, 315
Democracies, 326
Democratic Republicans, p213, 325
Denver, 298, m303, 318
Detroit
in Central Plains, 298, 299
manufacturing in, 317, p317
St. Lawrence Seaway and, 301
Diagrams, 15
Dias, Bartolomeu, p52, 58
Dickinson, John, 167
Diné, 34
Discovery, 80, 81
Discrimination against free blacks, 231
Disease
in American Revolution, 182
impact on Native Americans, 65, 92
Disposable income, 321
District of Columbia, p211
Dominican Republic, 63
Douglas, Marjory Stoneman, p301
Douglas, Stephen, 253
debate between Abraham Lincoln and, p250, p254–55, 255
in election of 1860, 257
Douglass, Frederick, 251, p251, 268
Draft in Civil War, 259
Dred Scott v. Sandford, p250, 254
Droughts, 309, 318
Dry farming, 25, 33, 34
Dutch, 107, 108
explorations of, 80
settlement of New Netherlands by, 107
See also Netherlands
Dutch East India Company, 80
Dutch West India Company, 107

Eastern Woodlands tribes, 40–45, p40, m41
Creek as, 42, p42
farming by, 41

Index

(br) The Granger Collection, New York; **136-137** (LesOp) The Colonial Williamsburg Foundation; **137** The Colonial Williamsburg Foundation; **138** Historical Picture Archive/CORBIS; **139** Michael Newman/PhotoEdit; **140** (inset) Atwater Kent Museum of Philadelphia, Courtesy of Historical Society of Pennsylvania Collection/Bridgeman Art Library; **140-141** (bg) The Granger Collection, New York; **141** (t) Schomburg Center/Art Resource, Inc., (c) The Colonial Williamsburg Foundation; **142** The Colonial Williamsburg Foundation; **144** amana images/Getty Images; **145** (UnitOp) Artist Robert Griffing and his Publisher Paramount Press Inc.; **146** (tl) POPPERFOTO/Alamy Images, (bl) Dan Guravich/CORBIS, (tr) The Granger Collection, New York, (br) The Granger Collection, New York; **147** (bl) The Granger Collection, New York, (br) The Granger Collection, New York, (tr) Réunion des Musées Nationaux/Art Resource, Inc., (tl) Bernstein Collection/CORBIS; **148** (bl) Culver Pictures/The Art Archive, (br) The Granger Collection, New York; **149** Culver Pictures/The Art Archive; **151** (t) The Granger Collection, New York; **152** (bl) The Granger Collection, New York, (br) General Wolfe Museum Quebec House/Eileen Tweedy/The Art Archive; **152-153** (LesOp) Artist Robert Griffing and his Publisher Paramount Press Inc.; **153** The Granger Collection, New York; **154-155** (bg) General Wolfe Museum Quebec House/Eileen Tweedy/The Art Archive; **155** (cl) SuperStock, (cr) The Granger Collection, New York; **156** (br) North Wind Picture Archives, (bl) Library of Congress, Prints & Photographs Division, [LC-USZC4-1583]; **156-157** (LesOp) Library of Congress, Prints & Photographs Division, [LC-USZC4-1583]; **157** The Granger Collection, New York; **158** North Wind Picture Archives; **159** (b) Culver/The Art Archive, (t) Library of Congress, Prints & Photographs Division, [LC-USZC4-1583]; **160** (bc) The Granger Collection, New York, (br) Phil E. Degginger/Mira.com, (bl) Bettmann/CORBIS; **160-161** (LesOp) Bettmann/CORBIS; **162-163** (t) The Granger Collection, New York; **164** SuperStock; **165** (t) Phil E. Degginger/Mira.com, (c) Bettmann/CORBIS; **166** (bl) NTPL / Christopher Hurst/The Image Works, Inc., (br) Bettmann/CORBIS; **166-167** (LesOp) SuperStock; **167** NTPL / Christopher Hurst/The Image Works, Inc.; **168** Bettmann/CORBIS; **169** (t) EPA/Tom Mihalek/Landov, (c) SuperStock; **170** (bl bcl) Painting by Don Troiani/Historical Art Prints, (br) The Granger Collection, New York, (bcr) SuperStock; **170-171** (LesOp) Painting by Don Troiani/Historical Art Prints; **171 172** Painting by Don Troiani/Historical Art Prints; **172-173** (bg) Fine Art Photographic Library/CORBIS; **173** (l) From the original painting by Mort Kunstler, Reading the Declaration of Independence to the Troops. 1975 Mort Kunstler, Inc. www.mkunstler.com, (r) Painting by Don Troiani/Historical Art Prints; **174** (r) The Granger Collection, New York, (bg) Massachusetts Historical Society, (l) SuperStock; **175** David Wagner; **176** (t) The Granger Collection, New York, (c) Painting by Don Troiani/Historical Art Prints; **178** (bl) Library of Congress, Prints & Photographs Division, [LC-USZCN4-159], (bc) Peter Bowden, (br) SuperStock; **179** (l) The Granger Collection, New York, (r) Library of Congress, Prints & Photographs Division, [LC-USZCN4-159]; **180** Ron & Diane Salmon/Flying Fish Photography; **181** (tl) Kathy McLaughlin/The Image Works, Inc.,(tr) Peter Bowden, (b) Independence National Historical Park; **182-183** (b) SuperStock; **184** (bl) The Granger Collection, New York, (bc) SuperStock, (br) Michelle & Tom Grimm/Buddy Mays/Travel Stock Photography; **184-185** (LesOp) Michelle & Tom Grimm/Buddy Mays/Travel Stock Photography; **185** The Granger Collection, New York; **186** SuperStock; **187** (t) Erich Lessing/Art Resource, Inc.; **188-189** (t) Cynthia Hart Designer/CORBIS; **189** (c) Michelle & Tom Grimm/Buddy Mays/Travel Stock Photography; **190** (t) Painting by Don Troiani/Historical Art Prints, (b) Victoria & Albert Museum, London/Art Resource, Inc.; **192** (t) Dave Mager/Index Stock Imagery, (b) The Granger Collection, New York; **193** (UnitOp) The Granger Collection, New York; **194** (tl) Chateau de Blerancourt/Dagli Orti/The Art Archive, (bl) Madeline Polss/Envision; **194** The Granger Collection, New York; **195** (tl) Burstein Collection/CORBIS, (bl) D. Boone/CORBIS, (tr) Private Collection, Christie's Images/Bridgeman Art Library, (br) SuperStock; **196** (bcl) The Granger Collection, New York, (bcr) Bettmann/CORBIS, (br) Stock Montage/Hulton Archive/Getty Images; **198 199** The Granger Collection, New York; **200-201** (b) John McGrail/John McGrail Photography; **201** (t) Bettmann/CORBIS; **202** (b) Stock Montage/Hulton Archive/Getty Images, (r) Stock Montage/Getty Images; **203** (c) John McGrail/John McGrail Photography; **204** (bl) Bettmann/CORBIS, (bcl) Danilo Donadoni/Bruce Coleman Inc., (bcr) Dennis Brack Photography, (br) The Granger Collection, New York; **204-205** (LesOp) Bettmann/CORBIS; **205** Comstock/PunchStock; **206** (r) Danilo Donadoni/Bruce Coleman Inc., (l) SuperStock; **206-207** (bg) PhotoLink/Photodisc/Getty Images; **207** Wendell Metzen/Bruce Coleman Inc.; **209** (t) The Granger Collection, New York, (b) Dennis Brack Photography; **210-211** (bg) The Granger Collection, New York; **211** (t) The Granger Collection, New York, (c) Danilo Donadoni/Bruce Coleman Inc.; **212** (bl) The Granger Collection, New York, (br) Detail of "Lewis and Clark at Three Forks" by E.S. Paxson, Oil on Canvas, 1912, Courtesy of the Montana Historical Society. Don Beatty photographer 10/1999; **212-213** (LesOp) The Granger Collection, New York; **213** The Granger Collection, New York; **214** (l) Independence National Historical Park, (r) National Historical Park, Independence, Missouri, MO, USA/Bridgeman Art Library; **214-215** (b) Detail of "Lewis and Clark at Three Forks" by E.S. Paxson, Oil on Canvas, 1912, Courtesy of the Montana Historical Society. Don Beatty photographer 10/1999; **215** (c) The Granger Collection, New York; **216** (bl) Patrick O'Brien / www.patrickobrienstudio.com, (br) Bettmann/CORBIS; **216-217** (LesOp) Patrick O'Brien / www.patrickobrienstudio.com; **217** Salt Lake Tribune/AP Images; **220** (t) Bettmann/CORBIS, (c) Patrick O'Brien / www.patrickobrienstudio.com; **222** (bl) The Granger Collection, New York, (br) Bettmann/CORBIS; **222-223** (LesOp) The Granger Collection, New York; **223** John G. Walter/Alamy Images; **225** (t) Bettmann/CORBIS, (c) The Granger Collection, New York; **226** (bl) The Granger Collection, New York, (bc) SuperStock, (br) Museum of the City of New York/CORBIS; **226-227** (LesOp) The Granger Collection, New York; **227** Bettmann/CORBIS; **228** SuperStock; **230** (c) Bob Daemmrich/PhotoEdit; **230-231** (bg) Museum of the City of New York/CORBIS; **231** (c) SuperStock; **232** (bl) Bettmann/CORBIS, (bc) National History Museum Mexico City/Dagli Orti/The Art Archive, (br) Snark/Art Resource, Inc.; **232-233** (LesOp) Bettmann/CORBIS; **233** (t) Texas State Library & Archives Commission, (b) National History Museum Mexico City/Dagli Orti/The Art Archive; **234** (inset) The Corcoran Gallery of Art/CORBIS; **234-235** (bg) National History Museum Mexico City/Dagli Orti/The Art Archive; **236** (c) Jules Frazier/Photodisc/Getty Images, (l) Courtesy of The Bancroft Library, University of California, Berkeley. [call number, 1905.16242.25]; **236-237** (t) Snark/Art Resource, Inc.; **237** (c) National History Museum Mexico City/Dagli Orti/The Art Archive; **238** (c) SuperStock; **240** Blend Images/PunchStock; **241** (UnitOp) Private Collection, Peter Newark Military Pictures/Bridgeman Art Library; **242** (tl) General Research & Reference Division, Schomburg Center for Research in Black Culture, The New York Public Library, Astor, Lenox and Tilden Foundations, (tr bl) The Granger Collection, New York, (br) Henry Fichner/Index Stock Imagery; **243** (br) SuperStock, (others) The Granger Collection, New York; **244** (bl) Ken Karp for MMH, (bc) The Granger Collection, New York, (br) Bettmann/CORBIS; **244-245** (LesOp) Scala/Art Resource, Inc.; **245** (r) Bettmann/CORBIS, (l) Ken Karp for MMH; **247** (t) The Granger Collection, New York, (c) Historic Deerfield, Photo by Penny Leveritt; **248** (l) Bettmann/CORBIS, (r) The Granger Collection, New York; **249** Thinkstock/PunchStock; **250 251 252** The Granger Collection, New York; **254** (t) The Granger Collection, New York; **254-255** (b) Private Collection/Bridgeman Art Library; **256 257** The Granger Collection, New York; **258** (bl) Private Collection, Peter Newark Military Pictures/Bridgeman Art Library, (bcl) Painting by Don Troiani/Historical Art Prints, (bcr) The Granger Collection, New York; **258-259** (LesOp) Private Collection, Peter Newark Military Pictures/Bridgeman Art Library; **259** David Muench/CORBIS; **260** (l) Painting by Don Troiani/Historical Art Prints; **260-261** (bg) Edward Owen/Art Resource, Inc., (fg) Alex Wong/Getty Images; **261** (r) Painting by Don Troiani/Historical Art Prints; **263** The Granger Collection, New York; **265** The Granger Collection, New York; **266** (bl) Library of Congress, Prints & Photographs Division, [LC-USZC4-1526], (bcl) Private Collection, Peter Newark American Pictures/Bridgeman Art Library, (bcr) The Granger Collection, New York, (br) CORBIS; **266-267** (LesOp) David Alan Harvey/Magnum Photos; **267** Library of Congress, Prints & Photographs Division, [LC-USZC4-1526]; **268** Private Collection, Peter Newark American Pictures/Bridgeman Art Library; **269** (t) The Granger Collection, New York, (b) Culver Pictures/The Art Archive; **270** From the original painting by Mort Kunstler, The Angle. 1988 Mort Kunstler, Inc. www.mkunstler.com; **271** From the original painting by Mort Kunstler, The Gettysburg Address. 1987 Mort Kunstler, Inc. www.mkunstler.com; **272** (tr) Bettmann/CORBIS; **272** (c) CORBIS, (tl) Library of Congress, Prints & Photographs Division, Civil War Photographs, [LC-USZC4-7983], (tr) C Squared Studios/Photodisc/Getty Images; **272-273** (bg) The Granger Collection, New York; **273** (tl) MPI/Hulton Archive/Getty Images, (tr) CORBIS, (c) David Alan Harvey/Magnum Photos; **274** (bl) Otto Herschan/Hulton Archive/Getty Images, (br) The Granger Collection, New York, (bc) Bettmann/CORBIS; **274-275** (LesOp) Painting by Don Troiani/Historical Art Prints; **275** Otto Herschan/Hulton Archive/Getty Images; **277** Bettmann/CORBIS; **278** The Granger Collection, New York; **279** (b) The Granger Collection, New York, (tl) National Archives Washington DC/The Art Archive, (tr) Painting by Don Troiani/Historical Art Prints; **280** (bl bc) The Granger Collection, New York, (br) Culver Pictures/The Art Archive; **280-281** (LesOp) The Granger Collection, New York; **281** The Granger Collection, New York; **282** Bob Daemmrich/Stock Boston/IPNstock; **283** The Granger Collection, New York; **284** (tr) Picture History, (tl) CORBIS; **284-285** (b) Culver Pictures/The Art Archive; **285** (c) The Granger Collection, New York; **286** CORBIS; **288** (t) Richard Hutchings/PhotoEdit, (b) The Granger Collection, New York; **289** Jean Brooks/Getty Images; **290** (t) The Granger Collection, New York, (br) Marc Muench/CORBIS, (bl) Shubroto Chattopadhyay/ CORBIS/PunchStock, (tr) Bettmann/CORBIS; **291** (tl) Time & Life Pictures/Getty Images, (bl) CORBIS, (tr) Getty Images, (br) Time & Life Pictures/Getty Images; **292** Robert Glusic/CORBIS/PunchStock; **294-295** (b) Dobbs Photography; **295** (r) Robert Glusic/CORBIS/PunchStock; **296** (bl) Craig

Tuttle/CORBIS, (bkgd) Ted Spiegel / The Image Works, (bc) Cathlyn Melloan/ Getty Images, (br) Sigrid Dauth Stock Photography / Alamy; **297** Earth Imaging/ Getty Images; **298** (t) Associated Press; **298-299** (bkgd) Craig Tuttle/CORBIS, (c) Crittenden Studio/Jupiter Images, (t) (c) David Zimmerman/Masterfile; **300** (b) Cathlyn Melloan/Getty Images; **301** Associated Press; **302** (t) Sigrid Dauth Stock Photography / Alamy; **304** (bkgd) Grant Faint/Getty Images, (bcl) Yann Arthus-Bertrand/CORBIS, (br) Danita Delimont / Alamy, (bl) Lowell Georgia/CORBIS; **305** Lowell Georgia/CORBIS; **306** (tr) GUILLEN PHOTOGRAPHY / Alamy, (tl) Roger Ressmeyer/CORBIS, (br) Photodisc/Punchstock, (bl) Yann Arthus-Bertrand/ CORBIS; **309** (b) Grant Faint/Getty Images, (tl) Burgess Blevins/Getty Images, (tr) Danita Delimont / Alamy; **310** (br) 2007 Clark James Mishler/AlaskaStock. com, (bkgd) Harald Sund/Getty Images, (bl) Mark Richards / PhotoEdit; **311** Mark Richards / PhotoEdit; **312** 2007 Clark James Mishler/AlaskaStock.com; **313** Harald Sund/Getty Images; **314** (bkgd) Thierry Dosogne/Getty Images, (bl) Stockbyte/PunchStock, (bc) DUNG VO TRUNG/CORBIS SYGMA, (br) Chuck Pefley / Alamy; **315** (t) CORBIS, (b) Stockbyte/PunchStock; **316** (bl) DUNG VO TRUNG/ CORBIS SYGMA, (t) Harald Sund/Getty Images; **317** (b) STAN HONDA/AFP/Getty Images, (t) Photo by Tim Boyle/Newsmakers; **318** Chuck Pefley / Alamy; **319** (b) Thierry Dosogne/Getty Images, (tl) Charles O'Rear/CORBIS; **319** (tr) Associated Press; **320** (bl) Creatas Images/Punchstock, (bkgd) David Young-Wolff/Photo Edit, (br) Jack Hollingsworth/Getty Images; **321** Creatas Images/Punchstock; **322** Jack Hollingsworth/Getty Images; **323** David Young-Wolff/Photo Edit; **324** (br) Bill Fritsch/Brand X/CORBIS, (bcl) AP Photo/State of Michigan, (bl) Mary Evans Picture Library/Alamy Images, (bkgd) (c)Bill Brooks/Masterfile; **325** (r) Mary Evans Picture Library/Alamy Images, (l) Historicus, Inc.; **326** (br) AP Photo/State of Michigan, (bc) Steven Clevenger/CORBIS, (bl) DigitalVision/ eStock Photo; **327** Kim Karpeles/Alamy Images; **328** (b) Mike Dobel/Alamy Images, (c) Paul Ridsdale/Alamy Images, (t) Charles O'Rear/CORBIS; **330** (l) Getty Images, (r) The McGraw-Hill Companies, Inc./Jill Braaten, photographer; **331** (t) Bill Fritsch/Brand X/CORBIS, (b) (c)Bill Brooks/Masterfile; **332** Burgess Blevins/Getty Images; **334** (t) Tony Freeman/PhotoEdit, (b) Lourens Smak/Alamy Images; BKCOV Pixtal/SuperStock; **R01** (b) Stockdisc/Getty Images, (t) CORBIS, (c) The Granger Collection, New York; **R03** Nathan Benn/CORBIS; **R05** Museo Real Academia de Bellas Artes, Madrid, Spain, Index/Bridgeman Art Library; **R07** James Hazelwood Photography; **R09** Painting by Don Troiani/Historical Art Prints; **R13-R15** The Granger Collection, New York; **GH2** (b) Panoramic Images/ Getty Images, (t) Peter Gridley/Photographer's Choice/Getty Images; **GH3** (t) Photolibrarycom/Getty Images, (c) CORBIS/PunchStock, (b) Larry Dale Gordon/ The Image Bank/Getty Images.

ACKNOWLEDGMENTS

Grateful acknowledgment is given to the following authors and publishers. Every effort has been made to trace the ownership of all copyrighted material and to secure the necessary permissions to reprint these selections. In the case of some selections for which acknowledgment is not given, extensive research has failed to locate the copyright holders.